WALKING WATERLOO

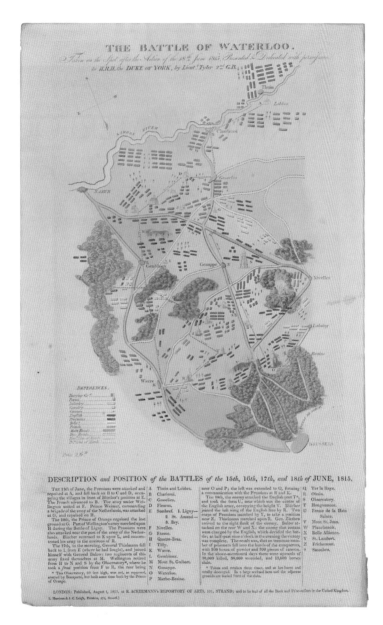

An early map of the Waterloo campaign showing each of its successive stages. In order to help its British audience to visualise the situation better, the normal polarity has been reversed.

WALKING WATERLOO
A Guide

CHARLES J. ESDAILE

Pen & Sword
MILITARY
AN IMPRINT OF PEN & SWORD BOOKS LTD.
YORKSHIRE ~ PHILADELPHIA

War Heritage Institute
Brussels

First published in Great Britain in 2019 by
PEN & SWORD MILITARY
An imprint of
Pen & Sword Books Ltd
Yorkshire – Philadelphia

ISBN 978 1 52674 078 6

A CIP catalogue record for this book is
available from the British Library

Typeset in 10/13 Palatino by Aura Technology and Software Services, India
Printed and bound by Replika Press Pvt. Ltd.

Pen & Sword Books Ltd incorporates the Imprints of Aviation, Atlas,
Family History, Fiction, Maritime, Military, Discovery, Politics, History,
Archaeology, Select, Wharncliffe Local History, Wharncliffe True Crime,
Military Classics, Wharncliffe Transport, Leo Cooper, The Praetorian Press,
Remember When, White Owl, Seaforth Publishing and
Frontline Publishing.

For a complete list of Pen & Sword titles please contact

PEN & SWORD BOOKS LTD
47 Church Street, Barnsley, South Yorkshire, S70 2AS, England
E-mail: enquiries@pen-and-sword.co.uk
Website: www.pen-and-sword.co.uk

Or
PEN & SWORD BOOKS
1950 Lawrence Rd, Havertown, PA 19083, USA
E-mail: Uspen-and-sword@casematepublishers.com
Website: www.penandswordbooks.com

CONTENTS

FOREWORD

As a Belgian citizen, Waterloo has a very special ring for me. First and foremost, this is because the venue of one of the most famous battles in history is situated in Belgium, under 30km from Brussels, location of the War Heritage Institute. However, also very important is the fact the battle testifies to a truly Belgian geographical reality: we are in the heart of Europe and at the crossroads of all the battles that have bloodied our regions over the centuries. Our institution's slogan indeed is *Belgium, battlefield of Europe*. Except for the two world wars, which other event but Waterloo so perfectly illustrates this concept?

That is precisely why we gladly and wholeheartedly accepted the invitation extended by Professor Charles Esdaile of the University of Liverpool. Collaboration between our two institutions could only be an enjoyable and rewarding adventure. First contacts between Liverpool University and the Royal Military Museum (integrated in the War Heritage Institute in May 2017) were laid in 2016. On our side Mr Patrick Nefors, PhD, historian and Head of the WHI Documentation Centre, supervised the exchanges. Scientific data was compared, first-rate photographic material offered and numerous archival sources made available, which all led to the creation of the *Walking Waterloo* e-guide.

This excellent app then quite logically gave birth to a paper version: the eponymous book you are presently holding. For Professor Esdaile, who had previously already authored both the compulsory *The Peninsular War* and the brilliant *Napoleon's Wars*, this seemed to be a dream come true. We are most happy to have been able to assist him in this endeavour.

I wish you pleasant reading.

Michel Jaupart,
Director-General of the War Heritage Institute (Brussels)

PREFACE

There are many, many books on Waterloo, and one may therefore well ask whether there is space for yet another. To this, the author would obviously answer in the affirmative, but, or at least so it is hoped, not without reason. Whilst there are various other guides to the battlefield, some of which are very good indeed, as witness for example David Buttery's excellent *Waterloo Battlefield Guide* (Barnsley, 2013), there is probably none that offers so much detail and certainly none that tries to render accessible the many hidden corners of the battlefield that are never seen by those who stick only to the main sights. In this respect, places like Hougoumont and La Haye Sainte are certainly evocative, whilst also witnesses to some of the most dreadful slaughter in the history of warfare, and yet they were not, as has so often been supposed, the keys to Napoleon's defeat. Still worse, viewed close to, it becomes apparent that they were not even especially useful as defensive positions – that they could not, indeed, have had the effect on the battle in which even the author of this work once believed. Walk the battlefield, then, and a very different Waterloo takes shape, a phrase that can be taken almost literally given the manner in which so many of those who have written about the battle have failed to spot that the most imposing terrain feature on the battlefield is neither the ridge occupied by Wellington nor the one occupied by Napoleon, but rather the roughly north-south watershed that linked their two positions and split the battlefield in two. With a new understanding of the battlefield comes space for reflection: to leave the crowds who cluster around the Lion Mound and head for Papelotte, or still more so, the empty hillsides where the outnumbered troops of Georges Mouton put up a defence more desperate and more prolonged than anything mounted by the Imperial Guard in the last moments of the battle, is to find a haunted beauty in which it is all too easy to envisage the horrors of a battlefield that saw slaughter on a scale that was barely rivalled even in the two World Wars: 1 July 1916 saw some 68,000 British and German soldiers fall killed or wounded in an area of roughly sixty square miles, but at Waterloo two-thirds of that number became casualties, along, sadly, with at least 5,000 horses, in an area little more than 5 per cent of the size.

Accompanying the various tours will be found a potted history of the battle. This makes no claim to originality, but it does seek to correct some of the many received ideas that appear with such monotonous regularity in the traditional narrative. The story of Napoleon spotting the Prussian army on the horizon at one o'clock, then, makes no appearance for the simple reason that there is not a single line of sight that would have allowed the emperor to see any such thing, just as the idea that the start of the battle was delayed so as to give the mud caused by the torrential overnight rain time to dry out has also been discounted: difficult though the task of shifting the French guns certainly was, anyone who goes to Waterloo in the wake of heavy rain will realize that such is the nature of the soil that a mere two hours of a damp and overcast morning would not have made a *centime* of difference. Lastly, gone too is the absurd notion that the great French cavalry charges were launched because Ney spotted large numbers of Allied troops apparently falling back from the ridge: as even a cursory visit to the battlefield should show, there was again nowhere from which Ney or anyone else in a position of authority in the French army could have seen such a thing. Take away a few other things that were either invented altogether – the fabled last stand of the Old Guard – or misplaced in the narrative – the captured Prussian hussar who was brought before Napoleon and confirmed the news of Bülow's arrival – and one gets a very different battle. Moreover, thanks to the wonders of modern technology, it is now one that can be explored in a very different way. Thus, thanks to the services of the Computer Services Department at the University of Liverpool, and, especially, the estimable Chris Rodenhurst, an electronic version of this book is available as a free downloadable app from both Apple and Android. For full details, please see < https://www.liverpool.ac.uk/csd/app-directory/waterloo/ >.

On a note of clarification, it may be useful to say something about usage. For reasons that I fail to understand, in so far as the principal French actors are concerned, it is customary to speak of Marshal Ney and Marshal Soult rather than the Prince of the Moscowa and the Duke of Dalmatia, and yet Georges Mouton is always referred to as the Count of Lobau and Jean-Baptiste Drouet as the Count of Erlon. In this work, however arbitrary it may seem, French commanders will all be denied their titles. Logically, of course, for the sake of consistency we should therefore probably refer to Wellington as 'Wellesley', but to insist on this would be a ridiculous conceit, not to mention one that might give rise to thoughts of referring to Napoleon throughout as 'Bonaparte'.

My debts are many. In the first place, there are the many people in the University of Liverpool's 'impact team', including, not least, Chris Williams and Kate Spicer, without whom this project would never have got off the ground in the first place, and, in addition, Catherine Macmanamon of the University's Sydney Jones Library who has continued to meet my demands for yet more Napoleonic memoirs with much grace and patience. In the second place, there is each and every member of staff at the Royal Army Museum in Brussels, but, especially, Patrick Nefors and Marc Brans. In the third place, there is my good friend and colleague, Rupert Harding, and all his team at Pen and Sword, a particular mention going here to the ever-patient Stephen Chumbley. In the fourth place, there are the various friends and colleagues who have offered advice and encouragement, especially Nick Lipscombe, Andrew Jones and Zack White. In the fifth place, there is the Belgian specialist, Bernard Coppens, who gave generously of his time and expertise and was a wonderful companion in the course of many visits to the battlefield. In the sixth place there is the tower of strength, knowledge and sheer endeavour that is Gareth Glover, who very kindly gave the author permission to use the maps in his excellent *Waterloo: Myth and Reality* as the basis for the ones in this book. In the seventh place there is my ever-patient family. And, in the eighth place, there are all those who fought and died at Waterloo: how sad it is that this book is being written at a time when the continental commitment that took so many British soldiers to Mont Saint Jean is being so wilfully thrown aside.

Charles J. Esdaile, Liverpool, 13 September 2017.

BATTLE MAPS

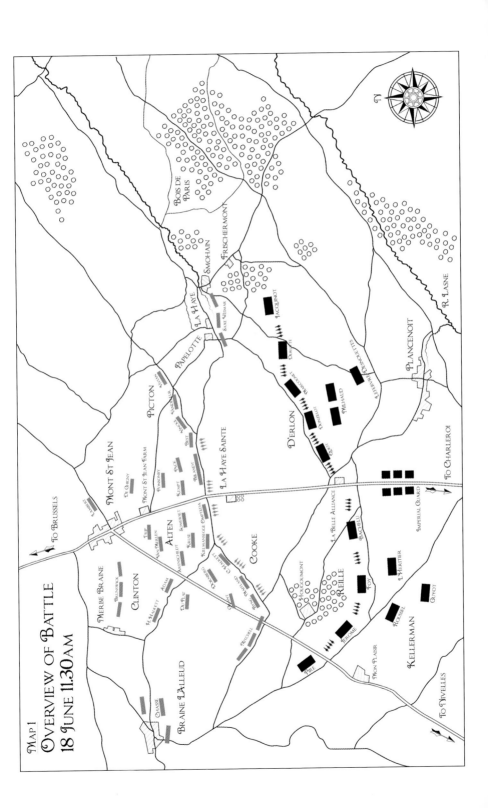

MAP 1

OVERVIEW OF BATTLE
18 JUNE 11.30AM

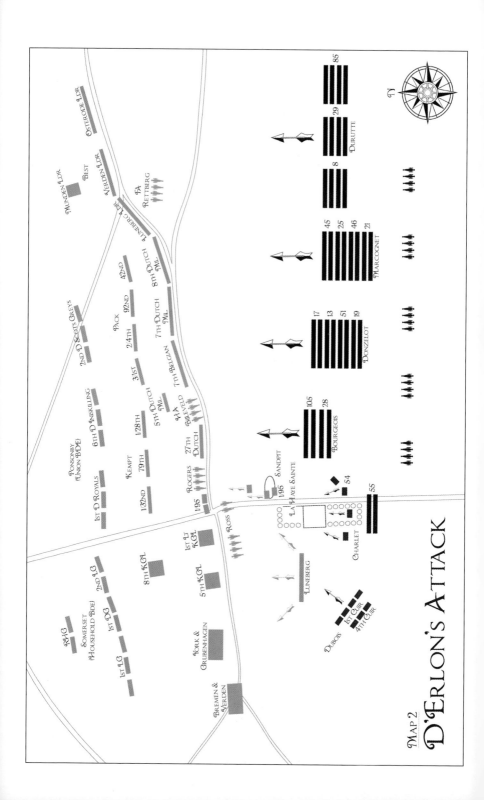

MAP 2
D'ERLON'S ATTACK

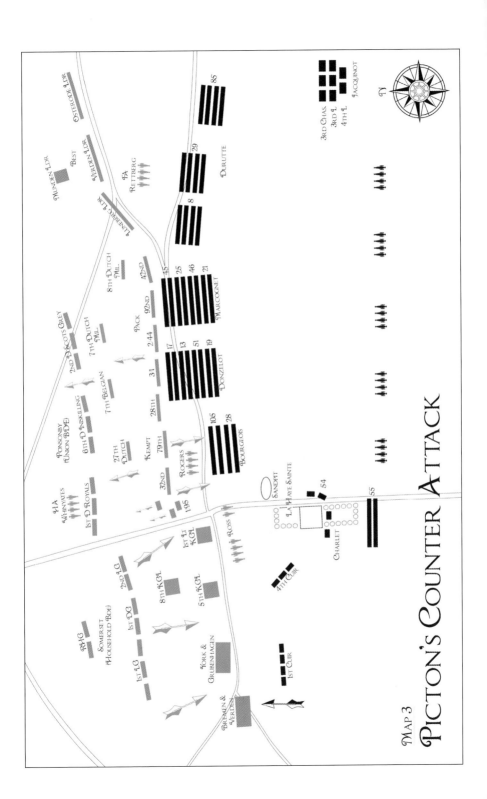

MAP 3
PICTON'S COUNTER ATTACK

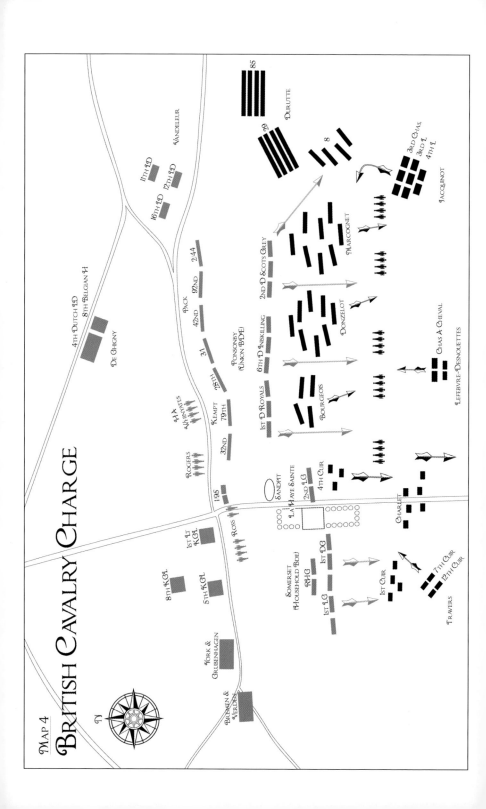

MAP 4
BRITISH CAVALRY CHARGE

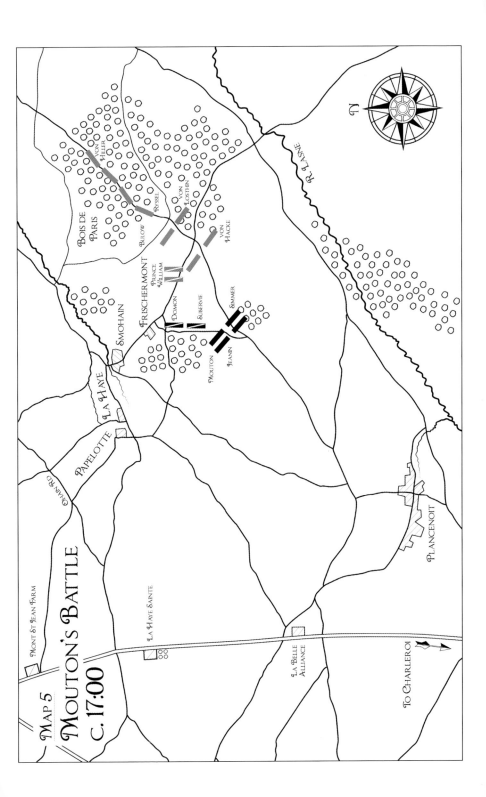

MAP 5

MOUTON'S BATTLE
C. 17:00

MONT ST JEAN FARM

BOIS DE PARIS

VON HILLER

BÜLOW

VON RYSSEL

VON LOSTHIN

VON HACKE

FRISCHERMONT

PRINCE WILLIAM

SMOHAIN

DOMON

SUBERVIE

SIMMER

MOUTON

JEANIN

LA HAYE

PAPELOTTE

OHAIN RD.

LA HAYE SAINTE

LA BELLE ALLIANCE

PLANCENOIT

R. LASNE

TO CHARLEROI

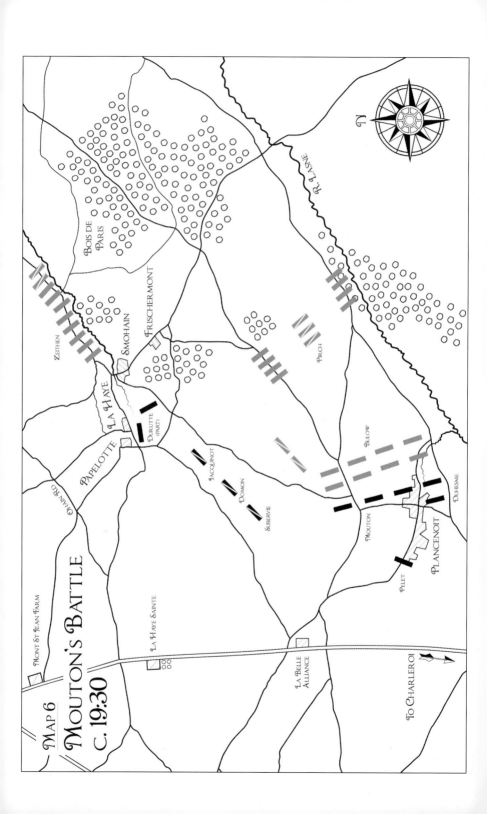

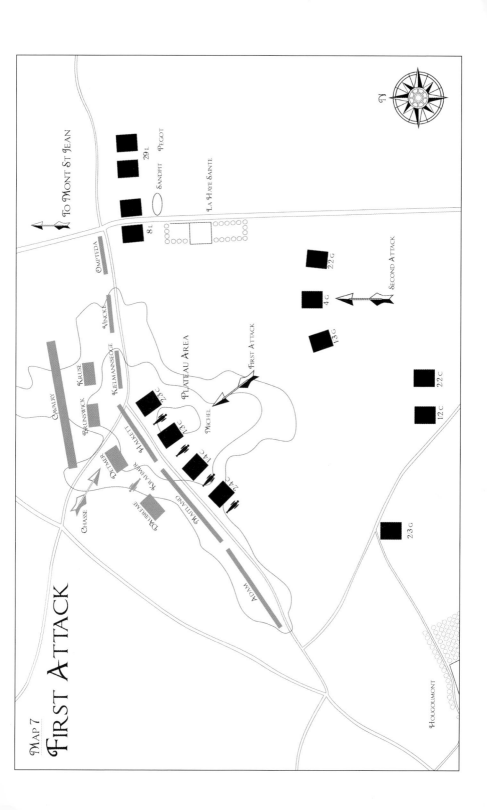

Map 7
FIRST ATTACK

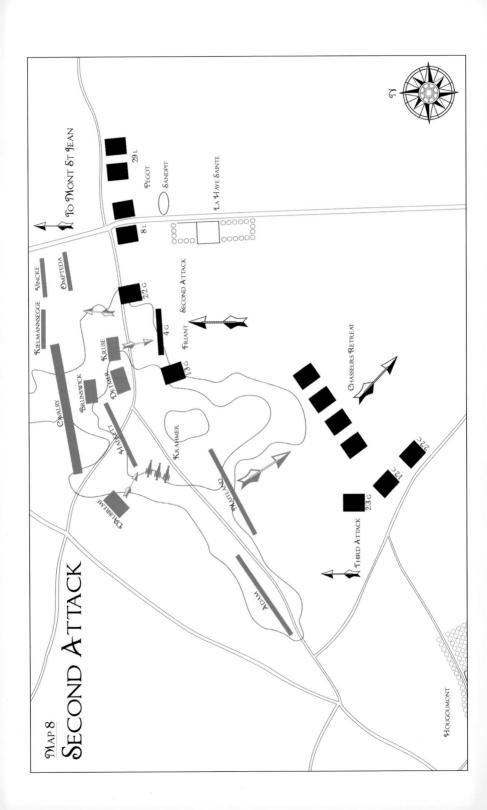

Map 8
Second Attack

To Mont St Jean

29 L

Pegot

Sandpit

La Haye Sainte

8 L

Vincke

Ompteda

Kielmannsegge

22 G

4 G

Second Attack

Friant

Kruse

13 G

Brunswick

Detmer

Cavalry

Halkett

Krahmer

Chasseurs Retreat

D'Aubreme

Maitland

22 C

12 C

23 G

Third Attack

Adam

Hougoumont

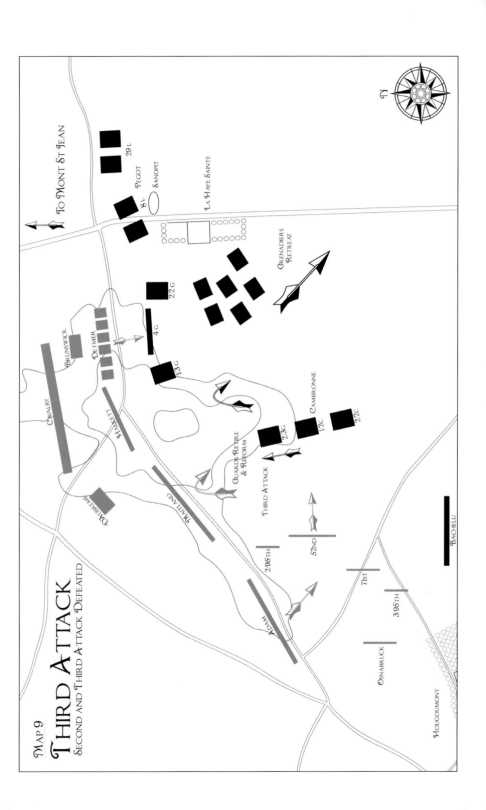

MAP 9

THIRD ATTACK
SECOND AND THIRD ATTACK DEFEATED

To Mont St Jean

29 L

PEGOT

SANDPIT

18 L

LA HAYE SAINTE

GRENADERS RETREAT

2/2 G

4 G

1/3 G

BRUNSWICK

DETMER

CAVALRY

HALKETT

MAITLAND

DAUBREME

GUARDS RETIRE & REFORM

2/3 G

CAMBRONNE

1/2 C

2/2 C

THIRD ATTACK

52ND

2/95TH

KWON

71ST

3/95TH

OSNABRUCK

HOUGOUMONT

BACHELU

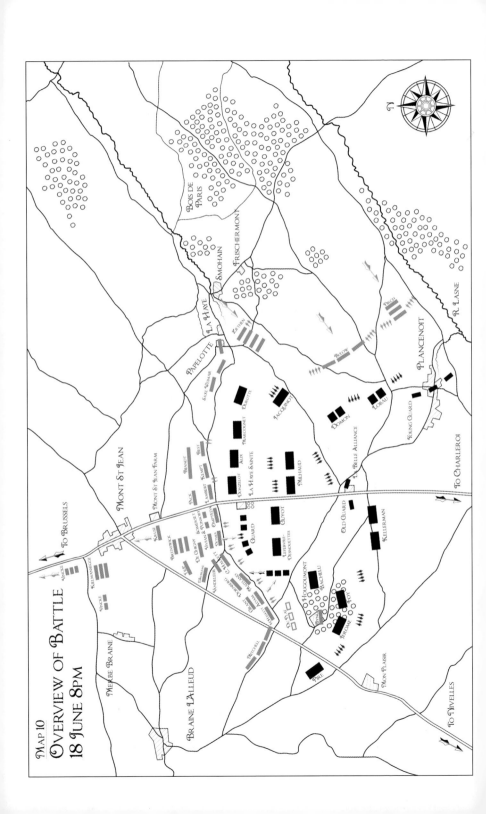

MAP 10
OVERVIEW OF BATTLE
18 JUNE 8PM

HISTORICAL CONTEXT

The battle of Waterloo is inextricably linked with the figure of Napoleon Bonaparte. A scion of an old Corsican family who had gained a commission in the French artillery in 1787, he was initially an avid supporter of Corsican independence, but in 1793 Napoleon and his entire family were forced to flee to France after falling out with many of the other factions on the island. Left with no other outlet for his dreams of becoming a great man – dreams which had been a fixation ever since his teenage years, if not before – Napoleon therefore threw himself into a policy of both wholesale collaboration with the Revolution and equally wholesale alignment with whichever faction held the balance of power at any given moment. Together with a certain amount of good luck, in 1796 this brought him command of the Army of Italy. Initially, Italy was seen as a minor front, but Napoleon struck it lucky in that the much larger French forces deployed elsewhere failed dismally, thereby throwing the string of dramatic victories which his undoubted – some would say unrivalled – talent as a general quickly gained him against the Austrians into sharp relief. By the end of 1797, then, he was a veritable 'power in the land', and, notwithstanding the failure of a colonial adventure in Egypt, in 1799 the convoluted state of French politics opened the way for him to take power in a military coup.

As ruler of France, Napoleon represented a paradox. Backing his coup, then, had been claims that he would end the ever-more exhausting wars which had cost France so much blood in the years since the outbreak of war in 1792, and at first it seemed that he would make good in this respect: by the end of 1801 all the states still at war with France had been forced either to surrender or at the very least open peace negotiations. Yet herein lies the paradox, for, if Napoleon had temporarily brought peace to Europe, he was anything but a man of peace himself. On the contrary, from his earliest youth, he had been fascinated by war, whilst it was above all through war that he had achieved power. To turn his back on war was therefore at best difficult for him, but there is little sign that Napoleon ever seriously tried to do so, it being quite clear that he regarded the general peace he secured as nothing more than a truce aimed at winning time for him to rebuild the much-battered French navy, strengthen the power and efficiency of the state and, above all, end the massive popular resistance to conscription that had been a millstone round the army's neck ever since 1793. Indeed, even the idea of a breathing space does not seem to have appealed to him that much for his actions essentially constituted an endless series of provocations which, entirely predictably, forced Britain back to war within a year.

The result, of course, was the Napoleonic Wars. Initially, Britain stood alone, but from 1805 onwards Napoleon, now emperor of France, was faced by a series of international coalitions of varying unity, composition and strength of purpose. At first one after another was beaten down in a series of great battles that by 1807 had transformed Napoleon into the veritable master of Europe, but in 1808 he made the fatal mistake of deposing the Spanish royal family and installing his brother, Joseph, on the throne in their stead, the result of this being that from then on he was faced by a long and debilitating war that skilful British intervention made winning at best a long and difficult task. This need not in itself have been a disaster – in the end the French could probably have won the Peninsular War – but in 1812 Napoleon's alienation of Alexander I led him to attack Russia, the net result of this action being to destabilize the position of his armies in Spain and, still worse, all but wipe out the 500,000 men who had marched across the frontiers of East Prussia. The campaign of 1812, as it is known, is often assumed to have set the Napoleonic empire on an irrevocable slide into ruin, but this is not the case. Though Prussia joined Alexander in his war on Napoleon, Austria stayed out of the fight while the emperor's German and Italian satellites ignored appeals to them to change sides. As a result a fresh army was got together in Germany, at the head of which Napoleon fought the Russians and Prussians to a standstill at the battles of Lützen and Bautzen. At this point, he might have had peace, for Alexander I and Frederick William III were so horrified by the slaughter they would have been willing to offer him a generous deal, but the chance was cast aside: rejecting an attempt at Austrian mediation that might have brought him terms that were still more generous, the emperor rather elected to fight on and that despite the fact that this decision led Austria in turn to declare war.

Napoleon, then, was risking disaster, and this duly struck in the form of defeat in the Battle of Leipzig, a terrible three-day struggle that dwarfed Waterloo in numbers of combatants and casualties alike. Yet, forced to retreat to the French frontier and deserted by every single one of his German allies, not to mention his brother-in-law Joachim Murat, since 1808 King of Naples, he continued to reject the peace overtures that were made to him, leaving the Allied armies no option but to march on Paris. In the resultant campaign the emperor worked wonders: marching from one danger spot to the next with great speed, he inflicted reverse after reverse on his assailants. Yet, setting aside the fact that every battle constituted a drain on his already wasting assets – assailed by years of economic crisis and utterly exhausted by demands for manpower that had become utterly intolerable, the populace had once more resorted to the wholesale draft evasion characteristic of the years before Napoleon came to power, while the local authorities were no longer willing to enforce the law – this very success was his undoing. In large part thanks to the influence of the Austrian chancellor, Metternich, who believed that it was very much in Austria's interests to retain a strong France, even now the Allies were ready to offer terms that would have kept Napoleon in power, but, buoyed up by his victories, the emperor elected to fight on. However, this last folly was the end: ignoring his futile attempts at diversionary operations, the Allies entered Paris, whilst on 6 April a group of senior marshals confronted their commander at his headquarters at Fontainebleau and forced him to abdicate.

The emperor, however, was not finished. We here come, of course, to the campaign of Waterloo. Napoleon secured generous terms in the wake of his abdication, including, most notably, the grant of a kingdom in the form of the miniscule Italian island of Elba, but it was probably unrealistic to expect such a man to allow himself to be confined to so small a sphere of activity. Indeed, encouraged by reports of widespread discontent in France, at the end of February 1815 he set sail for Provence at the head of the 1,000-strong personal bodyguard he had been allowed to take with him into exile. According to legend, the erstwhile emperor came back to a hero's welcome, but, whilst he quickly secured power, entering Paris in triumph on 20 March, this is so much myth. Driven to fury by the restored monarchy's treatment of the military, the army rallied to him *en masse*, but popular responses were muted. In some areas which had done well out of Napoleon, had particular reason to resent the Bourbons or suffered the full brunt of the invasions of 1814, there was a measure of enthusiasm, but elsewhere the news that he had returned was greeted with a mixture of fear and horror. Notably absent, too, were most of his old marshals: of the sixteen who were on the army's books in 1814, just seven rallied to Napoleon in 1815. In the event armed resistance was limited to the old heartlands of counter-revolution in the Vendée and Brittany, but only quick action on the part of troops who had gone over to Napoleon prevented further outbreaks elsewhere, while from one end of the country to the other there was a deep-seated sullenness and unwillingness to co-operate that was but little assuaged by a plan of political reform which in effect bolted the concessions which had already been made by Louis XVIII in 1814 to the structures of the empire.

From the very beginning, then, Napoleon found himself at a severe disadvantage. Inherent in the situation was a resumption of the wars of 1803–14: casting aside Napoleon's protestations that he only wanted peace as so many attempts to garner support at home and abroad, Britain, Austria, Prussia and Russia immediately declared the French ruler to be an outlaw and committed themselves to his overthrow. Nor did Napoleon enjoy the slightest support beyond the borders of France: pro-French risings came there none, while the French ruler's only ally – a Joachim Murat terrified that he was about to be removed from his Neapolitan throne – was quickly crushed when he tried to launch a war of liberation in Italy. With each of the powers mentioned promising to mobilize an army of 150,000 men, or, in the case of the British, provide an equivalent mixture of troops and finance, and still more troops likely to be forthcoming from Spain, Portugal and the minor German and Italian states, the odds against Napoleon would have been enormous even had he been able to count on more support at home, but that support was not forthcoming, the result being that the emperor had to forego conscription and for the most part rely on the troops that were already on the books in 1815. In theory, this was scarcely an inconsiderable force – the regular army numbered some 175,000 men and the National Guard another 280,000 – but the latter, a militia only mobilized in time of war, was lacking in training, equipment and above all motivation, little more than half the men concerned answering the call to arms and many of these going home at the earliest possible opportunity. Not to be able to draft fresh conscripts was therefore a disaster, whilst the attempt to get round the issue by calling up all the men who had been serving in the army in 1814 but had been demobilized following the coming of peace, or deserted in the course of the defence of France, was not much of a substitute: the 118,000 troops that should have been produced by this measure would have been insufficient even had they all come forward, but in the event only about two-thirds of them of them appeared. As for genuine volunteers, these probably numbered no more than 30,000, the vast majority of them veterans who had been discharged from the service prior to 1814, though many of the men concerned were too unfit to do anything other than serve as garrison troops. For Napoleon to triumph, then, it would require a miracle.

ARMIES AND GENERALS

In many ways, the armies that fought at Waterloo were very similar. Broadly speaking, they were dressed in a similar style, composed of the same types of troops and armed with weapons that were all but identical, while they also used very similar tactics on the battlefield. That said, they were yet very different forces, whilst their commanders could not have offered a greater contrast.

Beginning with the French army, this was by far the best of the three in terms of its quality: there was not a single man of the 125,000 men whom Napoleon took into Belgium who was not a veteran of at least one campaign and some of soldiers of the Guard in particular had records of service dating back to the days of the Revolution. Divided into six regular army corps, each composed of three or four infantry divisions, a division of cavalry and five or six artillery batteries; the Imperial Guard (three infantry divisions, two cavalry divisions, eight artillery batteries); and four corps of reserve cavalry, each of which had two divisions of cavalry and two batteries of horse artillery, this was truly an imposing force, while its morale was very high. As for its commanders, if there was a shortage of marshals, at the level of the corps, the division and the brigade, Napoleon could draw on a wealth of talent that had been tempered in its many campaigns. That said, there were still many problems. Thus, many of the men who had returned to service had not received proper uniforms or equipment; some of the artillery batteries were manned by sailors drafted in from the fleet; and, in the Guard many units had had to be put together from scratch, almost the entire force having been disbanded in 1814.

With some 90,000 men, the Allied Army of the Netherlands was a much more uneven affair. Organized into three corps, one of which was designated as a reserve, this was extremely multifarious in its composition: in terms of the foot alone, there were nine brigades of British infantry, two brigades of King's German Legion infantry, five brigades of Hanoverian infantry; two brigades of Brunswick infantry; two brigades of Nassau infantry; and six brigades of Dutch infantry.

Unlike in the Army of the North, the quality of Wellington's forces was open to serious question: if the best British units – in general, those which had fought in the Peninsular War – were excellent, many others were composed of raw recruits who had never fired a shot and in some cases had been in the army only a few weeks. As for the rest, though originally very good, the King's German Legion had long since lost its character of, in effect, the Hanoverian army in exile and was now in large part a mass of foreign deserters and erstwhile prisoners of war, whilst the other German contingents and the Dutch were mostly either very raw or composed of militiamen who had only been called up on the return of Napoleon to power. That said, the officers were in most cases very experienced, though the fact that most of them had gained that experience fighting for Napoleon in the armies of one or other of his satellite states or even in the forces of France herself rendered even this qualification more than somewhat dubious (in fairness, however, it should be pointed out that persistent British fears of wholesale defections to the French proved unfounded: even among the Belgians, a nationality which had escaped annexation by France only to handed over to its much disliked Dutch neighbours, the idea of a return to rule by Napoleon was thoroughly hated). At the same time, this was an army that was seriously under-gunned: at Waterloo Wellington could put only 157 guns into line compared with 246 for the French, whilst his largest pieces were only 9-pounders as opposed to the 12-pounders that equipped at least six of the twenty-nine French batteries present on the field (in compensation, however, it should be noted that only British guns were equipped with the deadly anti-personnel shrapnel shell, and, equally uniquely, that at least five battalions of infantry were armed with the highly accurate Baker rifle). In so far as he could, Wellington had tried to create mixed divisions in which experienced British brigades could shore up less experienced foreign ones, but political considerations meant that it was hard to take this beyond a certain point, the Brunswickers and the Dutch insisting on maintaining independent formations of their own. Meanwhile, politics had also supervened at the level of the high command, Wellington having had no option but to accept the Prince of Orange – the teenage heir to the Dutch throne – as commander of I Corps despite the fact that his only previous service had been as an *aide de camp*.

Last but not least, we come to the Prussian Army of the Lower Rhine. Here, too, there were many difficulties. Organized in four corps, Blücher's 122,000 men were at least as mixed as their counterparts in the Army of the Netherlands. Some, certainly were veterans of the campaigns of 1813–14, but others were raw conscripts (and in many instances not very willing ones) recently called up from the large areas of Germany that had been awarded Prussia in the wake of the fall of Napoleon; troops who had been in the service of other armies that had been forcibly transferred to the Prussian service; or militiamen called out in time of war alone who had received only the most basic level of training. Standards of armament and uniform varied dramatically, while there were also tremendous deficiencies with the army's organization. In the Prussian army divisions were known as brigades and brigades as regiments, but far more serious than this difference in nomenclature was the fact that no provision was made for a separate force of mounted troops on the basis of those that existed in both the Army of the North and the Army of the Netherlands: instead, the Prussian cavalry, much of it of notoriously poor quality in the first place, was allocated piecemeal to the different corps, this being an arrangement that could not but harm its striking power.

What, then, of the commanders? Here we cannot but begin with the figure of Napoleon. Regarded by many as the greatest general of all time, the emperor was beyond doubt a master of the operational art, as witness, indeed, the plans he drew up for the invasion of Belgium, whilst he was also adept at winning the love and devotion of his soldiers. That said, far too given to believing his own propaganda, he was a poor strategist whose thinking in 1815 bordered, as on a number of occasions before, on the delusional, whilst by the time of the Hundred Days he was, if not chronically ill – of this there is no firm evidence one way or the other – then certainly seriously overweight and in poor physical shape. Meanwhile, at heart he was a servant of nothing but his own glory, this completely marking him out from the Duke of Wellington who, by contrast, regarded himself, above all, as a servant of the state. At the same time, the British general was a very different commander who was unfailingly as sparing as he could be of the lives of his soldiers, a master of battlefield tactics and, last but not least, a strategic genius, the long series of campaigns that he had waged in Spain and Portugal between 1808–14 representing an extraordinary masterpiece that left many of the French generals who had had to face him distinctly overawed, for proof whereof one has only to cite the repeated warnings of his prowess voiced by Soult and various others on the morning of Waterloo. And, finally, there was Blücher, a flamboyant figure who was little good for anything more than leading heroic charges and, if not actually drunk for much of the time, then certainly a serious alcoholic, but who yet was loved by his soldiers, hated Napoleon beyond all things and retained enough sense to place himself completely under the guidance of his far more cerebral chief of staff, Auguste von Gneisenau.

To conclude, then, none of the armies who met in the campaign of the Hundred Days possessed all the advantages, but none of them possessed all the disadvantages either. In short, it was not the cards that mattered, but how the cards were played, and in this Wellington and Blücher were to prove to be infinitely superior.

THE CAMPAIGN

With war inevitable, Napoleon faced a herculean task. Much fatter and more unfit than he had ever been before, aided by his new Minister of War, Marshal Davout, he yet threw himself into the task with all his old energy: around the country, hundreds of workshops were set to the task of producing weapons, uniforms and equipment; the veterans who had returned to the colours were fed into the army so as to bring the regiments up to strength; fortresses were provisioned and refurbished; the Imperial Guard rebuilt – reduced to a mere two regiments of infantry and four of cavalry, this was now to consist of twenty-four regiments of infantry, five regiments of cavalry and seventeen batteries of guns, plus detachments of engineers, sailors and transport troops – and no fewer than seven armies set up to defend France's frontiers or take the war to the enemy. What, though, should he do with his soldiers? In so far as this was concerned, there were only two courses of action: either stand firm and await the inevitable enemy attack, or strike hard at the only Allied forces in reach – the British, German, Dutch and Prussian troops in modern-day Belgium under the Duke of Wellington and Field Marshal Gerhardt von Blücher – in the hope that victory would so shake the coalition forming against France that it would fracture or even disintegrate altogether. Both courses of action offered real possibilities: whilst standing on the defensive would buy time for the completion of French rearmament, allow Napoleon to build the numerous French fortresses into his strategy, offer the possibility of operating on interior lines against his assailants and help to convince the population that the emperor was devoid of aggressive intentions, taking the offensive would capitalise on the offensive spirit of the army and encourage (or so it was hoped) national insurrections in Belgium, Poland, Italy and Germany. However, Napoleon being Napoleon – a commander who lusted after glory and had been denied it for far too long – only the latter would do, and on 11 June he took the field at the head of the 125,000-strong Army of the North, leaving the rest of the country to be defended by no more than 73,000 regular troops, plus whatever elements of the National Guard had been got together.

In so far as Napoleon's plan of campaign was concerned, it was quite simple: launch a surprise attack at the spot marking the demarcation line between the area occupied by Wellington's forces to the west and Blücher's forces to the east – essentially the city of Charleroi and the highway leading from there to Brussels – drive the two Allied commanders apart and use the bulk of his troops to crush one or the other of them before the other could intervene. However, the emperor was greatly hampered by the fact that his great chief-of-staff, Marshal Berthier, had responded to his return by fleeing into exile in Germany. In his place, there had for political reasons been little choice but to appoint Marshal Soult, but it is generally agreed that the latter was not especially gifted at staff work whilst he was hated by many senior commanders, including, not least, the only other member of the pre-1814 marshalate who turned out to be available for the campaign in Belgium, namely the hot-headed and impetuous Michel Ney. Hardly had the three columns of troops into which the Army of the North got off the mark at dawn on 15 June, then, than things began to go badly wrong: units took wrong turnings, failed to move at the appointed time or became jammed in the narrow country lanes leading to the frontier.

Fortunately for the French, the situation was not at its best in the Allied camp either. For ease of subsisting the troops, the armies of Wellington and Blücher alike were spread over a wide expanse of southern Belgium, while the two commanders were not expecting an attack in the slightest. Immediately confronted by the French vanguard around Charleroi, most of the Prussians got moving straight away and began to concentrate around the village of Ligny a few miles north-east of that city, though a combination of stubbornness and misunderstanding meant that the furthest away of the four corps, each of some 30,000 men, of which they consisted – that of Friedrich Bülow von Dennewitz – delayed setting off for more than twenty-four hours. However, amongst the British, Dutch, Hanoverians, Brunswickers and Nassauers commanded by Wellington, it was a different story. Intelligence from the frontier was very slow to reach the British general, while he was in any case convinced that, if the

French were coming at all, it would not be via Charleroi but rather one of several alternative routes much further west. In consequence, it was well into the night of 15 June before the Army of the Netherlands began to get on the road, though in one important instance a march was stolen on the French by the steps taken by a number of Dutch officers to secure the important crossroads at Quatre Bras, a vital link between Wellington and Blücher whose loss would have made it very difficult for them to assist one another. Famously, however, Wellington himself remained in Brussels where he had spent part of the evening at a ball hosted by the Duchess of Richmond, although this was not the act of complacent insouciance sometimes suggested, but rather a calculated move aimed at reassuring the increasingly nervous populace.

By the early morning of 16 June, then, battle was imminent. To the north and west the Army of the Netherlands was for the most part heading for the initial concentration point represented by the town of Nivelles, a compromise position from which Wellington, who was still not convinced that French would not suddenly switch their main thrust to the west rather than marching directly on Brussels, could move swiftly in any direction; to the south the Army of the North had captured Charleroi and pushed several miles towards Brussels; and to the east the Army of the Lower Rhine was massing around Ligny. Yet, curiously enough, with their only hope achieving a smashing victory before the Allies could concentrate their forces, the French proved slow to get moving. In part, true, this was because their forces were exhausted from a day of long marches and sporadic fighting with the Prussian troops holding the Charleroi area, but many units were still strung out along the roads leading back to the French frontier. Now separated into two wings, of which that on the left had been given at the last minute to Marshal Ney and that on the right to the newly-promoted Marshal Grouchy, the French army did not advance until the late morning, and by then it was too late: having ridden from Brussels to investigate the situation at Quatre Bras, Wellington had at last woken up to the fact that the main thrust was coming straight up the axis of the Brussels highway and therefore ordered the bulk of his forces to concentrate there forthwith, whilst he had also been given time and opportunity to ride over to Blücher's headquarters and promise that, providing that the French did not attack him (something that no-one anticipated at this stage), he would march to his support.

When what became the twin battles of Quatre Bras and Ligny began in the early afternoon, then, the Allies were in a much better situation than might have been expected. On the former battlefield, the Dutch division of Henri Perponcher-Sedlnitzky was holding a defensive line anchored on a large walled farm called Gemioncourt, whilst a brigade of Dutch light cavalry and the first units of Wellington's troops – Sir Thomas Picton's Fifth Division – were only a mile or two away to the north. And, on the latter, 83,000 Prussian troops were holding the line of a little brook that curved along the foot of a broad ridge and was dotted with a series of villages, the most notable of which were Wagnelée, La Haye, Saint Amand, Ligny and Sombreffe, which had all been barricaded and crammed with as many troops as they could hold. There followed an afternoon of slaughter. At Quatre Bras Ney launched attack after attack on the Allied positions and on a number of occasions almost reached the crossroads, only every time to be forced back by the arrival of a fresh wave of British or German reinforcements, and by the end of the day the marshal had been forced to retire to his start line (it might here be noted that, in yet another symbol of the way that the Hundred Days stood at a turning point in the history of warfare, amongst the 8,000 casualties suffered by the two sides was the Duke of Brunswick, the last ruler of a European sovereign state not only personally to command his army on the battlefield, but to be killed in action doing so). Meanwhile, at Ligny a much bigger battle raged to and fro around the various villages held by the Prussians until, at length, Blücher's men were forced to retreat from the field when the Imperial Guard were unleashed against their centre amidst the thunder and lightning of a terrible storm.

June 16th 1815 might have been a day that Napoleon secured a great victory, but it was not to be. Marshal Ney, who had only been given command of a wing at the last minute, is often blamed for this on the grounds that he should either have captured Quatre Bras on the evening of 15 June or at the very least early the next day, but, useful though this might have been, he in fact received no orders to do anything of the sort till perhaps eleven o'clock on the morning of 16 June, and, thanks to the delays in French movements the previous day, was not in a position to launch an attack until the early afternoon anyway. Had he been allowed to press on with all the troops at his disposal he might well have obtained a considerable victory, but in doing this he was prevented by none other than Napoleon himself. Thus, correctly divining that the right flank of the Prussian position was completely in the air, in the midst of the fighting the emperor suddenly decided that, rather than pushing on towards Brussels as the marshal had originally been told to do, he should rather go over to the defensive. Still strung out along the road from Charleroi, meanwhile, Jean-Baptiste Drouet's I Corps was ordered to march east and envelop Blücher's right flank and that despite the fact that it had been assigned to Ney's command. The result was chaos: never properly informed of what was going on, the marshal fell into a violent rage and sent orders to Drouet, who by this time had all but reached the battlefield of Ligny, to retrace his steps and head for Quatre Bras once more, the consequence being that I Corps ended up by intervening in neither action. Had things gone otherwise the French would probably either have won as big a victory at Quatre Bras as they actually did at Ligny, or smashed Blücher altogether. That such a result would have made any difference in the long term is doubtful, but it would have certainly won Napoleon much time and given his army a much-needed injection of confidence. As it was, however, Wellington's men could legitimately feel that they had won a victory at Quatre Bras, whilst at Ligny the bulk of the Prussians were able to slip away into the night.

What happened at this point was crucial. Blücher was missing, having had his horse shot from under him whilst leading one last desperate cavalry charge. Responsibility for the conduct of operations had therefore fallen on the shoulders of the chief of staff, August von Gneisenau. Never fond of the British and all but completely unaware of events at Quatre Bras, Blücher's deputy was furious at Wellington's failure to appear the previous day, whilst the many deficiencies of the Prussian army had been laid bare in the most cruel fashion. In the circumstances, then, it would have been all too easy for Gneisenau to order a retreat to the safety of Rhine, but, to his eternal credit, he instead ordered a retreat northwards, a move that kept open the possibility of co-operation with the Army of the Netherlands. Whilst Gneisenau was taking the right decisions, meanwhile, Napoleon was taking the wrong ones. Elated by his victory, he jumped to the conclusion, first, that the Prussian army was far more badly beaten than was actually the case and, second, that it was indeed heading east rather than north. Despite the fact that the emperor had large numbers of cavalry with him who had played no part in the battle, no attempt was made to pursue the Prussians that night, while the following morning, when some units of horse did finally get on the road, they marched on the town of Gembloux rather than the concentration area Gneisenau had selected at Wavre. As for Napoleon, he spent the morning in a state of compete inaction, touring the battlefield and making a show of ensuring the best possible medical care for his many wounded.

Only around midday did the situation change. The emperor had assumed that, in the wake of Ligny, Wellington must have withdrawn on Brussels, but this was not the case: the British commander had remained completely in the dark as to the situation of the Prussian army until well on into 17 June, and had therefore kept his forces at Quatre Bras, where he was joined in the course of the morning by most of the troops who had missed the battle the previous day including all his British cavalry. Very belatedly gaining wind of his presence, Napoleon suddenly realized that the campaign was his for the taking and sent half his forces – specifically, Mouton's VI Corps and the Guard – rushing to envelop the Army of the Netherlands' left. Yet it was already too late: finally hearing of Blücher's defeat, Wellington had immediately ordered his men to head north with all the haste they could muster, and by the time Napoleon arrived there was nothing left but a cavalry rearguard, Ney having in the meantime failed to do anything to impede the Anglo-Dutch retreat. If Ney was at fault, however, Napoleon committed a still more egregious error. According to all the information he had in his possession, not to mention his own very strong assumptions, the Prussians were in full retreat. Why Napoleon should at this point have ordered Grouchy to take 35,000 men to pursue them therefore beggars belief: if they were out of the fight, they were out of the fight, and logic therefore dictated the concentration of every possible man against Wellington. Still worse, inherent in the decision was the serious risk of a major setback in that Grouchy was being sent to march into the unknown in the face of forces that were potentially three times the size of his own, matters being complicated by the fact that two of the six cavalry divisions that should by rights have been attached to the four corps which constituted his command had been given to Ney in exchange for one of VI Corps' three infantry divisions. Why Napoleon acted as he did is unknown, but one can only conclude that in his innermost self he suddenly lost confidence in his own assumptions and decided that the Prussians might not be out of action after all. Whatever the reason, it was a classic case of half-measures, and one that could not but have the most serious of effects on the campaign.

Meanwhile, said campaign went on. Desperate to make up for lost time, Napoleon now hurried the forces assembled at Quatre Bras northwards. Just as his troops set off, a massive storm that had been threatening all day burst upon the area. That this slowed down movement cannot be doubted, but Wellington's forces were faced by exactly the same conditions as their opponents, and so the vagaries of the weather cannot be blamed for what happened. The fact was that Army of the Netherlands was simply too far ahead to allow the French a chance of inflicting serious damage. By the time that darkness fell, then, the whole of the forces that had fallen back from Quatre Bras were filing into the position which Wellington had already chosen as his fighting ground should he be forced to retire on Brussels. It had not been a good day for the French army, but Napoleon was pleased enough: finally offered the chance of a pitched battle against Wellington, he felt certain of victory.

Was that confidence merited, however? Though he only outnumbered Wellington very slightly, the emperor had far more guns than the British general did, whilst his troops were overall of much higher quality: to this extent, then, victory was by no means beyond his grasp, and that despite the fact that the Army of the Netherlands' positon was extremely strong. Yet it was not just the situation on the prospective battlefield that mattered. Also to be considered was the Prussian army. Badly battered though it was, it had escaped the clutches of a Grouchy hampered by the attitude of his two corps commanders, Vandamme and Gérard, both of whom deeply resented his promotion to the marshalate and elevation to the position of a wing commander, and succeeded in concentrating in its entirety at Wavre, whilst its morale had been greatly boosted by the unexpected reappearance of Blücher, who had been ridden over by his own fleeing cavalry and badly bruised, but saved from capture by a faithful aide. As for Grouchy, he had still not discovered the crucial fact that the entire Prussian army had fallen back parallel with Wellington. True though it was that he had at least spotted that a strong force of Prussians were at Wavre, he was so far away from that town that he had no means of preventing them from joining Wellington whenever they wanted to, not that this dissuaded him from sending a letter to Napoleon assuring him that he would do just this. As the rain continued to pour down, then, the emperor was oblivious of the growing danger in which he stood, whereas Wellington, by contrast, was increasingly confident: not only were the Prussians just ten miles away, but in the small hours he had received a note from Blücher assuring him that he would come to his aid with his entire army. Before the day of 18 June had even dawned, then, the stage was set for a great Allied victory.

THE BATTLEFIELD

The battlefield of Waterloo is commonly envisaged as a simple matter of two parallel ridges with a shallow valley in between. Rather,what one has is a rolling upland pitted with a variety of dips, valleys and indentations, all the high ground being pretty much of a similar elevation. Having emerged from the forest of Soignies and passed through Waterloo, where Wellington had his headquarters, the Brussels–Charleroi highway rose gradually for the two miles that it took to reach the battlefield. After perhaps three-quarters of the distance at a small hamlet known as Mont Saint Jean, a second highway branched off to the south-west in the direction of Nivelles, whereupon the Charleroi highway ascended a steep slope culminating in a long east-west ridge: known, like both the hamlet and the substantial walled farm half-way up the hill, as Mont Saint Jean, it was this that provided Wellington with his main fighting position, and here, too, that the upland we have spoken of begins. At the crest, meanwhile, the highway was crossed at ninety degrees by a lane stretching left and right, the junction being marked by a solitary elm tree. To the east this lane, which ran from the town of Braine l'Alleud two miles to the north-west to the village of Ohain, was lined on both sides by thorn hedges, but to the west the ground was completely open. In the immediate vicinity of the crossroads, meanwhile, both the Charleroi highway and the Ohain road were deeply sunken, the banks rising to as much as ten feet on either side, whilst the forward slope of the ridge to the east of the highway was broken by a prominent knoll, immediately beneath which there was a shallow quarry.

In so far as the ground was concerned, to the east the battlefield was much as it has generally been portrayed: across a shallow valley perhaps half a mile across, a second ridge ran from east to west more-or-less parallel to Wellington's position. However, several hundred yards to the west, rising a little as it did so, a broad ridge jutted out diagonally in the direction of the French lines which it reached in the

The Charleroi highway looking north from the crossroads in the direction of La Belle Alliance. The knoll held by the First Battalion of the Ninety-Fifth can be seen on the left whilst La Haye Sainte nestles in its hollow halfway down the hill. (War Heritage Institute, Brussels)

vicinity of the spot where they were crossed by the Charleroi highway; an important local watershed, this cut the battlefield completely in two and rendered it quite impossible for troops posted to the east of the highway to see what was going on to the west and *vice versa*. To the right of this feature, meanwhile, there was a deep hollow which after half a mile opened out into a broad north-south valley through which ran the dead-straight Nivelles highway, said hollow being crossed diagonally at its eastern end by a lane that ran in a roughly south-easterly direction from the Ohain road and joined the Charleroi highway just a little short of the spot where it reached the French ridge, this last being much more prominent to the east of the highway than it was to the west.

Even this passage does not exhaust the complications offered by the battlefield. As the Charleroi highway rose towards the French positions, then, it passed through a deep cutting occasioned by the presence of a significant swell in the ground (referred to in this work as the intermediate ridge) that ran parallel with the French position for much of its length, and was separated from it on both sides of the watershed mentioned above by a shallow valley. Behind the French right, meanwhile, there was a much deeper depression and then a ridge that connected the upland crossed by the Charleroi highway with a further mass of high ground known as the Heights of Agiers, this last feature thrusting a pronounced shoulder southwards that all but merged with the ridge that marked the French front line and hid a deep re-entrant that angled sharply back uphill from the valley beneath Wellington's positions and was home to the hamlet of Smohain (today La Marache).

From Smohain a lane ran southwards up the side of the re-entrant and at the top of the slope this crossed what was to turn out to be the most important channel of communications on the battlefield, namely a country road that led westward from Wavre to Braine l'Alleud. Having crossed a small river some distance to the west at the village of Lasne, this ascended the heights of Agiers via a thick wood called the Bois de Paris, and then ran due west along the ridge parallel to the French front line to a spot above a second and far more substantial village called Plancenoit situated in a deep valley to the left, at which point it turned sharply to the south and ran uphill to the high ground crossed by the Charleroi highway. Turning sharply to the west once more, having crossed the highway, it then dropped down into the dip behind the intermediate ridge from whence it followed a generally north-westerly course in the direction of the Nivelles road and, ultimately, Braine Alleud. To its left, meanwhile, the ground was undulating, the most important feature being a pronounced hill just beside the Charleroi highway, but it generally sloped upwards to a further area of high ground that marked the northern edge of the upland on which the battle was fought.

With the exception of the need to note that, except for the Bois de Paris, patches of woodland either side of the Wavre–Braine l'Alleud road at the eastern end of the ridge above Plancenoit and various features at Hougoumont and La Haye Sainte (see below), the battlefield was almost treeless, and, further, that it was mostly given over to the cultivation of cereal crops grown in broad open fields, there is little more that needs to be said about the physical geography. As for the human geography, this was limited. Setting aside the two villages and the farm of Mont Saint Jean, on the French side of the battlefield the course of the highway was marked successively by two wayside taverns, of which the first was known as La Belle Alliance and the second owned by a man named De Coster, and, a mile to the south near the further edge of the upland, a house called Rossomme. In the rear of the French left beside the Nivelles road was a large country-house called Mon Plaisir, and, more-or-less opposite it at the other extreme of the battlefield on the slopes overlooking Smohain, the chateau of Frischermont. However, the most important buildings on the battlefield by far were the four complexes that dotted the forward slope of Wellington's position, from east to west these being the farms of La Haye, Papelotte and La Haye Sainte and the chateau of Hougoumont.

Beginning with the first two, these stood side by side a few hundred yards from Smohain, though La Haye was a mere cluster of buildings whilst Papelotte was a stoutly built courtyard farm. Meanwhile, another courtyard farm, screened to its south by a small orchard, La Haye Sainte constituted a compact rectangle built on a north-south axis immediately beside the Charleroi highway perhaps

The farm of Papelotte. Defended throughout the battle by troops from the Duchy of Nassau, despite repeated claims to the contrary it never fell into the hands of Napoleon's forces. (War Heritage Institute, Brussels)

250 yards south of the crossroads. And, finally, situated deep in the hollow beneath the watershed in advance of Wellington's right flank, Hougoumont was a much larger affair than any of the rest, comprising the chateau itself (a three-storey building surrounded by a series of barns, stables and store sheds); a large formal garden protected on its southern and eastern sides by a high wall; a kitchen-garden; two orchards; a paddock; and a large wood that stretched southwards all the way to the summit of the intermediate ridge. Much of the perimeter was surrounded by a dense hedge and ditch, while a further hedge separated the orchard from the paddock.

Hougoumont was linked to the Ohain road by a lane lined by a row of poplars, whilst other lanes besides the ones already mentioned criss-crossed the battlefield in various directions (for example, from Hougoumont to La Belle Alliance; from Papelotte to La Belle-Alliance; from Smohain to Plancenoit; from Plancenoit to the Charleroi highway; and from Rossomme to the Nivelles road), but, though occasionally deeply sunken, particularly in the vicinity of Papelotte, they were to play little role in the battle. With the exception of the Charleroi highway and the Nivelles road, meanwhile, all the roads were mere country lanes with no paving of any sort, the heavy rain therefore meaning that that they were all deep in mud even before the fighting began. Indeed, with the whole of the battlefield composed of a thick clay soil, the going was everywhere at best heavy and, in places, completely impossible.

The view of the Hougoumont estate that confronted Foy's division on the morning of 18 June 1815. Thanks to the intermediate ridge, even the extent of the wood is impossible to gauge. As for the existence of the chateau, this came as a complete surprise to the French army. (War Heritage Institute, Brussels)

THE BATTLE

Although the rain stopped at first light, dawn on 18 June 1815 was a damp and miserable affair, whilst many of the French troops had yet even to reach the field. For some little time, then, there was no chance of anything happening, and it was not in fact till about half-past eleven that the battle began. In consequence, the Army of the Netherlands was able to deploy without the slightest haste, its order of battle showing the British general's mind all too clearly. Thus, believing that the Prussians would arrive very quickly, Wellington left his left flank but thinly held: from the crossroads to Smohain, there were but the equivalent of seven brigades of infantry, of which only two were British, and three brigades of cavalry. By contrast, from the crossroads to the Nivelles road, there were six infantry brigades, of which four were either British or King's German Legion, and seven cavalry brigades, and from the Nivelles road to Braine l'Alleud seven infantry brigades, of which three were either British or King's German Legion, most of the troops in this last section of the line being held well back so as in effect to create a refused flank. Obviously enough, then, it was felt that the real danger rather lay in the relatively open ground in front of Braine l'Alleud, Wellington being so concerned about his right that he posted a further 10,500 men well to the west at Hal in case the emperor should try a wide outflanking movement. Quite why he should have thought this was a possibility, however, it is hard to see, for, even if successful, an attack on his right flank would only drive him towards the Prussians, this being precisely the object which Napoleon was least likely to desire.

In assessing Waterloo, Wellington's many admirers have made much of the strength of the position which he adopted. This last was certainly far from bad, but nor was it impregnable. If the ridge certainly offered protection from artillery fire, not to mention complete concealment, in very few places were its slopes a serious obstacle to movement, while Hougoumont, La Haye Sainte and Papelotte-La Haye were of less use than is sometimes suggested.

Best of all was probably the often neglected Papelotte-La Haye as this offered its defenders an excellent field of fire in all directions, but the value of the other two were more dubious. Situated in a deep hollow and almost entirely masked by trees, Hougoumont was near useless unless troops could hold the outer perimeter, whilst the layout of La Haye Sainte was very inconvenient in that troops trying to defend the orchard at its southern end could neither retire nor be reinforced within any ease for want of any gate or door in the southern wall. Still worse, there were few apertures in the walls on either side; the outer door of the main barn had been taken for firewood; and, unlike at Hougoumont (see below), almost nothing had been done to prepare the buildings for defence. On the bright side, neither position was especially helpful to troops attacking the ridge as they offered no view of the defenders' positions and could easily be pounded by artillery should they be taken, but the keys to victory they most certainly were not, the real importance of both La Haye Sainte and Hougoumont being simply that they denied the French the space they needed for the combined operations that were their best chance of breaking Wellington's line and then only in a sector which was far from uppermost in Napoleon's thoughts.

Contrary to Wellington's expectation, in fact, the emperor was not initially planning to attack his right wing at all: believing that the Prussians were out of the fight though he might, he did not wish to do anything that would increase the chances of the British commander linking up with Blücher. As his troops came up, they were arrayed in a convex line stretching from beyond the Nivelles road to the slopes opposite Papelotte and in this manner placed so as to threaten the whole length of their opponents' position – in brief, the three divisions of Reille's II Corps held the sector from the Nivelles Road to La Belle Alliance and the four of Drouet's I Corps that from La Belle Alliance to Papelotte with their respective light cavalry divisions on their outer flanks, whilst each one of them was backed by three divisions of cavalry with the three divisions of Guard infantry, the two cavalry divisions detached from Grouchy and the severely understrength VI Corps stationed still further back as a central reserve – but the aim was by no means simply a head-on attack, and it is therefore likely that the sheer symmetry of the Army of the North's initial disposition was a trick designed to obscure Napoleon's real intentions (see Map 1). Thus, abjuring the cluttered terrain to the west in favour of the open hillsides to the east, the emperor planned to launch a massive attack on Wellington's left with I Corps – it was no mistake that this was both the largest and the freshest of his formations – whilst keeping back the Guard, VI Corps and most of his cavalry for the final *coup de grâce*. With the benefit of hindsight, of course, it can be argued that an attack on Wellington's left was foolhardy indeed, as it effectively meant that a good half of the French army would in effect be marching into a trap, but it cannot be emphasised strongly enough that on the morning of 18 June, the emperor did not have the slightest reason to believe that Blücher was coming: that there was a strong force of Prussians at Wavre, he knew full well, but Grouchy had only the previous night assured him that he could deal with the problem and that there was no need to worry.

Setting aside a few shots that rang out when some French cavalry chased off a few German infantry who had been sent to garrison Smohain and Frischermont, it was not on the eastern half of the battlefield that the battle began, however. On the contrary, realizing that his great right hook needed to be secured against a spoiling attack, Napoleon sent orders for Reille to dispatch some troops to occupy the extensive wood in his front. This was, of course, the same wood that masked Hougoumont, but the fact that it concealed a strong and well-garrisoned fortified post – unlike at La Haye Sainte, the 1,300-strong garrison, almost all at this point either Hanoverians or Nassauers, had had time to build firing steps, barricade some of the gates and knock extra loopholes in the walls – was entirely lost on Napoleon, for the buildings were entirely invisible to him. This should have made no difference, for, to carry out their orders, Reille's men needed only to seize the wood and the orchard, but in command of the attackers was Napoleon's younger brother, Jérôme. A headstrong and foolish individual who was ever out for glory, having almost literally bumped into the chateau, he resolved on its capture at all costs, and the result was a prolonged struggle that negated the position's value as a firebase and pulled in the bulk of a particularly valuable British Guards brigade, but at the same time came permanently to absorb fully one-half of Reille's corps.

The struggle for Hougoumont was marked by many famous incidents, of which the most well-known is the episode in which a large party of French troops burst in through the north gate, only to be cut down almost to the last man when the gate was forced shut behind them. In the end, however, horrific though it was – towards the end, many of the buildings caught fire with the loss of many wounded who had been sheltering inside – the fight was but a side issue. Far more crucial were events further east. Here Napoleon's aim, as we have seen, was to crush Wellington's left. Available for the assault were the four infantry divisions of Drouet's I Corps, namely those of Quiot, Donzelot, Marcognet and Durutte, but before they were sent forward a sustained attempt was made to soften up the defenders with the three heavy artillery batteries attached to I, II and VI Corps. Together composed of eighteen 12-pounder guns and six heavy howitzers, these pounded the area around the crossroads from La Belle Alliance for more than an hour, but, unbeknownst to the French, they inflicted little damage: not only did many of the projectiles simply bury themselves in the waterlogged ground, but the infantry had been ordered to lie down and the cavalry to dismount. Casualties, then were limited, but this did not mean that the assault was not a major threat. On their left flank the assault forces – some 20,000 men – were supported by a brigade of cuirassiers, while the two divisions in the centre of the array – those of Donzelot and Marcognet – were drawn up in an unusual formation that saw the eight battalions of which they were each composed drawn up in line one behind the other, the idea being that they could match the firepower of any troops who confronted them whilst yet maintaining the manoeuvrability of a column (on either side, by contrast, the divisions of Quiot and Durutte appear to have been deployed in standard brigade or battalion columns of a much more flexible nature; see Map 2).

Drouet's assault, then, was by no means just a matter of brute force. Nor did the careful thought that went into it go unrewarded. First to feel the weight of the assault were the defenders of La Haye Sainte, the rifle-armed Second Light Battalion of the King's German Legion commanded by Major Georg Baring. Overwhelmed by the enemy skirmishers, the soldiers whom Baring had placed to hold the orchard were forced to flee into the open fields to the west where they were succoured by a Hanoverian unit (the Lüneburg light battalion) that had been sent down from the ridge above to cover their retreat. This last decision, however, proved a grievous error: to their horror, the riflemen and Hanoverians alike suddenly found themselves assailed by the cuirassier brigade mentioned above. Being closer to the farm, most of Baring's men managed to make it back inside, but the Hanoverians were completely routed and effectively ceased to exist as a fighting unit. Still worse, a King's German Legion battalion sent forward to cover their retreat (the Eighth Line) was also caught by the French cavalry and driven back with the loss of a colour. On the other side of the farm, meanwhile, things were just as bad: if the troops of Quiot's division were unable to break into the buildings, they did overrun the knoll and quarry a little further up the highroad, the defenders of which – several companies of the first battalion of the famous 'Ninety-Fifth Rifles' – fled in disorder, whilst the sudden appearance of cuirassiers on the slopes above La Haye Sainte caused a panic that saw the whole battalion fall back to the rear. Only once they had breasted the knoll and reached the sunken Ohain road did Quiot's men experience any check. Setting aside the Ninety-Fifth, the front line of the defenders was composed of the Dutch brigade of Willem van Bylandt. Having suffered very heavy casualties at Quatre Bras, the troops concerned were in no condition to resist an assault by four French divisions and, after a brief fight, they too turned and fled. Behind them, however, were the two veteran British infantry brigades of Sir James Kempt and Sir Denis Pack, and, notwithstanding the terrible losses they too had endured at Quatre Bras, these immediately launched a counter-attack. On the right, under the personal direction of their divisional commander, Sir Thomas Picton, Kempt's three remaining battalions (the Ninety-Fifth appears not yet to have rallied from its earlier disorder) scored an immediate success in that, suddenly leaping up from behind the crest of the ridge, they checked Quiot's division with a single volley followed by a bayonet charge. That said, Picton himself was shot dead, while, to the left, Pack's brigade had been less fortunate. Thus, advancing to attack Marcognet's division, it was thrown back by a massive volley and completely checked (see Map 3).

For a moment, then, it looked as if the French had broken through, but there now followed one of the most dramatic episodes in the battle. Behind Picton's troops was the heavy cavalry brigade of Sir William Ponsonby, whilst across the Charleroi highway in a similar position was that of Sir Edward Somerset (by chance composed of one English, one Irish and one Scottish regiment, the former quickly nicknamed itself 'the Union Brigade', just as the fact that the latter was largely drawn from the Life Guards and Royal Horse Guards gained it the sobriquet of the 'Household Brigade'). Apparently at the personal initiative of the commander of the British cavalry, Lord Uxbridge, these two brigades launched a dramatic charge that took them through the crumbling Allied front line and into the oncoming enemy (see Map 4). Initially, success was complete: taken by surprise, the French recoiled in disorder and in many instances turned to flee altogether, the spoils of the victorious cavalry including two eagles and perhaps 3,000 prisoners. However, drunk on glory, the two British brigades now got out of control, galloping down into the low ground below Wellington's position, and in some instances even getting up onto the intermediate ridge where they rode down a number of I Corps' divisional batteries, these last having advanced to occupy the obvious position which it offered. The result was disaster: French cavalry under Travers, Lefebvre-Desnouettes and Jacquinot moved against the milling horsemen from right, left and centre alike, and slaughtered them in great numbers, less than half their number eventually making it back to their original positions and many of them only doing so at all thanks to a timely charge on the part of the British light cavalry brigade of Sir John Vandeleur near Papelotte.

The survivors of the brigades of Ponsonby (himself among the dead) and Somerset were for the time being out of the battle, but through their actions they had thwarted what was probably Napoleon's best chance of victory. Nevertheless, the emperor was far from finished. On the right Durutte's division had not been much affected by Uxbridge's counter-attack, and had therefore continued to press forward, thereby inaugurating what became a long and bitter battle for La Haye and Papelotte. Entirely composed of Dutch and Germans who had lost many men at Quatre Bras, the defenders were pressed ever backwards and were eventually driven from La Haye altogether, the French ruler therefore resolving to exploit their success by sending in the VI Corps of Georges Mouton which had hitherto been sitting out the battle far to the rear in the vicinity of Rossomme, the idea being that this would push down through the valley in which Smohain was situated and swing round the Allied left flank.

Also given the support of the two cavalry divisions detached from Grouchy's command, such a move seemed to promise every success, but until it could be brought to fruition there was a major problem in that much of Napoleon's front line was in complete disarray: on the left Reille continued to be bogged down at Hougoumont, while on the right the three divisions caught by the British cavalry were still badly shaken.

It is in this context that what happened next has to be understood. In brief, virtually all the available cavalry were flung into a massive assault on Wellington's right-centre. According to the traditional version, this was the work of a Ney mistakenly convinced that the Anglo-Dutch forces were retreating, but all the evidence suggests that the author of what happened was rather Napoleon. Given the emperor's determination to shift the blame elsewhere, we can only speculate as to why he acted as he did, but the most probable explanation is that he was concerned that, with much of his army shaken and off-balance, there was a serious danger that his opponent might launch a general assault. As massed cavalry charges had proved a very effective way of staving off disaster in some of his earlier battles, the remedy was obvious, and thus it was that, while as many French guns as possible continued to pound the Allied line, about four o'clock the first of the units involved moved forward along the axis of the watershed ridge.

There followed extraordinary scenes. Advancing on Wellington's line at a pace no better than a lumbering trot (the ground was far too waterlogged for anything else), the cuirassiers of Milhaud and Kellermann, not mention to mention the two divisions of cavalry belonging to the Imperial Guard, crowded into the narrow front offered by the gap between La Haye Sainte and Hougoumont under a hail of artillery fire. Reaching the crest, they overran most of the batteries which lined it, but then hit an insuperable obstacle. Thus, all the way from Hougoumont to the Charleroi highway, the Allied infantry had been deployed in two lines of squares. So long as the defenders held their nerve, such formations were impervious to cavalry, and the result was that the horsemen milled about them in confusion whilst at the same time suffering heavy losses to musketry. Nor was this an end to their travails, for the squares were backed by numerous regiments of British and Dutch cavalry, and these counter-charged the discomforted French horse and drove them back over the crest, only immediately to gallop back to their original positions to reform.

For the next two hours the same process was repeated over and over again with the increasingly desperate French cavalry losing heavy casualties each time they returned to the charge and achieving almost nothing in return for their efforts. That said, the defenders did not go unpunished: forced to remain in square and in some cases deprived of the shelter of the ridge (the worst sufferers here were Adam's brigade, this last having been deployed in the open fields to the east of Hougoumont in an effort to safeguard communications with the chateau), in between the French charges they suffered very badly from artillery fire. Had a mass of infantry been available to follow up the cavalry attacks, then, something more might have been obtained, but when the division and a half of Reille's corps that were the only troops available in the sector for such a task were finally ordered forward, they were flung back with enormous losses.

At this point in the battle, Napoleon still possessed substantial reserves in the form of the three divisions of infantry belonging to the Imperial Guard. That they were not forthcoming brings us to a dramatic development in the narrative. As we have seen, during the night Wellington had received assurances from Blücher that he would march to his assistance with his entire army at first light. Completely unmolested by Grouchy, who was still many miles to the south, the Prussian commander proceeded to do just this, but a variety of issues, including, not least, the terrible state of the only roads available, slowed his rate of march dramatically, and it was therefore well past four o'clock before the first Prussian troops reached even the Bois de Paris. Contrary to all the usual accounts of the battle, however, the French were completely unaware of their presence, the fact that Mouton's corps was on hand to deal with the new arrivals being pure happenstance.

In consequence, when Prussian forces – the advanced guard of Bülow's IV Corps – suddenly emerged from the Bois de Paris at about half past four in the afternoon, it came as a complete shock, so much so, indeed, that Napoleon initially put the firing that suddenly erupted on his extreme right down to an accidental clash between Grouchy's men and those of Mouton. In the circumstances, then, the latter did extremely well in that they managed to form a solid defensive line between the woods flanking the road from Lasne to Braine l'Alleud, while the various units of light cavalry that had been attached to them launched a series of charges designed to slow down the progress of the enemy. However, tough and determined though Mouton was, he could not hope to prevail against the ever-greater numbers by which he was faced, and, with substantial Prussian forces beginning to push through the low ground to his right, he was forced to conduct a fighting retreat that eventually took him to a position running north from Plancenoit (see Maps 5–6). Securing this last place with one of his four infantry brigades, he then turned at bay, but the Prussians soon drove his men from the outskirts of the village, thereby creating a real crisis: were Plancenoit to fall, the whole French position would become untenable.

It was this fresh danger that prevented Napoleon from making any use of the sacrifice of so many of his cavalry, for, rather than sending the three divisions of Imperial Guard infantry that constituted his last reserve to attack Wellington, he was forced to use the whole of the Young Guard to drive back the Prussians. This they did with aplomb, but, having once advanced into Plancenoit, they could not be withdrawn, Bülow's men showing not the slightest sign of slackening the pressure.

If help was at last at hand, the Army of the Netherlands was barely aware that this was the case: situated in a deep hollow as it was, Plancenoit was all but invisible from Mont Saint Jean. Indeed, the situation of Wellington's forces now deteriorated dramatically. Having personally taken part in the cavalry charges, Ney now organized a fresh assault on La Haye Sainte. Unfortunately, successively reinforced though it may have been, the garrison was running short of ammunition, and in consequence it was soon overwhelmed. Much encouraged, the troops who had driven it out pressed forward to the crest of the ridge and assailed the defenders with heavy fire, while they also for a second time gained the knoll held by the Ninety-Fifth and in addition brought up a number of guns, including some that they stationed on the highest point of the watershed in a position in which they could wreak terrible damage on the defenders. Frantic to redeem the situation, the inexperienced Prince of Orange ordered Christian von Ompteda's King's German Legion infantry brigade to retake La Haye Sainte, but only one battalion – the Fifth Line –

was still in a state to fight, and this was immediately cut down by a force of cuirassiers that had gone unperceived in the thick smoke that now cloaked the whole battlefield, Ompteda himself being killed by French infantry in the farm's kitchen garden. In short, Wellington's army was in serious difficulties, but the decisive blow that might have settled the issue never came, for, when an exultant Ney sent to Napoleon for fresh troops, the emperor refused point-blank to send him any, and that despite the fact that he still had the two divisions of infantry of the Old Guard within a few yards of his position at La Belle Alliance (for much of the day, he had remained far in the rear at his command post overlooking the farmhouse of Rossomme, but at some point in the afternoon he had come forward to observe the progress of the battle at first hand).

The decision not to send in the Guard at this point was fatal, for a concentrated blow might well have broken through and forced Wellington to withdraw. Yet, once again, Napoleon appears to have lost his nerve, backing away from the final gamble that was his only hope of obtaining even a marginal victory (that it would be no more than this was guaranteed by the fact that his cavalry were no longer in any state to pursue Wellington). Instead, he became bogged down in organizing a counter-attack by a mere two battalions at Plancenoit, and it was not until another hour had passed that he finally relented and released a part of the Guard to follow up Ney's success (see Maps 7–9). By now, however, it was almost certainly too late, for Wellington had rushed in his last reserve – the Dutch division commanded by David Chassé previously stationed at Braine l'Alleud – to shore up his centre as well as bringing in some of the forces that had hitherto been guarding his left. Still worse, only ten battalions of the fifteen that might have been employed in the attack actually took part in it, whilst even they lost their cohesion as they advanced across the muddy and much encumbered ground, and therefore struck Wellington's line at three different places and anything but in unison. Supported by the troops who had seized La Haye Sainte and led by Ney himself, the right-hand-most elements of the attack succeeded in driving back or putting to flight altogether a number of units that had been hard hit in the course of the day, but even they were thrown back by the fresh troops of Chassé, while the rest of the assault force did not even achieve that much in the way of success, but was routed by a classic British combination of volleys and bayonet charges, the *coup de grâce* being delivered by the Fifty-Second Foot which wheeled forward from its position on the ridge and took the last French troops still in the fight in the flank. Seeing his advantage, Wellington immediately ordered the right wing of his army to advance and large numbers of troops therefore swept forwards towards La Belle Alliance. Their spirit utterly crushed at the sight of the Guard fleeing in panic, all the French troops in the area broke and ran, the only resistance of any sort being put up by three battalions of the Guard that had unaccountably been left in the rear.

According to British accounts, it was the Guard's defeat that shattered Napoleon's army. This, however, is only partially true. Due to the configuration of the ground, few of the French troops who were fighting to the east of the Charleroi highway had any view of the western half of the battlefield, and, if they turned and fled at virtually the same moment in time, it was for an entirely different reason. Thus, for hours many more Prussian troops had been pouring onto the battlefield, but the majority of these had been fed into the fight for Plancenoit. At length, however, a further force that had marched from Wavre by a different route, namely the corps commanded by Hans von Ziethen, reached Smohain, where it had been temporarily delayed by a firefight with some German troops who had managed to creep back into the village and mistook the blue-coated Prussians for fresh enemies. The noise of this fighting greatly cheered the French troops in the vicinity: not surprisingly, they assumed that Grouchy, who in fact had ignored the sound of the guns at Waterloo and continued to follow the orders that he had received to march on Wavre where he became engaged in a bitter battle with a Prussian rearguard, had come (indeed, desperate to spur his troops on to one last effort, Napoleon had spread the idea that Grouchy had arrived across the entire battlefield). All too soon, however, delight turned to dismay: at almost exactly the same time that the Guard was being routed at the other end of the line, Ziethen's men launched a massive attack that immediately broke Durutte's division and soon saw thousands of infantry and cavalry heading for La Belle Alliance.

Given that Plancenoit finally fell at around the same time, all was now lost for Napoleon, who, after a short delay, left the battlefield in his personal carriage. The few units of the Guard that were still intact tried to cover the retreat, but the army as a whole streamed southwards in a state of complete panic. Meanwhile, despite the myth-making with which the battle has been surrounded, there was no heroic last stand: to purloin a famous phrase supposed to have been uttered by a senior officer of the Guard as the rest of the army collapsed, the Guard neither died nor surrendered, but rather was swept away in the flood.

So ended Waterloo. At a minimum of 18,000 for the Allies and 24,000 for the French, casualties had been enormous. Yet had it all been anything other than a glorious irrelevance? Probably not: even had Napoleon triumphed in the Waterloo campaign, there would have been no change in the political situation, and it may therefore safely be assumed that the war would have gone on, and that the Allied superiority in numbers would have prevailed in the end. That said, Waterloo did ensure that the war came to an end with a minimum of bloodshed: there was some minor fighting as the Allies closed in on Paris, but Napoleon had been so comprehensively beaten that he was left no choice but to abdicate, the provisional government that had taken over power in his stead thereupon promptly rushing to secure the best terms that it could. With the erstwhile emperor soon on his way to Saint Helena, truly it was the end of an era.

TOUR 1: GRAND WATERLOO

Time: five hours (breaks excluded); at least eight hours if visits to the Mémorial 1815, the Panorama, the Butte du Lion and Hougoumont are added to the itinerary. Going: mostly metalled roads or well-maintained tracks, the latter with some patches that may be waterlogged in wet weather; moderate slopes with occasional steeper stretches (see Map 1).

1. Begin the tour at the display panel in the south-western angle of the crossroads (A).

A. The Crossroads
The spot where the visitor is situated marked the centre of Wellington's line and is, by tradition, his principal headquarters

Wellington surveys the battlefield at the head of his staff from the vicinity of the crossroads. Whereas Napoleon ran the battle from the rear of his army, his British counterpart chose rather to superintend operations in person. (War Heritage Institute, Brussels)

and point of observation. In 1815 the very busy highway was the main route from Brussels to Charleroi, while the side-road crossing it at right angles was the Ohain road (i.e. the sunken lane that for most of its length marked Wellington's front line). Lamentably, however, this crucial spot is the most altered section of the battlefield and one of the least rewarding viewpoints that it has to offer. The solitary elm tree that stood in the south-western angle was cut down in 1817; all the northern lip of the Ohain road between the Charleroi highway and the Butte de Lion was scraped away to provide the earth needed for said monument; the cluster of buildings at the crossroads was not there in 1815 (ditto the trees lining the main road); and still more clutter is added by the so-called Hanoverian, Gordon and Belgian memorials. However, some impression of the original ground level may be derived from the mound on which the Gordon monument stands, while the slope down to La Haye Sainte – the farm beside the main road 300 yards to the south – remains surprisingly steep: although the distance is very short indeed, the crossroads is at least on a level with the farmhouse roof; in 1815 it is probable that the inclination of the slope rose very sharply, thereby creating something approaching a natural rampart: advantageous enough when the Ohain road marked the front line, following the fall of La Haye Sainte French skirmishers were able to use it as a fire-base from which they inflicted heavy casualties on the troops still holding the sector.

Basil Jackson, aide-de-camp to Sir William de Lancey:
    As few can have any idea of the number of persons usually attached to the headquarters of a large army, it may be as well to state that the Duke's tail at Waterloo comprised at least forty officers. There was his personal staff consisting of his military secretary and six or eight *aides de camp,* the Adjutant and Quartermaster-Generals, each with a suite of half a dozen officers, [and] the commanding officers of engineers and artillery with their following. Besides our own people, we had Generals Alava, Muffling and Vincent, attended by their *aides de camp,* so that we formed an imposing cavalcade . . . Wherever there was an attack, thither went

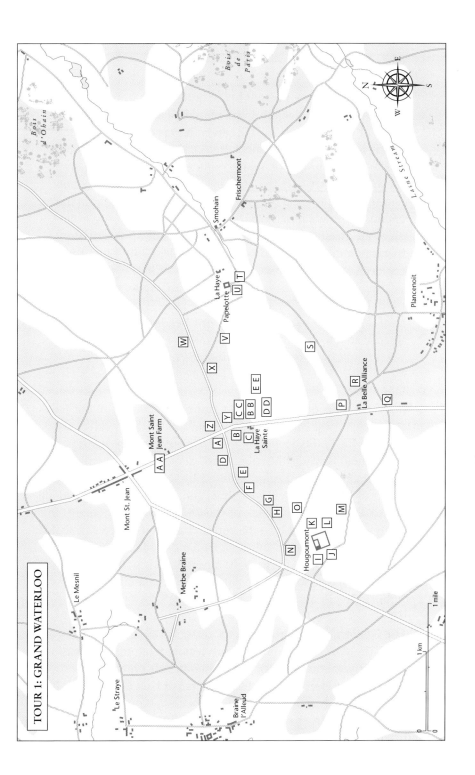

TOUR 1: GRAND WATERLOO

the Duke, exposing himself to the hottest fire . . . Indeed, his escaping without a wound was marvellous. On one occasion especially, I trembled for his safety. It was during an attack on the left of La Haye Sainte between three and four o'clock, when he remained for many minutes exposed to a heavy fire of musketry. All the staff except a single *aide de camp* had received a signal to keep back in order not to attract the enemy's fire: we remained, therefore, under the brow of the elevated ground, and, the better to keep out of observation, dismounted. As I looked over my saddle, I could just trace the outlines of the Duke and his horse amid the smoke . . . bearing a resemblance to the statue in Hyde Park when partially shrouded by fog, while the balls – and they came thickly – hissed harmlessly over our heads. It was a time of intense anxiety, for, had the Duke fallen, Heaven only knows what might have been the result of the fight.[1]

2. Take the track that parallels the Charleroi highway and follow it along the line of trees to the Gordon memorial. In the fields immediately to the right took place several of the most dramatic episodes of the battle, including the charge of the right-hand part of the Household Brigade, the counter-attack of the Fifth Line Battalion of the King's German Legion ordered by the Prince of Orange in the wake of the fall of La Haye Sainte, and, most dramatically of all, the second phase of the attack of the Old and Middle Guard, this last only being repelled by a desperate charge on the part of Dutch troops drawn from the Third Netherlands Infantry Division of General David Chassé. To the left, meanwhile, it will be noted that the highway has to ascend the slope by dint of a cutting: this was both much deeper and much narrower in 1815.

B. The Gordon Memorial

Erected in 1817 by his family and restored on many occasions subsequently, this monument commemorates Sir Alexander Gordon, an aristocratic officer of the Third Regiment of Foot Guards who had served Wellington as one of his principal *aides de camp* throughout the Peninsular War. Struck from his horse by a cannonball while trying to rally a battalion of Brunswick troops during the attack of the Guard, he was carried to the farm of Mont Saint Jean where his right leg was amputated by a Doctor John Hume late in the evening. Taken from thence to Waterloo, he was installed in Wellington's own bed in the inn that had constituted the Duke's headquarters the night before, but died of loss of blood at half-past three in the morning. Told of his death, Wellington 'said . . . in a voice tremulous with emotion, "Well, thank God, I don't know what it is to lose a battle; but certainly nothing can be more painful than to gain one with the loss of so many of one's friends."' Touching though such details are, however, the view from the monument is no better than it is from the crossroads and in some respects even worse.

> *August von Kruse, colonel, First Regiment of Nassau*:
> Napoleon's Guard reached the plateau with our infantry withdrawing only 100 paces. A violent fire fight broke out, and showing as much courage as foresight, the Crown Prince . . . attempted to put an end to it with a bayonet charge. For this honour he thought of the Nassauers. Thus, he brought up the second battalion and led it in column. The remainder of the first battalion joined up with them and the attack was carried out with great bravery. I saw . . . the French Guard start to waver when, perhaps because the Prince of Orange was wounded, a wave of panic hit the young soldiers, and at the moment of their greatest victory, the battalion fell into confusion and retreated. The remaining battalions in the first line soon followed, leaving only small bodies of brave men on the plateau. I had the *landwehr* battalion and the remainder of the second battalion join them, but in such a way that the enemy fire could have little effect on them.[2]

3. Return to the crossroads and turn left. After a hundred yards a track will be found running downhill towards La Haye Sainte. A notice at the gate declares the land to be private, but, so long as they make no disturbance, keep to the track and do not approach the buildings – over the years, the owner and his family have been much bothered by large groups of visitors invading their privacy – it is probably all right for small parties and, more especially, individuals, to enter the area. Walking down the track even a few

The fields south-west of La Haye Sainte. It was in this area that the Luneburg battalion was wiped out by Dubois' cuirassiers. (Author's collection)

yards produces a much better view, especially towards La Belle Alliance (the white building silhouetted by the clump of trees on the southern skyline). At the end of the track, it swings towards the farm buildings: do not follow it any further, but, instead, carry straight on towards the small patch of rising ground at the edge of the field to the right.

C. La Haye Sainte (western face)
From this spot a good impression may be obtained of the rolling nature of the slopes beneath Wellington's centre. Meanwhile, take especial note of the rising ground in front: a cross-ridge running diagonally from the area of the Butte de Lion to La Belle Alliance, this completely blocks the view towards Hougoumont and also offered perfect cover for the cuirassier brigade that destroyed the Luneburg battalion when it was sent to succour the defenders of the farm during the attack of I Corps in the early afternoon. As for La Haye Sainte, the spot offers an excellent view of its western face, though it will be observed that the lack of windows meant

that the number of men who could fire was very limited, even granted the fact that the doors at the western end of the barn (the southernmost of the buildings) had been torn down for firewood. When the farm was finally assaulted, this spot was the scene of particularly desperate fighting and the gateway is described as having been literally barricaded with the bodies of the dead and wounded. To the right, the hedged orchard that extended the property to the south is no more (though, at the time of writing, a replacement for the orchard, at least, is springing up). Move to the outer edge of the new orchard and it will become clear that from this spot the garrison would have had an excellent field of fire over much of the centre of the battlefield, though the trees and cottages that line the road mean that it is difficult to appreciate just how good it was.

> *Georg Baring, major, Second Light Battalion, King's German Legion*:
> I was sent to the farm of La Haye Sainte in order to occupy it. We built defensive positions during the remainder of the daylight hours and as far as the rain allowed us, and laid down in expectation of an attack the next morning. The farm . . . lies, as is well known, close by the side of the high road which lead from Brussels to Genappe . . . The dwelling house, barn and stables were surrounded by a rectangular wall, forming a court in the interior. Towards the enemy's side was an orchard surrounded by a hedge, and in the rear was a kitchen garden, bounded by a small wall towards the road, but on the other side by a hedge. Two doors and three large gates led from the court to the exterior, but, of these, that of the barn had been unfortunately broken and burned by the troops. The battalion consisted of six companies, which did not number 400 men: I posted three companies in the garden, two in the buildings and one in the garden. Important as the possession of this farm undoubtedly was, the means of defending it were very insufficient, and, besides, I was ordered, immediately on arriving there, to send off the pioneers of the battalion to Hougoumont, so that I had not even a hatchet, for unfortunately, the mule that carried the entrenching tools was lost the day before.[3]

The reverse slope looking north from the Ohain Road. To the right can be seen the farm of Mont Saint Jean. (Author's collection)

4. Return along the track to Ohain road, noting on the way how effective the reverse slope would have been and, in particular, how little warning the cuirassiers who had just ridden down the Luneburg battalion would have had of the charge of the Household Brigade. At the Ohain road cross over to the other side and ascend the low bank to the level of the field. Note that a little further along this is as much as ten feet above the level of the carriage-way: in 1815 a similar bank would have run along the southern side of the road.

D. The Reverse Slope

From here an excellent view can be obtained of La Belle Alliance and the whole sweep of the French centre. To the north, meanwhile, the broad field stretching down to the motorway is much the same as it was in 1815 and marks the position occupied by the Household Brigade prior to its famous counter-attack, as well, of course, as a number of other units, including most notably the Dutch heavy cavalry brigade of General Tripp. At the same time, standing on the verge of the Ohain road, the visitor is at the spot which marks the final French advance's greatest success: it was here that the second wave of the Guard routed the remnants of the brigades of Christian von Ompteda, Friedrich von Kielmansegg and Sir Colin Halkett (the first King's German Legion, the second Hanoverian, and the third British) and, immediately afterwards, the Brunswick contingent and the independent First Regiment of Nassau, the defeat of the latter unit being in part precipitated by the wounding of the Prince of Orange. Finally, a short walk along the hedge beside the Hotel 1815 will show both how well the reverse slope operated and also, if it is at all wet, how heavy-going the battlefield was on the day of the battle: after even a few yards, the visitor will find their footwear caked with a thick layer of mud that is all but impossible to remove and inclined to make walking very difficult.

Anonymous British officer:
   To say that, where the battle raged most furiously, the ground was actually covered with the dead and the dying; that arms and appointments of all sorts were scattered throughout the field; that numbers of horses were seen in every direction, some only having lost their riders, others smarting under wounds and wild from pain . . . that the cavalry of the enemy and our own, repeatedly charging over the same ground, trampling indiscriminately on the wounded of both armies . . . brought ten-fold sufferings upon the miserable men whose wounds were too severe to allow of their seeking safety in the rear; and that the terrors of the scene were heightened by the constant bursting of shells, and, at times, even the explosion of . . . an ammunition wagon, is but to give . . . a faint idea of what actually took place during those tremendous hours of destruction and death, the impression of which can never be effaced from those who had the good fortune to escape. On the fall of the hill behind our line, every hole, every little irregularity of ground, was filled with the wounded whose strength had enabled them to crawl thus far in hopes to find shelter from the short and shells of the enemy. And here, horrible to relate, were often to be seen followers of the army, both men and women, venturing so far and risking their lives for plunder. Even some soldiers appeared, forgetting their honour in their thirst after pillage, and actually stripping their companions almost before life was extinct.[4]

La Haye Sainte viewed from the Ohain Road. It was in this area that the second echelon of the Guard struck Halkett's brigade. Meanwhile, the ground had also been much fought over earlier in the battle: the slope leading up to the Ohain Road had been the scene of the destruction of the Fifth Line Battalion of the King's German Legion following the fall of La Haye Sainte, and, before that still, it had been crossed by the Household Brigade in the first stages of the British cavalry attack. (Author's collection)

5. Taking care not to trample any crops, walk along the bank above the Ohain Road towards the cluster of buildings grouped at the foot of the Butte du Lion. It was across this stretch of road that the Household Brigade charged the French cuirassiers who had ascended the ridge in support of Drouet and just destroyed the Hanoverian Luneburg battalion. Just before the buildings are reached, a particularly good view may be obtained of the positions held by the French centre.

E. Halkett's Position
Situated at the very foot of the Butte du Lion, the area beside which the visitor is now standing witnessed one of the great crises of the battle, indeed, perhaps the greatest crisis of the battle. Having already seen much fighting during the French cavalry charges, in the attack of the Imperial Guard the slopes to the left were ascended by the second echelon of the French assault force, namely the First

Battalion of the Third Regiment of Foot Grenadiers, the Fourth Regiment of Foot Grenadiers and the Second Battalion of the Second Regiment of Foot Grenadiers (note that, despite habitual references to the attack of the Old Guard, both the first two units were drawn not from the Old Guard, but rather the hastily improvised Middle Guard, essentially several battalions of Guard grenadiers and *chasseurs* flung together from men who had been disbanded in 1814 but had now returned to the colours). Facing them were only the depleted remnants of the brigades of Ompteda, Kielmansegg and Sir Colin Halkett but these had suffered terribly in the course of the day and now fled in disorder. An attempt to plug the gap with the Brunswick contingent and the First Regiment of Nassau breaking down in confusion, the French would therefore beyond doubt have broken through had it not been for Detmers' brigade of Chassé's Third Netherlands Infantry Division, this striking diagonally across the crest of the ridge through the area occupied by the present-day Hameau du Lion and sending the three French battalions fleeing back towards La Belle Alliance.

> *Johannes Koch, captain, Seventeenth Battalion, Netherlands Militia*: We advanced on the enemy at attack speed. To keep it together, the colonel was to the right and I to the left of the column . . . The artillery that was accompanying the column caught the enemy properly with canister, and then we attacked with the bayonet . . . Our losses were considerable: I well remember a woman who had not wanted to leave her husband and had marched with him in his company being shot in half, together with an officer. At the same time a shell exploded in the midst of our drummers and fifers; almost none of them being left alive, the drum-major hung a drum around his neck and beat the attack himself.[5]

6. Return to the Ohain road and turn right into the Hameau du Lion.

F. Hameau du Lion
The cluster of buildings at the foot of the Butte du Lion is known as the Hameau du Lion. Visitors might be amused at the caution displayed by the café/restaurant across the road from the mound: housed in the

building which was the battlefield's very first museum and visitor centre, namely Edward Cotton's Waterloo Hotel, this simultaneously proclaims itself to be 'Le Wellington' and 'Le Bivouac de l'Empereur'! Less amusing is the statue of Napoleon that stands in its forecourt: it is not the emperor who should be commemorated at this spot but the Dube of Wellington. To the left, meanwhile, the Rotunda houses the famous 'Panorama', this being a somewhat misleading depiction of the French cavalry charges. As for the 141-foot-high Butte du Lion, thrown up in 1826 to glorify the Dutch part in the battle, this offers a view that is oddly disappointing: certainly the whole of the battlefield can be seen at once, but the ground appears much smoother than is actually the case. On the whole, then, if time is short, it is better to spend it in the 'Mémorial du Waterloo', the brand-new museum opened for the bicentenary. In the course of its construction a complete skeleton of a soldier of the King's German's Second Line Battalion was discovered, and, controversially perhaps, this is now on display in a prominent position in one of the galleries. A hunchback, the man had been killed by a musket ball that struck him in the chest, and was subsequently identified as 23-year-old Friedrich Brandt. The unit he was serving with only coming within musket range of the French while in the vicinity of Hougoumont in the later part of the afternoon, it can be assumed that he was carried to the rear after he had fallen, only to die at some improvised aid station.

Thomas Morris, private, Seventy-Third Regiment of Foot:
Hitherto we had only acted against cavalry, but now Napoleon was leading up his infantry in masses, and, as our brigade was literally cut to pieces, the remnant formed up in line four-deep. But the French infantry that were advancing were now so overwhelming in numbers that we were forced to retire. While doing so, General Halkett received a ball through his cheek and, falling from his horse, was taken to the rear. The fire from the French infantry was so tremendous that our brigade divided and sought shelter behind some banks . . . Captain Garland, on whom the command of the regiment now devolved . . . invited us to follow him in an attack upon about 3,000 of the French infantry. About a dozen of us responded to the call and such was the destructive fire to which we were exposed, that we had

not advanced beyond six or seven paces before every one of the party, except me and my brother, was either killed or wounded.[6]

7. From the Rotunda take the track that follows the hedge enclosing the Butte du Lion. This track marks the front line of Wellington's right-centre and, in particular, the line occupied by the squares formed by the British brigades of Halkett and Maitland during the cavalry charges. The fields to the right were occupied by the Allied cavalry and saw much fighting, those enemy horsemen who managed to get past the squares being repeatedly counter-charged and driven back over the ridge, whilst the lane led to the hamlet of Merbe Braine and with it the positions initially occupied by the divisions of Chassé and Clinton. It will be noticed that for some distance the road is raised above the field to the right, the result being that in effect it runs along an embankment: this is mentioned in several accounts as having been utilized by the troops as a source of cover immediately prior to the final French assault. Continue along the lane till the visitor reaches a memorial stone to one Augustine de Mulder.

G. The De Mulder Memorial
An officer of the Fifth Cuirassiers wounded at Eylau, Aspern-Essling and Hanau who stayed on in the French army after the fall of Napoleon in 1814, De Mulder was of Belgian origins, and, not just that, but a native of nearby Braine l'Alleud. However, the presence of De Mulder, and, not just him, but a number of other Belgian officers, in the ranks of the French forces, should not be taken as evidence that the Belgians were unreliable in 1815. Whilst young men like De Mulder who had forged a career in the French army may have chosen to stay on in its ranks in 1814 and then to have rallied to the cause of Napoleon, few Belgians serving in the Dutch army deserted to him, while Belgian units served with more distinction in the campaign than they have generally been credited with.

Thomas Morris, private, Seventy-Third Regiment of Foot:
     A considerable number of French cuirassiers made their appearance on the rising ground just in our front . . . and came at a gallop down upon us. Their intrepid bearing was well calculated . . . to inspire a feeling of dread. None of

them under six feet, defended by helmets and corselets made pigeon-breasted to throw off the balls . . . they looked so truly formidable that I thought we could not have the slightest chance with them. They came up rapidly until within about ten or twelve paces of the square when our rear ranks poured into them a well-directed fire which put them into confusion, and they retired: the two front ranks, kneeling, then discharged their pieces at them . . . The next square to us was charged at the same time, and, being unfortunately broken into, retired in confusion . . . but the Lifeguards, coming up, the French in their turn were obliged to retrograde . . . About this time a large shell fell just in front of us, and, while the fuse was burning out, we wondered how many of us it would destroy. When it burst . . . seventeen men were killed or wounded by it: the portion which came to my share was a piece of rough cast-iron about the size of a horse-bean which took up its lodging in my left cheek; the blood ran down copiously inside my clothes and made me rather uncomfortable.[7]

8. Continue along the lane to a memorial stone marking the position occupied by Captain Alexander Mercer's troop of the Royal Horse Artillery. Note that it is only when one gets beyond the memorial stone that Hougoumont comes into sight, this being a situation that would not have been so very different in 1815.

H. Mercer's Position.
Composed of five 9-pounder guns and one 5.5in howitzer, Mercer's troop was moved to the position the visitor is currently occupying in the course of the afternoon, and distinguished itself during the cavalry charges by (literally) sticking to its guns throughout and flaying the oncoming horsemen with discharge after discharge of canister (the usual practice was for the gunners to abandon their pieces and take shelter in the nearest square). A gifted writer, its commander later published one of the most detailed British accounts of the battle, albeit one marred by a considerable degree of embellishment and inaccuracy. From the memorial stone, meanwhile, the view to the south is much the same as it was in 1815. Note, however, how the cross-ridge jutting out in the direction of La Belle Alliance obscures

Mercer's monument (note La Belle Alliance in the distance) looking along the watershed. French horse artillery posted in the middle distance inflicted heavy losses though Mercer's battery escaped much more lightly than he suggests in his memoirs. Also false, meanwhile, is the story that at the end of the battle it was fired on by Prussian guns which had supposedly occupied the ridge ahead. (Author's collection)

THIS STONE MARKS THE LAST POSITION
OF G TROOP ROYAL HORSE ARTILLERY
COMMANDED BY CAPTAIN A.C. MERCER
DURING THE BATTLE OF WATERLOO
18 JUNE 1815. FROM HERE THE TROOP
TOOK A CONSPICUOUS PART IN DEFEATING
THE ATTACKS OF THE FRENCH CAVALRY.

the view in the direction of La Haye Sainte whilst at the same time affording the French horse artillery brought up to support, first the cavalry and later the Imperial Guard, a position from which they could do terrible damage to the whole span of Wellington's centre-right (including, not least Mercer's battery). Finally, the brigades of Halkett and Maitland having closed up to the left and formed into line four deep, it was in the area between this spot and the road to Merbe Braine that the five battalions of the Guard that constituted the first wave of the last assault were famously repelled by a dramatic bayonet charge orchestrated by Wellington himself.

Alexander Mercer, captain, Royal Horse Artillery:
We suddenly became sensible of a most destructive flanking fire from a battery which had come, the Lord knows how, and established itself on a knoll somewhat higher than the ground we stood on, and only about 400 or 500 yards a little

in advance of our left flank. The rapidity and precision of this fire were quite appalling. Every shot, almost, took effect, and I certainly expected we should all be annihilated. Our horses and limbers, being a little retired down the slope, had hitherto been somewhat under cover from the direct fire in front, but this plunged right amongst them, knocking them down by pairs and creating horrible confusion. The drivers could hardly extricate themselves from one dead horse before another fell or perhaps themselves. The saddle-bags in many instances were torn from the horses' backs and their contents scattered over the field. One shell I saw explode under the two finest wheel horses in the troop: down they dropped . . . The whole livelong day had cost us nothing like this. Our gunners too – the few left fit for duty of them – were so exhausted that they were unable to run the guns up after firing; consequently at every round they retreated closer to the limbers . . . The fire continued on both sides, mine becoming slacker and slacker, for we . . . were so reduced that all our strength was barely sufficient to load and fire three guns out of our six.[8]

9. Carry on along the track: the stretch which the visitor is now walking along marks the sector of the line initially held by the Guards brigade of Sir Peregrine Maitland. Later, however, it was held by Adam's brigade of the Sixth Division and it was from here that the Fifty-Second Foot wheeled forward to take the third wave of the assault of the Imperial Guard in the flank. After a short distance, a turning is reached to the left: visitors who wish to shorten the tour may here turn off here and follow it across the battlefield to La Belle Alliance. Otherwise, follow the track into the wood (a feature that was not present in 1815), noting on the way the stretch of ground immediately to the left: it was here that Adam's brigade was positioned during the cavalry charges. Continue through the wood until the vicinity of the motorway at which point the track angles sharply to the south. After several hundred yards, it emerges from the trees whereupon the complex of Hougoumont will be seen spread out in the low ground to the left. Follow the track to the north gate (the scene of desperate fighting when a group of French soldiers who had managed to get round to the rear of the chateau rushed the

A general view of Hougoumont taken from the vicinity of the north gate. The complete destruction of the main building and the stables that lined the eastern face of the complex mean that the scene is very different from what the same view would have looked like in 1815. (Author's collection)

gateway and entered the courtyard) and then walk along the right-hand side of the buildings to the entrance.

I. Hougoumont

For many British visitors especially, Hougoumont will be the highlight of any visit to Waterloo: the scene of desperate fighting for virtually the whole of the day, it has often been represented as the key to Wellington's whole position, whilst one cannot but be moved by the fate of the unfortunate wounded who were dragged into the shelter of the buildings, only to be burned to death when the latter were set on fire by French shells. Visitors wishing to visit the complex will find an excellent museum, a monument to the British troops who closed the gates in the crisis mentioned above, stretches of the very cobbles trodden by the soldiers of 1815, and, perhaps above all, the private chapel built on to the side of the great house. Whether any of the forty-five men crammed inside survived the flames that spared their hiding place is unknown, however – the smoke alone should by rights have been enough to suffocate them – while the terror they must have endured as the flames closed in is barely imaginable, and so this is very much a place for a moment of quiet reflection, and all the more so as the crucifix hanging over the door is the very one that hung there in 1815.

Edward Cotton, sergeant-major, Seventh Regiment of Light Dragoons: Hougoumont . . . was then a gentleman's seat with farm, out-buildings, walled garden, orchard and wood. The latter has been since cleared in consequence of the injury the trees sustained in the battle. The buildings are more than 200 years old and were erected for defence: many of the stone loop-holes made in the garden walls when first built are still quite perfect. The hedges were all banked up, and, with the ditches on the inner side, formed excellent breast works. A ravine, or hollow-way, [which] runs along the northern boundary of the premises . . . during the battle frequently served as a covered communication with the walled enclosures and the buildings, as also for a rallying point and cover . . . The chateau, farm, walls, etc., were at the time of the battle of a substantial nature. The garden, or park, was walled on the east and south sides, where our troops made additional loop-holes, and, in the inside of the front, or south, wall, they cut down a portion of the buttresses for the purpose of erecting a scaffolding to enable them to fire over the top of the wall . . . Loop-holes were also made in the stables joining the south gate, and a scaffold was erected against the west wall that ran from the stables to the barn. The flooring over the south gateway was partly torn up to enable our men to fire down upon the enemy should they force the gate, which had been blocked up.[9]

10. Continue along the western wall of Hougoumont in the same direction as before, passing an open area to the right which was a kitchen garden in 1815. Within a few yards a small yard is reached.

J. South Gate of Hougoumont
The yard in which the visitor is standing was the scene of desperate fighting which saw French infantry make repeated attempts to smash their way in through the gate to the left. Despite the plaques dedicated to the memory of the Scots Guards, throughout the battle

The south face of Hougoumont. During the battle the gates were kept firmly barred whilst the archway behind them was barricaded with a variety of agricultural implements. Throughout the day the buildings shown in the picture were held not by British guardsmen but rather troops from the First Regiment of Nassau. (Author's collection)

the gate-house was held by three companies of the First Battalion of the green-coated Second Nassau Regiment. A well-known print that has often been reproduced shows bodies being buried beneath the very spot on which the visitor is now standing, while a plaque just round the corner on the garden-wall recalls the death of the commander of the first brigade to assault the walls, Pierre Bauduin. At the southern edge of the yard, meanwhile, will be observed three ancient sweet-chestnut trees: these are the only survivors of the wood that in 1815 completely covered the southern aspect of the chateau and stretched as far as the crest of the slope that can be seen beyond them; so badly damaged was said wood that it was cut down in 1817. Between the wood and the south wall of the garden, meanwhile, there was a lane: described as one of the worst killing grounds on the entire field, this was lined on its right-hand side by a hedge so thick that it was described as being all but impenetrable. All trace of this last is now gone, but the line it followed is marked by the wire fence along the edge of the field.

Théobald Puvis, sub-lieutenant, Ninety-Third Regiment of Line Infantry:
  We threw ourselves as skirmishers into a wood with tall trees that was on our left and arrived in front of . . . a vast construction (the Hougoumont farm), fortified at every point and defended to the utmost by tall hedges protected . . . by profound cuts in the terrain. Traversing these cuts . . . we arrived at a hedge defended with the greatest vigour by the enemy. In vain we attempted to take this hedge . . . Our losses were enormous: the lieutenant of my company was killed near me. A musket ball hit the peak of my shako and struck my cheek, the shock to my head being so great that I believed myself to be injured. However, there was no blood and I soon recovered.[10]

11. Follow the wire fence and at the end turn sharp left and follow it northwards to the line of bushes.

The remains of the sunken lane that lined the northern face of the Hougoumont estate looking west. In 1815 the ground to the left was occupied by the smaller of the property's two orchards. (Author's collection)

K. The Lane to Hougoumont

The gully stretching right and left in 1815 was a sunken lane linking the north gate of Hougoumont to the lane leading from the Ohain road to La Belle Alliance: bordered by a thick hedge, this served to give shelter to the defenders of the orchard that bordered the formal garden at its eastern end on the many occasions that they were forced to abandon it by the enemy, Note, meanwhile, that soldiers manning the walls would have been incapable of firing at targets more than a few yards away as the heavy foliage of midsummer would have blocked their view entirely; had they been able to hold the leading edge of the orchard and the wood, it would have been a different matter, but the defenders were too few to do so for any length of time, the result being that they were for the most part unable to deliver flanking fire on troops moving up to attack Wellington's centre. From this it follows that the French could very easily simply have masked Hougoumont – the plan that Napoleon seems to have had had in mind for the area – rather than throwing away hundreds of lives in vain attempts to subdue it. At the same time a glance at the terrain is enough to suggest that, even had it fallen, the French would have been little better off: not only was the chateau complex too tangled an area to offer an easy approach to Wellington's positions, but it was completely dominated by the high ground beyond. If a major struggle developed at Hougoumont, then, it was only because the emperor lost control of his subordinate commanders.

Sylvain Larréguy de Civrieux, cadet, Ninety-Third Regiment of Line Infantry:
    The division of the erstwhile King of Westphalia having melted away in the face of the enemy fire, that of General Foy was sent forward to replace it . . . All round the place the ground was piled high with thousands of dead and wounded, and, of these, we quickly doubled the number, ripped apart in our turn as we were by the canister of the English . . . Soon our feet were bathed in blood: in less than half an hour, our ranks had been reduced by more than half. Everyone stoically awaited death or horrible wounds . . . and yet our courage remained at the highest possible degree of exaltation. Albeit in a voice that was becoming ever weaker, my captain, who had been struck by two

musket balls and was losing a lot of blood, kept encouraging us until he succumbed in the midst of that immortal hecatomb.[11]

12. From the sunken lane, visitors should retrace their steps until they reach the south-east corner of the formal garden. At this point turn left and walk along the edge of the field of crops: in 1815 the path marked the southern edge of the orchard, the field to the right then as now being open ground (the eastern edge of the wood extended no further than the line of the garden wall). After some 200 yards the path angles sharply to the left: at this point the visitor is standing at the site of the south-western corner of the orchard, the eastern face of which ran straight across the field in parallel with the garden wall until it intersected with the sunken lane leading to the north gate of the chateau. Meanwhile, a gap in the hedge and ditch surrounding the orchard that gave access to the open ground to the left made this a particularly difficult spot to hold, many of the defenders being shot down by skirmishers hidden in the tall crops.

The remains of the hedge at the northern edge of the main orchard of Hougoumont looking towards the French positions: lining the sunken lane that ran along the northern boundary of the complex, this came to constitute an important defensive position. To the right can be seen the wall of the garden: this afforded the garrison the perfect means of enfilading any French troops who attempted to penetrate the orchard. (Author's collection)

L. The Orchard of Hougoumont

No more than 300 yards wide in each direction, the square of ground facing the visitor was bitterly contested. Held at the start of the battle by the three companies of the First Battalion of the Second Regiment of Nassau that had not been sent to hold the chateau, together with 200 men of the Hanoverian Feldjäger, Grubenhagen and Luneburg light infantry battalions, the outer edges of the orchard offered an excellent field of fire to the east and south-east. At first the men defending them were not directly threatened, but they were outflanked by the French troops pushing through the wood and had to retire to the sunken lane, where those men who had not run away altogether were joined by the light companies of the First and Second Battalions of the First Regiment of Foot Guards. Commanded by Lord Saltoun, the newcomers drove the French back through the orchard, only to be driven back themselves when Jérôme Bonaparte reinforced the original attackers with the division of General Foy. Forced retire to the lane, the survivors of Saltoun's force then received fresh reinforcements in the shape of two line companies of the Third Regiment of Foot Guards. Having by now suffered heavy casualties, they were withdrawn from the front line and replaced by three more companies of the same unit. The latter then launched a fresh counter-attack and drove back the French only to be forced to retire themselves by the division of General Bachelu. This same sequence of events being repeated shortly afterwards, in the end the orchard was lost, regained and lost again at least four times over.

Rees Gronow, ensign, First Regiment of Foot Guards:
   Early in the morning on the day after the battle of Waterloo, I visited Hougoumont in order to witness with my own eyes the traces of one of the most hotly contested spots of the field of battle. I came first upon the orchard and there discovered heaps of dead men in various uniforms: those of the Guards in their usual red jackets, the German Legion [*sic:* actually Nassauers] in green, and the French dressed in blue, mingled together. The dead and the wounded positively covered the whole area of the orchard: not less than 2,000 men had there fallen. The apple trees presented a singular appearance: shattered branches were seen hanging about their mother-trunks in such

profusion that one might almost suppose the stiff-growing and stunted tree been converted into the willow. Every tree was riddled and smashed in a manner which told that the shower of shot and shell had been incessant. On this spot I lost some of my dearest and bravest friends, and the country had to mourn many of its most heroic sons.[12]

13. At a second angle in the path visitors should take the narrow path between two fields leading uphill in the general direction of the French position. After approximately 300 yards a concrete manhole is reached.

M. The Intermediate Ridge
Positioned on the crest of the so-called 'intermediate ridge' – the swell of ground running east-west in the very centre of the

Reille's position viewed from the intermediate ridge from the vicinity of the south-eastern corner of the site of the wood of Hougoumont. At the start of the battle the French troops were in the dead ground beyond the crest-line in the middle distance. Finally, the coppice to the left is a post-1815 addition to the scene. (Author's collection)

battlefield – the manhole marks the south-eastern corner of the Hougoumont estate, and constitutes an excellent spot from which to survey both the line occupied by the French left wing and to look back over Hougoumont: the hollow in which the latter sits is very clear as is the fact that French artillery could not possibly have bombarded it from the direction of the main French position, the guns that set it afire rather enfilading it from positions in the vicinity of the Nivelles highway to the west. By contrast, of course, troops holding the edge of the wood, not to mention the hedged enclosure that ran beside the path, would have had an unrivalled field of fire, the only problem being that Wellington's forces were driven from the area at the start of the battle and never succeeded in regaining the ground they had lost for any length of time. Please note, meanwhile, that, like the wood above Hougoumont, the copse immediately to the east did not exist in 1815: this is, alas, a landscape in which there are many trees where there should be none and no trees where there should be many.

Sylvain Larréguy de Civrieux, cadet, Ninety-Third Regiment of Line Infantry:
For a long time my regiment was left in a very difficult position: while out of range of infantry fire, it could still be hit by the enemy cannon. The latter's balls came flying at us after having been flung up by a fold in the terrain, and we could easily judge their likely course before they spread destruction in our ranks. In this situation, our spirit of abnegation was put to the hardest of proofs: it was beyond desperate to have to stand there waiting for the end in the most absolute inaction surrounded by mutilated corpses and the screams of the dying.[13]

14. Retracing their steps to the spot marking the south-eastern corner of the orchard, visitors should now follow the path they originally took from Hougoumont to the right. In a short distance the track running downhill from the ridge above the chateau in the direction of La Belle Alliance is reached once more. Turn to the left and ascend the slope to the Ohain road.

The area south of the Ohain Road occupied by Adam's brigade during the French cavalry charges viewed from the track to La Belle Alliance. Unlike most of the rest of Wellington's army, so long as they were stationed in this area the troops concerned had no protection from French artillery fire. (Author's collection)

N. Adam's Position

The sector of the battlefield on either side of the track which the visitor has just ascended is chiefly associated with the light-infantry brigade commanded by Sir Frederick Adam. Made up of the first battalion of the Fifty-Second Regiment of Foot, the First Battalion of the Seventy-First Regiment of Foot, and the Second and Third Battalions of the Ninety-Fifth Regiment of Foot, this unit had originally been in reserve near Merbe Braine, but in mid-afternoon it was brought forward to strengthen the line, and, in particular, hold the tract of land between the Ohain road and the northern edge of the orchard of Hougoumont. Thus posted, it was among the first of Wellington's troops to be assailed by the French cavalry reserve when it attacked the ridge from about four-o'clock in the afternoon onwards.

William Leeke, ensign, Fifty-Second Regiment of Foot:
  Immediately on descending the slope of the position towards the enemy, the regiment . . . formed two squares.

I remember that, when we formed these two squares, we were not far from the north-eastern corner of the Hougoumont enclosure and on the narrow white road which, passing within one hundred yards of that point, crosses the interval between the British and French positions in the direction of La Belle Alliance . . . The old officers who had served during the whole of the Peninsular War stated that they were never exposed to such a cannonade as that which the Fifty-Second squares had to undergo on this occasion . . . The only interval that occurred in the cannonade was when we were charged by the French cavalry, for [the French artillery], of course, could not fire on our squares for fear of injuring their own squadrons . . . After we had been stationed for an hour or so down in front of the British position, a gleam of sunshine, falling on them, particularly drew my attention to some brass guns which appeared to be placed lower down the French slope and nearer to us than some of the others. I distinctly saw the French artilleryman go through the whole process of sponging out one of the guns and reloading it. I could see it was pointed at our square, and when it was discharged I caught sight of the ball which appeared to be on a direct line for me . . . It did not strike the four men in rear of whom I was standing but the four poor fellows on their right.[14]

15. The visitor should now retrace his steps to the path by which he arrived at the track to La Belle Alliance *en route* from Hougoumont.

O. The Slopes of Mont Saint Jean

From this position the most obvious item of interest is the fashion in which the crest of Mont Saint Jean completely obscures any view of the proverbial 'other side of the hill'. However, the importance of the cross-ridge linking the ridge above Hougoumont and La Belle Alliance is also all too obvious: not only did it preclude any chance of the garrisons of La Haye Sainte and Hougoumont subjecting the approaches to Wellington's centre and right to sustained crossfire, but it also offered a perfect position from which the various batteries of French horse artillery brought up later in the charges could bombard the British squares from close range. As for the spot where the visitor

The northern slopes of Mont Saint Jean east of Hougoumont. The line of the Ohain Road is marked by the lone tree on the crest of the ridge. (Author's collection)

is standing, for at least two hours it would have witnessed thousands of French horsemen surging to and fro in the course of their desperate attempts to break Wellington's line. As the French cavalry charges were dying away, meanwhile, it was here that Adam's brigade, which had since been withdrawn to the crest of the ridge, was attacked by the division of General Bachelu. Finally, perhaps an hour later, the same spot witnessed the repulse of the third wave of the so-called 'attack of the Old Guard'. Like the second of its two predecessors, this headed for Maitland's brigade, only to be struck in flank by that of Adam, the latter having wheeled forward from the ridge so as to occupy the angle constituted by the Ohain road and the track to la Belle Alliance.

> *William Leeke, ensign, Fifty-Second Regiment of Foot:*
> When the leading battalion of the . . . Guard was about 400 yards from . . . Maitland's brigade . . . Sir John Colborne. . . moved forward the Fifty-Second in quick time directly to its front. As we passed over the . . . crest of our position, we plainly saw . . . two long columns of the Imperial Guard . . . advancing . . . in the direction of Maitland's brigade, stationed

on our left . . . As the Fifty-Second moved down towards the enemy, it answered the cries of 'Vive l'empereur!' with three tremendous British cheers. When the left of the regiment was in a line with the leading company . . . the word of command 'Right shoulders forward!' came down the line . . . The movement was soon completed and the . . . line became parallel to the left flank of the leading column of the French Guard . . . The regiment opened fire on the enemy without halting . . . Here I saw Winterbottom badly wounded in the head . . . Diggle, commanding No. 1 Company . . . desperately wounded . . . Lieutenant Dawson . . . shot through the lungs; Anderson [lose] a leg; Major Love . . . wounded in the head Lieutenant Campbell . . . severely wounded in the groin . . . Sir John Colborne . . . grazed in the hand and on the foot . . . about 140 of our men . . . killed or wounded . . . in the course of five or six minutes. As we closed toward the French Guard, they did not wait for our charge, but at first somewhat receded from us, and then broke and fled.[15]

16. Follow the track in the direction of the French positions. After approximately 500 yards a crest is reached: ahead La Belle Alliance can now be seen on the skyline, along with the positions occupied by Reille's corps at the start of the battle (these stretched right and left from the vicinity of the small wood dead ahead) while to the rear there is an excellent view of Wellington's centre-right: a large part of the artillery attached to Reille's corps was posted at this spot and from it did terrible damage to the brigades of Adam and Du Plat when they were brought forward to maintain communications with Hougoumont and keep enemy skirmishers away from the main ridge. Carry on to La Belle Alliance, noting that the cross ridge stretches right across the space between the two armies, and that it is quite impossible to see anything beyond the Charleroi high road. To the right, meanwhile, is the spot where the last two battalions of the Old Guard formed up in square to resist the oncoming Allies, though their resistance did not last very long. At the same time, it was somewhere in the vicinity of the spot where the track reaches the Charleroi highway that the French general Cambronne was overtaken and captured by the commander of the

The lane that runs diagonally across the battlefield from the Ohain Road to La Belle Alliance. French artillery posted at this spot inflicted heavy damage on Adam's brigade and other units. (Author's collection)

Third Hanoverian Brigade, Hugh Halkett: whilst he may well have uttered a certain expletive, the idea that he uttered the words 'The Guard dies, but never surrenders', let alone that he went down fighting in the midst of a defiant French square, is a complete myth. On reaching La Belle Alliance (now called Le Retro) cross the road via the pedestrian crossing: despite this facility, it is advisable to proceed with extreme care.

P. La Belle Alliance

In 1815 La Belle Alliance was a tavern, the name of which commemorated the marriage of the widow of the original owner to the man who had taken over the business in the wake of the death of her first husband. Though in essence the same building as the one which existed at the time of the battle, its appearance has been much altered: for example, a Denis Dighton watercolour painted shortly after the battle shows that the whitewash and plaster of today should be discarded in favour of faded brickwork, while the large block at the northern end of the building was added at some point in the nineteenth century). Traditionally, it is the scene of the much-pictured meeting that took place between Wellington and Blücher at the close of the battle but it is probable that the encounter actually took place a mile or more to the south. Be that as it may, delighted with the symbolism of the name, Blücher wanted the battle to be named after the inn, but Wellington rather insisted on following his usual practice and calling it after the place where he had spent the previous night, i.e. Waterloo. During the battle, the building was used as a hospital while the area provided an ideal position from which heavy artillery – specifically, the three 12-pounder batteries attached to I, II and VI Corps – could batter the Anglo-Dutch lines. Note, however, that the reverse slope on the further side of Wellington's position cannot be observed at all: whatever the reason for the French cavalry charges, it was certainly not that Ney spotted masses of troops heading for the rear.

Basil Jackson, aide-de-camp to Sir William de Lancey:
Crossing to the left of the *chaussée*, I found myself involved with Prussian infantry streaming from the direction of Frischermont in no military order whatever as they swept onward bayoneting every wounded Frenchman they came upon . . . The disorder of the Prussians . . . was so great that I was glad to push on, and soon overtook our Fifty-Second Regiment and with it our glorious commander, but thinly attended . . . Very soon our bugles sounded the halt, and the Fifty-Second formed up in line, as quiet and orderly as at the termination of a review. It was commanded by Colonel Colborne . . . a splendid soldier who had distinguished himself in the Peninsula. The Duke remained for a short time talking with Colborne . . . Certainly it was a moment when even the Iron Duke might feel excited. I heard him say to Colborne as he shook hands on departing that he would endeavour to send some flour for his men. He then turned his horse towards Waterloo, followed by five persons only. On nearing the farm of La Belle Alliance, a group of horsemen were seen crossing the fields on our right. On seeing them, the Duke left the road to meet them. They proved to be Marshal Blücher and his

suite. The two great chiefs cordially shook hands, and were together about ten minutes; it was then so dark that I could not distinguish Blücher's features, and had to ask a Prussian officer whom the Duke was conversing with.[16]

17. From La Belle Alliance walk a short distance along the highway. After 200 yards the visitor will reach the monument to Victor Hugo.

Q. The French Monuments
A gigantic column whose design was much influenced by masonic beliefs, the Hugo monument commemorates not so much the battle itself as Hugo's endeavours to romanticise the story of the French defeat through, for example, his invention of the image of the French cavalry being defeated not by the unshakeable resistance of Wellington's infantry but rather the accident of the sunken lane. A little further on on the other side of the highway, meanwhile, will be found the so-called 'Monument of the Wounded Eagle'. This is supposed to mark the site of the last stand of the remnants of the Old

La Belle Alliance. The area in the foreground was occupied by one of the three batteries of heavy artillery that were deployed to batter Wellingrton's centre. (Author's collection)

Guard, but this incident is in large part invention: placed on either side of the highway, three battalions of the Guard did hold out for a short while in this vicinity as the rest of the army disintegrated around them, but they did not fight to the end, instead withdrawing from the field in as good order as they could manage. Finally, if the visitor wishes to extend the tour a little perhaps 400 yards beyond the Victor Hugo monument and on the same side of the highroad there stands a nondescript house of a brownish colour with a red-tiled roof. Even more nondescript in 1815 – the upper storey of the section nearer the observer was added in the early twentieth century – this was the house of Jean-Baptiste Decoster, the local man pressed into service as a guide by Napoleon's headquarters staff.

Hyppolyte Mauduit, sergeant, First Regiment of Foot Grenadiers of the Imperial Guard:
     The two battalions of my regiment . . . grew ever more angry at the terrible confusion that marked the battlefield. On all sides our view was obstructed by hundreds of soldiers of every rank . . . searching frantically for some . . . refuge. The drummers had been ordered to beat the grenadier march in the hope that this might offer the army something around which to rally, and at this sound . . . our unfortunate comrades had come surging towards us . . . However, with the interior of our two squares already encumbered with generals and other officers whose men had been killed or run away, we were very soon reduced to the cruel necessity of denying access to anyone who sought to enter so as to ensure that we did not become the victims of our generosity . . . As for the battery of 12-pounder guns belonging to the artillery of the Guard that had for the past two hours been flaying Bülow's corps with canister fire . . . it was completely wiped out before our very eyes, all of the gunners choosing a glorious death rather than . . . take shelter in our square, thereby letting the English cavalrymen in with them. 'No quarter! No quarter!' That was what those savages were crying, but . . . their ranks shattered on our bayonets, and for fifty paces around the ground was soon covered with their corpses . . . Subjected to a hail of fire from three sides though we were, we were therefore able to begin our retreat in the midst of the general disorder.[17]

18. Take the track directly opposite the Wounded Eagle monument. At the end turn left. A short walk will then bring the visitor to a hedged enclosure which marks the spot where Napoleon is reputed to have spent much of the latter part of the battle.

R. Napoleon's Command Post

Whether Napoleon actually used the spot where the visitor is standing as his command post is a moot point: for one thing, the view of Wellington's positions is more complete from the vicinity of La Belle Alliance. However, the knoll does command a good view of the area from which the Prussians were attacking Plancenoit, so it is certainly plausible that the emperor was there at some point. Also important to note is the fact that on a fine day the position offers a view of a small portion of the heights on the far bank of the river Lasne that Bülow's

The rear of Drouet's position viewed from Napoleon's supposed headquarters looking east in the direction of the Heights of Agiers. At the end of the battle the fields in the foreground and middle distance witnessed desperate fighting as the remnants of Mouton's troops sought to hold off Ziethen. Meanwhile, the first Prussian forces to appear on the battlefield advanced along the ridge in the far distance on the right-hand side of the photograph. (Author's collection)

corps had to cross on its way to the battlefield from Wavre. Whilst the balance of informed opinion is now that the story that Napoleon spotted the Prussian advance in the distance at about one o'clock is a fabrication, that such an event did occur is therefore at least theoretically a possibility. That said, whether the very distant and very small area of ground in question could actually be seen on the rather murky day that was 18 June 1815, or even that the road that the Prussians were following actually crossed it is another matter, as is the question of Napoleon's whereabouts at the decisive moment: in so far as is known, he was at Rossomme and from there there is no such view.

Jean de Crabbé, aide de camp to Marshal Ney:
Marshal Soult . . . summoned me. He told me that the emperor had confided his ultimate reserve, all that remained of the Guard, to Marshal Ney to make a decisive attack on the English lines. He had asked for an experienced officer of his headquarters to carry supplementary orders. I reached the rise near the farm [*sic*] of La Belle Alliance where the emperor was located. He was surrounded by a squadron of the Guard Chasseurs à Cheval, jackets and trousers green trimmed with red, and shabraques of the same . . . From this position one could see the whole of the battlefield . . . The emperor was on a chair in front of a table on which some maps were spread . . . General Count Drouot and two *aides de camp* were at his side. He wore his usual grey riding coat over his uniform of a colonel of *chasseurs* and on his head his legendary hat. Slumped in his chair, he appeared to me both exhausted and angry. One of the *aides de camp* informed him of my arrival. Without even turning to me he said, out of the blue, 'Ney has acted stupidly again. He has cost us the day! He has destroyed my cavalry and is about to destroy my Guard. He manoeuvres like a good-for-nothing. He attacks the plateau obliquely instead of assaulting right at the centre. Go at best speed and order him to modify his march and pierce the centre of the English position in a compact mass'.[18]

19. Retracing his steps to La Belle Alliance, the visitor should next take a dirt-track angling to the right between the Plancenoit road and the Charleroi highway. Just past a small copse, this brings the

visitor out onto a broad spur jutting forward from the French ridge which offers an excellent view of the whole of the eastern half of the battlefield. Immediately in front lies La Haye Sainte, though only its roof may be seen, together with the eastern half of the intermediate ridge: in the course of Drouet's assault, this last was occupied by the six batteries belonging to I Corps, these having advanced alongside the infantry and then deployed to give them covering fire (it was these guns that were overrun by the Union Brigade in its famous charge across the valley). To the right, meanwhile, can be seen the high ground known as the heights of Agiers: completely covering, as these did, the movements of the Prussian army, the latter would have remained invisible to the French troops deployed against Wellington and for that matter the men opposing them until Bülow's corps attacked Mouton south of Frischermont. Finally, looking to the left, it will be seen that the western horizon is constituted by the cross-ridge leading to Mont Saint Jean: as a result, French troops stationed in this area could not possibly have seen, or even been aware of, either the advance or the retreat of the Imperial Guard, what produced the collapse of Napoleon's forces in this sector rather being the eruption of Ziethen's corps from the direction of Papelotte.

The crest of Drouet's initial position looking east towards Frischermont. (Author's collection)

S. Drouet's Front Line

The track which the visitor has followed to reach this spot marks the original front line of Napoleon's forces, and, more particularly, the position from which Drouet's corps set off to attack Wellington's centre-left. To its rear there is an extensive area of dead ground, but, seemingly intent on overawing the Anglo-Dutch army with his massed ranks, the emperor made no attempt to make use of the reverse slope with which he was thus presented in the same fashion as Wellington, the result being that his men suffered significant losses from artillery fire before they had advanced even a single step in the direction of the enemy. All the more was this the case given the defective formation adopted by Drouet, the battalions of his two centre divisions being formed in line one behind the other with little or no distance between them: not only were such targets hard to miss, but each Allied cannon-ball struck down as many as a dozen men. On the other hand, the ridge did offer a perfect position for the French artillery, and one can only surmise that the decision that was taken to move so much of it forward to the intermediate ridge reflected the fact that the batteries concerned were all armed with 6-pounder guns and were therefore essentially all but out of range. That said, this ensured that Drouet's men had little artillery support for much of their advance, whilst, being somewhat lower than its predecessor, the new position offered even less chance of hitting troops hidden behind the reverse slope.

Louis Canler, corporal, Twenty-Eighth Regiment of Line Infantry:
Towards noon we took up our positions on the plateau of [La Belle Alliance], where a battery of eighty guns was deployed, and next they had us descend into the ravine of the same name, where we were sheltered from a formidable battery the English had established during the night . . . which fired continuously . . . Pretty soon, our guns fired back and the result was a terrifying duel between some 200 guns, the balls and shells of both sides shrieking by just over our heads. After half an hour . . . Marshal Ney gave the order to attack . . . We formed in columns of closed battalions . . . Once the columns were formed, General Drouet . . . placed himself in the centre . . . and in a voice that was both loud

and clear shouted, 'It is today that we will conquer or die!' Upon this brief speech from all mouths there came the reply, 'Vive l'empereur!', and, with arms supported and drummers beating the charge, the columns set themselves in motion.[19]

20. Continue along the track in the same direction as before. After several hundred yards a substantial wood is passed: ahead and to the right can be seen the slopes where VI Corps tried to delay Bulöw, while straight on, the horizon is dominated by the heights of Agiers (a substantial ridge that made it almost impossible for the French to spot the advance of the Prussians). Note, meanwhile that, like so many of their fellows, the various copses that dot the area were not there in 1815. Also in view is the farm of Papelotte with its distinctive tower (a nineteenth-century addition). In the early afternoon it was from this area that the Scots Greys were struck by Jacquinot's brigade of lancers. Meanwhile, the track the visitor is following marks the axis of advance followed by Ziethen's troops at the close of the battle. Follow the track downhill and it progressively becomes more sunken (sadly, the highly atmospheric cobbles post-date the battle). Swinging sharply to the left, continue past a turning on the right that leads to Plancenoit, and at length arrive at a metalled road just opposite a lane leading uphill to the farm of Papelotte.

T. The Valley beneath Papelotte
Though not much visited, the sector of the battlefield the visitor has just traversed is, perhaps, one of the most evocative. Almost completely unchanged from 1815, for much of the day the sunken lane leading to Papelotte would beyond doubt have been crammed with wounded men and stragglers seeking refuge from the fighting. In the event, thanks to Mouton's two divisions being detained by the need to hold back Bülow, few French troops – no more, indeed, than the single division of Durutte – penetrated as far as the road beside which the visitor is standing, but even so the area was marked by fierce fighting. Held by the brigade of Prince Bernhard of Saxe-Weimar, the line of the road was cleared by Durutte's men as soon as they reached the area, while the latter went on to advance up the hill and establish a lodgement in some of the outer dependencies of Papelotte, whilst at the same time

Wellington's position viewed from a position c. 300 yards north-east of La Belle Alliance. The intermediate ridge is the fold in the ground running across the middle of the photograph. (Author's collection)

getting control of La Haye. Casualties on both sides were very heavy, and fighting raged from hedge to hedge, before finally dying down in the middle of the afternoon. At around half-past seven in the evening, however, fighting began again as a torrent of Prussians from Ziethen's newly arrived corps broke through the single brigade that was all that the French had left to hold the area (Durutte's other brigade had in the meantime been sent to support the French troops fighting at La Haye Sainte) and swept across the opposing hillside in the direction of Papelotte and La Belle Alliance.

Carl von Rettberg, captain, Second Nassau Regiment:
Between eleven o'clock and twelve o'clock, the enemy columns and artillery drew up before us. One of the first cannon balls wounded Major Hegmann, and Captain Frensdorff took command. Between twelve o'clock and one

o'clock, a line of enemy skirmishers moved towards Papelotte. The Prince of Saxe-Weimar sent me with my company . . . against them. Shortly thereafter a detachment of the Orange-Nassau Regiment occupied the village of Smohain and also La Haye, and I linked up with them . . . I was then able to drive back the enemy skirmishers to the furthest hedge on the edge of the valley meadow between our position and the enemy's and even took a few small houses there.[20]

21. Walk up the lane to Papelotte, whilst at the same time taking in the view of La Haye across the field to the right; the gradient, it will be noted, is surprisingly steep.

U. Papelotte
Badly damaged in the battle and today run as a riding stable, Papelotte was reconstructed in the course of the nineteenth century, one of the chief features that was added being the imposing tower over the

The courtyard of the farm of Papelotte. By the end of the battle the buildings were crammed with wounded. (Author's collection)

main gate; that said, the overall appearance of the courtyard, at least, has probably not altered very much from what it would have been in 1815. Persistent stories that the French occupied the whole complex in the course of the fighting are untrue, but it is not impossible that they got into the southern wing (note that the isolated building in the extreme south-west corner of the complex did not exist in 1815).

Carl von Rettberg, captain, Second Nassau Regiment:
Between three and four o'clock the reinforced enemy skirmish line advanced once more, and in support followed considerable infantry columns. Forced to vacate my position, I was thrown back upon Papelotte, which I now quickly turned into a redoubt. On receiving a request for reinforcements, Captain Frensdorff gave me the command of the Tenth, Eleventh and Twelfth Companies, these being joined by the Flanker Company of the Second Battalion of our regiment. The enemy column was checked by the fire from Papelotte and the small houses [La Haye?], where the occupants bravely resisted, and was now thrown back by a swift bayonet attack and pursued as far as the . . . outer [hedges]. Here an enemy battery welcomed us at barely 500 paces with canister. Although our losses were considerable – the third Flanker Company lost two officers . . . and melted away to half strength by the end of the battle – the enemy nevertheless did not attempt another serious attack, but instead limited himself to a lively skirmish fire from behind a [hedge] at the other side of the meadow.[21]

22. At the gateway, take the cobbled lane running directly away from the farm and follow it through two right-hand bends to reach a metalled road running up the hillside from the valley below. Turn right and follow the road uphill until it reaches a sharp left-hand bend.

V. Vandeleur's Charge
The spot where the visitor is standing is the site of the charge launched by the light cavalry brigade of Sir John Vandeleur in an attempt to rescue the survivors of the Union Brigade as they tried to escape from the valley (it will be observed that the slope here forms a re-entrant which would have provided an ideal route for a

The intermediate ridge looking south-west from the lane to Smohain. La Belle Alliance is the white building in the far distance. Vandeleur's brigade charged across the lane into the fields in the foreground. (Author's collection)

cavalry charge). Consisting of the Eleventh, Twelfth and Sixteenth Light Dragoons, the brigade struck south-westwards across the slope from its position north and a little east of Papelotte at the very left-hand end of Wellington's line. Despite being much slowed and disordered by the very heavy going on the hillside, it sliced into Jacquinot's light cavalry, but, like the Union and Household Brigades before them, Vandeleur's men went out of control and suffered heavy casualties, eventually having to be rescued by the Dutch light cavalry brigade of Charles Ghigny. Among the casualties was the commander of the Twelfth Light Dragoons and cousin of the William Ponsonby who commanded the Union Brigade, Lieutenant Colonel Frederick Ponsonby, who was badly wounded in both arms and carried deep into the French position when his horse bolted. Eventually cut down by a French horseman and then stabbed in the back by a lancer as he lay on the ground, he was to remain prostrate all day, at one point even being used as cover by a French skirmisher.

William Hay, captain, Twelfth Regiment of Light Dragoons:
Just in our front were . . . several squadrons of the French cavalry composed of lancers and light dragoons. We had no time for reflection: on we went at a gallop, sweeping . . . over the skirmishers who were running in all directions . . . to seek shelter . . . In an instant we were engaged hand to hand . . . Having made good our charge, the colonel said to me, 'Hang it! What can [be detaining] our centre squadron? I must get back and see. Lead the men out of this and tell off the squadron behind the infantry.' These were the last words, poor fellow, he uttered that day . . . According to his directions, I . . . stopped to see the last man down the sloping and deep banks of the lane [and] out of danger, and, while my attention was quite absorbed in the duty . . . a shell . . . burst under my horse and hurt his leg so severely that he sat down as a dog would do. At [that] moment I did not know the cause and used my spurs, but it was to no purpose, [and] I had therefore to let myself slide over his tail . . . When trying to kick him up, some men in the hollow shouted, telling me to take care of myself. On glancing round I saw two lancers coming full tilt at me. One instant more and both their lances would have been in the small of my back, [but] one spring into the hollow deprived them of their prey.[22]

23. Continue uphill along the lane. To the right there is a good view of the fields leading up to the line occupied by Vincke's brigade of Hanoverian militia, and to the left an equally good one of the slopes climbed by Drouet's centre and left in the great attack of the early afternoon. At the road junction at the top of the hill, having noted the monument to Marcognet's division, double back to the right and walk along the lane labelled 'Chemin de la Croix'. This is the Ohain road once more and just past the private house on the right the visitor reaches will find a wonderful panorama of the whole of the western part of the battlefield. The large building on the left, meanwhile, is a convent erected in 1929 in defiance of laws protecting the battlefield.

The Ohain Road looking east taken from the vicinity of the Frischermont convent: whilst the convent is a twentieth-century addition, in this area the lane is more-or-less in its original condition. Meanwhile, Vinck's brigade held the hedgeline in the middle distance. (Author's collection)

W. Vincke's Position

Almost entirely unchanged since 1815 – the surface is unpaved, the banks on either side up to six feet high and some of the hedges still in place – the stretch of lane stretching from the point where the visitor is currently standing to the lane that leads back down to Papelotte was held at the start of the battle by the Fifth Hanoverian Infantry Brigade of Colonel Ernst von Vincke. Composed of just four *Landwehr* battalions, it was perhaps the weakest formation in the whole of Wellington's army and it was therefore just as well that the arrival of the Prussians forestalled Napoleon's plan for VI Corps to punch through Wellington's extreme left and roll up his front line. Further to the left, meanwhile, the line was continued by Vivien and Vandeleur's light cavalry brigades.

> *George Farmer, private, Eleventh Regiment of Light Dragoons:*
> By and by an order arrived to take ground to the right where we enrolled ourselves in brigade with the Twelfth and Sixteenth

[Light Dragoons] . . . The place where we were directed to execute this formation chanced to be particularly favourable for obtaining a view over the whole field of battle . . . and never have these eyes of mine rested on a more imposing scene . . . As far as the eye could reach I beheld endless columns of the French . . . infantry, as it were, interlaced with artillery, while in the rear were masses of cavalry . . . Then again, on our side I beheld horse and foot and guns, all in admirable order, hidden in some degree from the enemy by the swell of the ground . . . while, both on our side and that of the French, staff officers . . . were galloping hither and thither . . . But the vision was like that which the sleeper obtains when, for a moment, the gates of fairy-land are opened before him. From the hundreds of cannon which [quickly] sent forth death on each side such a cloud of smoke emerged as soon rendered objects indistinct . . . From the instant the firing became general, all was to me dark and obscure beyond a distance of a few hundred yards from the spot on which I stood: indeed it was only by the ceaseless roar, or the whistling of shot and shell round me, that I knew at times that I and those round me were playing a part in the grave game of life and death.[23]

24. Return to the junction with the road ascended earlier.

X. Bylandt's Position

At the moment that the battle began, the stretch of line between the convent and the crossroads was held by Bylandt's Dutch brigade with immediately to its rear the British ones headed by Sir Denis Pack and Sir James Kempt. Already badly shaken at Quatre Bras and deployed in a long thin line with no supporting units from their own brigade in their rear, the Dutchmen fell back in the face of Drouet's assault. In the vicinity of the convent, this placed the onus for saving the day on Pack's brigade, but a counter-attack on the part of the latter succeeded in no more than checking the advancing French. Fortunately, however, just at this point, having been ordered to charge by Lord Uxbridge, Sir William Ponsonby's Union Brigade (so-called because it happened to contain one English regiment, one Scottish regiment and one Irish regiment) arrived on the scene. Achieving complete tactical surprise –

The Ohain Road and the crest of Wellington's position looking east from the knoll near La Haye Sainte. Already badly hit at Quatre Bras, Bylandt's brigade was in a difficult position: whilst its front was protected by the sunken lane, it was strung out in a long line perhaps half a mile long and had no supports of its own in its rear. It is therefore little wonder that it crumbled in the face of Drouet's assault. (Author's collection)

the smoke was so dense that the already somewhat disordered French infantry did not see them coming until the last moment – Ponsonby's men rode straight into the enemy masses and put them to flight. Situated on the left-hand end of the line, the brigade's Scottish unit – the Scots Greys, or, more properly, Royal North British Dragoons – happened to pass through the light company of the Ninety-Second Foot, or Gordon Highlanders, some of whose members grabbed the stirrups of various horsemen to save themselves from being ridden down and trampled underfoot, an action later misconstrued as a heroic attempt physically to take part in the charge.

James Hope, lieutenant, Ninety-Second Regiment of Foot:
    With their drums beating [and] colours flying . . . the enemy advanced in solid column . . . As they ascended the ridge, the Belgians poured on them a very destructive fire of musketry

. . . The French having almost gained the ridge, the Belgians partially retired from the hedge. These troops were induced to return again . . . but . . . at length the whole corps ran as fast as their feet could carry them . . . The post abandoned by the Belgians was ordered to be occupied by the Third Battalion, Royals [i.e. the Royal Scots], and the Second Battalion, Forty-Fourth. These two corps retarded the advance of the French, who, although they saw themselves opposed by fresh adversaries, still pressed forward . . . The two British battalions retired on the approach of the enemy who, no doubt, imagined that they would meet with no further opposition . . . but they were soon undeceived . . . Sir Denis Pack . . . perceiving the urgent state of affairs, galloped up to the Ninety-Second, and . . . said, 'Ninety-Second! You must charge! All the troops in your front have given way.' The regiment. . . formed in line . . . moved forward, and, with cheers, approached their veteran enemy. For some time they seemed quite determined to meet our assault, but, when we were about twenty paces from them, they, panic-struck, wheeled about, and in the utmost confusion attempted to escape. But it was too late. Sir William Ponsonby, perceiving the disorderly manner in which the enemy retired, rushed forward with the First, Second and Sixth Regiments of Heavy Dragoons, and cut his way through them.[24]

25. From the road junction, follow the lane along the crest of the ridge. Along this section of the road, the French side of the bank that lined it in 1815 has been smoothed away by generations of intensive farming, but sufficient remains of it on the British side for it to be possible to gain some impression of the obstacle it would have represented at the time of the battle (that said, it was lined on both sides by fairly dense hedges that, whilst passable enough, were all the same capable of causing considerable disruption to troops attempting to get through them). On both sides of the road there are excellent views, whilst the knoll which the Ninety-Fifth occupied is particularly clear. Just before the crossroad is reached, on the left will be encountered the monument to General Picton with, just opposite, one to the Twenty-Seventh Regiment of Foot, otherwise known as the Inniskillings.

Y. Picton's Monument

Sir Thomas Picton was not a pleasant character: notoriously rough and brutal in his disposition, he had earned a reputation for extreme cruelty during a term as governor of the newly-conquered island of Trinidad. Such a perspective should not be forgotten, yet it is but justice to admit, first, that he was also one of Wellington's best subordinate generals, and, second, that his leadership at Waterloo was exemplary: though suffering terrible pain from a glancing wound to his hip that he had suffered at Quatre Bras, he had refused to abandon his command and on 18 June continued in the saddle throughout the day until struck down by a musket ball to the temple while leading the counter-attack that stalled the advance of Drouet's corps prior to the charge of the Household and Union Brigades; meanwhile, the fact that he fought both Quatre Bras and Waterloo dressed in a civilian frock-coat and top-hat did nothing to damage his charisma. This last seems, indeed, to have been considerable: his last words were 'Charge! Hurrah! Hurrah!'

Unknown British officer, Kempt's brigade:
    After having tried the right and found it strong, Bonaparte manoeuvred until he got forty pieces of artillery to play on the left where the Fifth Division, a brigade of heavy dragoons and two companies of artillery were posted. Our lines were formed behind a hedge with two companies of the Ninety-Fifth extended in front to annoy the enemy's approach. For some time we saw that Bonaparte intended to attack us, yet as nothing but cavalry were visible, no-one could imagine what were his plans. It was generally supposed he would endeavour to turn our flank, but all on a sudden his cavalry turned to the right and the left and showed large masses of infantry who advanced . . . in the most gallant style to cries of 'Vive l'empereur!' while a most tremendous cannonade was opened to cover their approach. They had arrived at the very hedge behind which we were – the muskets were almost muzzle to muzzle and a French mounted officer had seized the colours of the Thirty-Second Regiment – when . . . Picton ordered the charge of our brigade, commanded by Sir James Kempt. When the French saw us rushing through the hedge

and heard the tremendous hurrahs which we gave, they
turned . . . and allowed themselves to be butchered without
any material resistance. Poor Picton was killed at the head of
our division while advancing.[25]

26. Cross the Ohain road to the Inniskilling monument.

Z. The Inniskilling Monument

Part of Lambert's Brigade, the Twenty-Seventh, or Inniskilling,
Regiment of Foot arrived on the battlefield in the course of the
afternoon after a forced march from Brussels and was immediately
deployed in the rear of the Ohain road immediately to the east of
the Charleroi highway. For much of the time deployed in square
on account of the danger of French cavalry attacks, along with
the rest of the brigade it was subjected to so terrible a pounding
by the French artillery brought up to the crossridge that it lost 103
killed and 360 wounded out of 730 officers and men present on the
field, this being the highest percentage loss suffered by any British
battalion in Wellington's army. For the men concerned, the sufferings
they endured can only be imagined – the torment of being forced
to endure prolonged artillery fire without the means to hit back is
widely recorded by soldiers of not just the Napoleonic Wars but
those of more modern conflicts as well – and it is remarkable that the
battalion did not disintegrate under the pressure.

John Kincaid, captain, Ninety-Fifth Regiment of Foot:
    The loss of La Haye Sainte was of the most serious
consequence as it afforded the enemy an establishment within
our position. They immediately brought up two guns on
our side of it and began serving out some grape to us, but
they were so very near that we destroyed their artillerymen
before they could give us a second round . . . For the two or
three succeeding hours, there was no variety with us but one
continued blaze of musketry. The smoke hung so thick about
that, although not more than eighty yards asunder, we could
only distinguish each other by the flashes of the pieces. A good
many of our guns had been disabled and a great number more
rendered unserviceable in consequence of the unprecedented

close fighting . . . I felt weary and worn out, less from fatigue than anxiety. Our division, which had stood upwards of 5,000 strong at the commencement of the battle, had gradually dwindled down into a solitary line of skirmishers. The Twenty-Seventh Regiment were lying literally dead in square a few yards behind us . . . I had never yet heard of a battle in which all were killed, but this seemed likely to be an exception as all were going by turns.[26]

27. Continue along the Ohain road and after a very short distance take a path that runs northwards in a direction roughly parallel with the Charleroi highway. After a several hundred yards, this intersects with the highway. Across the road there near this spot stood a small cottage which was occupied by a number of officers of the Rifles on the night before the battle. Continue beside the highway to reach the farm of Mont Saint Jean. From the summit of the ridge to the farm the whole road was swept by French roundshot ricocheting from the points on which they had come down on the reverse slope, while the danger was increased by French howitzer shells bursting overhead, the result being that many of the wounded were struck again as they tried to make their way to the rear or were being carried to safety.

AA. Farm of Mont Saint Jean
Today a working brewery whose products are reputedly extremely good, the farm of Mont Saint Jean has recently been extensively renovated, a task that involved the complete reconstruction of the pigeon loft that stands above the main gate (probably weakened by the ever increasing volume of traffic passing along the highway, this last collapsed in 1990), and there are plans afoot for a museum to be added to the complex. As a plaque on the outer wall records, on 18 June the building was requisitioned as a hospital by the Surgeon-General of I Corps, John Gunning (1773–1863). Amongst the many patients operated on by Gunning was Wellington's military secretary, Fitzroy Somerset (later Lord Raglan): his right arm having been hit by a musket ball towards the end of the day, it had to be amputated, but Somerset bore the pain without a word and had the presence of mind after the operation had been concluded to demand

The plateau in the rear of Wellington's left-centre looking towards the farm of Mont Saint Jean. It was in this area both that Picton was killed and the Inniskillings were decimated. (Author's collection)

the amputated member back again so that he could remove a ring his wife had given him.

George Simmons, lieutenant, Ninety-Fifth Regiment of Foot:

The next place I found myself in was where the men and officers had been collected for the surgeon. A good surgeon, a friend of mine, instantly came to examine my wound. My breast was dreadfully swelled. He made a deep cut under the right pap, and dislodged from the breast-bone a musket ball. I was suffocating with the injury my lungs had sustained. He took a quart of blood from my arm. I now began to feel my miseries. Sergeant Fairfoot was also here, wounded in the arm. He got me everything he could, and said he would go and knock some French prisoner off his horse for me in order to get me off. The balls were riddling the house we were in. He got me a horse. They tried to lift me upon it but I fainted: some other officer took it. In consequence of a movement the

French made with all their forces, our people were obliged to retire. If I stayed I must be a prisoner and being a prisoner was the same as being lost. Poor Fairfoot was in great agitation. He came with another horse. I remember some Life Guards . . . helped me on. Oh what I suffered! I had to ride twelve miles . . . The motion of the horse made the blood pump out, and the bones cut the flesh to a jelly.[27]

28. Return to the Ohain Road by the same route. Passing the Belgian monument to the right, carry straight on across the road and take the track through the fringes of the clump of trees beside the high road (like so many others of the trees on the battlefield, these did not exist in 1815). After a short distance the path swings to the right and enters a shallow cutting. At this point, ascend the bank to the left and walk along the edge of the field keeping the line of bushes to the right.

La Haye Sainte viewed from the knoll held by the First Battalion of the Ninety-Fifth. The loss of the farm to the French in the late afternoon is generally represented as a major blow to Wellington, but in fact the loss of the knoll was far more serious as troops posted there could fire into the ground beyond the Ohain Road. (Author's collection)

BB. The Knoll

The visitor is now standing on the knoll occupied by elements of the First Battalion of the Ninety-Fifth until the fall of La Haye Sainte and then used as a fire-base by the French. In 1815, it was bare of scrub and undergrowth alike, though a short length of hedge, the remnant, perhaps, of some enclosure grubbed up long before the battle, crowned its summit. The views across the ground in front of Wellington's position are excellent, while the intermediate ridge on which much French artillery was stationed for the whole of the afternoon and evening is very clear. Particularly striking is the open nature of the terrain, it being all too obvious, first, how helpless the French infantry were in the face of the British cavalry, and, second, how easy it was for the latter to get out of control.

George Simmons, lieutenant, Ninety-Fifth Regiment of Foot:
    Under cover of their guns, four columns . . . made their appearance . . . They moved steadily towards us. We formed a sort of line and commenced a terrible fire upon them which was returned very spiritedly, they at the same time advancing [to] within a few yards. I had an impression I would not be touched, and was laughing and joking with a young officer . . . I was a little in front of our line, and, hearing the word 'charge', I looked back at our line and received a ball which broke two of my ribs, went through my liver, and lodged in my breast. I fell senseless in the mud, and some minutes after found our fellows and the enemy hotly engaged near me . . . Most of the men with me were killed, so it was some time before any officer noticed me and not until I had been trampled over many times.[28]

29. Return to the path and turn left. After a few yards the visitor will come upon a small parking-area: this marks the site of the sandpit held by advance elements of the Ninety-Fifth at the start of the battle and, with it, by tradition at least, that of one of the largest mass graves on the battlefield. In the parking area is a monument to the French Eighth Regiment of the Line which claims that it overcame the Fifth Line Battalion of the King's German Legion under Colonel Christian von Ompteda: this claim is probably true – at the climax of the battle,

the unit concerned was certainly attacked and driven from the field by units that were not members of the Guard – but the fighting concerned did not take place where the monument is placed but rather in the vicinity of the restaurant in the north-western angle of the crossroads. At first the reference to Durutte's division is puzzling, for this was deployed in the Papelotte sector, but the regiment concerned belonged to the brigade of General Jean Pégot, this being transferred from the right flank following the fall of La Haye Sainte. From the lay-by, meanwhile, a short walk back along the road brings the visitor to the monument to the dead of the King's German Legion.

CC. Hanoverian Monument

Situated on the western fragment of the knoll, the so-called Hanoverian monument actually commemorates the thirty-eight officers of the King's German Legion who were killed at Waterloo, including, not least, the commander of the Fifth Line Battalion, Colonel Christian von Ompteda, who died at the northern edge of the garden of La Haye Sainte while leading a desperate counter-attack on the captured farm at the behest of the Prince of Orange. Just across the road is the Gordon monument, the mounds on which the two sites are situated being highly suggestive of the cutting which hemmed in the main road at this point in 1815.

Edmund Wheatley, ensign, Fifth Line Battalion, King's German Legion:

Colonel Ompteda ordered us instantly into line to charge with a strong injunction to 'walk forward until I gave the word.' When within sixty yards, he cried 'Charge!', and we ran forward huzzaing . . . I ran by Colonel Ompteda, who cried out, 'That's right, Wheatley!' I found myself in contact with a French officer, but, 'ere we could decide, he fell by an unknown hand. I then ran at a drummer, but he leaped over a ditch through a hedge in which he stuck fast. I heard a cry of 'The cavalry! The cavalry!' But so eager was I that I did not mind it at that moment, and, when on the eve of dragging the Frenchman back . . . I recollect no more. On recovering my senses, I . . . found myself in a . . . ditch with a violent headache. Close by me lay Colonel Ompteda on

La Haye Sainte viewed from the area of the sandpit beside Charleroi highway looking south. Stoutly defended, the farm was only taken when the garrison ran out of ammunition. (Author's collection)

his back, his head stretched back with his mouth open and a hole in his throat.[29]

30. Return to the main road and walk southwards until opposite main gate of La Haye Sainte. The traffic being extremely heavy, it is unwise to cross the road for a closer view: whilst there are various plaques on the walls, they are not of sufficient interest to risk life and limb for, whilst there is no access to the farm. Indeed, the owners of La Haye Sainte having in the past had to endure a great deal from thoughtless tourists, visitors to the battlefield are urged to make particular attempts to respect their privacy.

DD. La Haye Sainte (eastern face)

The eastern face of La Haye Sainte is much as it was in 1815, while the defence of the farm by Major Georg Baring's Second Light Battalion of the King's German Legion was an epic affair that is particularly well chronicled. Prior to the action a few loopholes had been cut in the length of wall facing the road, while other men fired from the roof of the piggery to the right of the gate, the windows of the farmhouse and a number of apertures that had been cut in the roof of the barn. For the first half of the battle, too, much support was received from the Ninety-Fifth from their positions on the knoll and in the sandpit. Yet it is quite clear that the position was in fact one that was extremely difficult to defend. An *abatis* made of broken branches that was placed in the road at the south-eastern corner of the farm was seemingly no obstacle at all, whilst men holding the excellent firing positions offered by the orchard were likely to find themselves cut off from safety as they had no direct access to the courtyard. Finally, as if this was not enough, by keeping close to the hedges that lined the orchard, the French could get very close to the buildings with scarcely a single shot being fired at them by the defenders: hence their ability, as mentioned in several accounts, to rush forward and seize hold of the rifles of Baring's men, amongst whom ammunition was in any case an increasing problem.

Friedrich Lindenau, private, Second Light Battalion, King's German Legion:
Running around near us were some wounded English horses . . . I called out to one of them, [and] it stood still and let me lead it into the farm where I brought it to Major Baring. Soon after this, the farm was stormed again . . . and my captain ordered me to remain by the gateway. This time the battle lasted longer as ever more columns advanced. We soon ran short of cartridges, so that as soon as one of our men fell, we immediately went through his pockets. Major Baring, who constantly rode round the farm, reassured us that fresh ammunition would soon arrive. Soon afterwards I got a bullet through the back of my head, which I informed my captain about as he stood above me on the platform. He ordered me to go back. 'No', I answered, 'so long as I can stand, I stay at my post.' Meanwhile, I undid my scarf . . . and asked one of my comrades to put rum into the wound and tie the scarf around my head . . . Soon after that I heard a cry at the door of the barn: 'The enemy mean to get through here!' I went there and had scarcely fired a few shots . . . when I noticed thick smoke under the beams. Major Baring

and Sergeant Reese . . . immediately hurried in with kettles that they had filled at the pond . . . The loopholes . . . were now weakly manned, and the French maintained a heavy fire on us through them.[30]

31. From the main gate of La Haye Sainte, take the track that leads into the middle of the field opposite the farm.

EE. The Charge of the Household Brigade

Composed of the First and Second Regiments of Life Guards, the Royal Regiment of Horse Guards and the First Regiment of Dragoon Guards, Lord Edward Somerset's so-called Household Brigade was the most prestigious unit in Wellington's army, and was superbly equipped, mounted and uniformed. Having burst through the area between the crossroads and La Haye Sainte in the course of the great counter-attack launched by Lord Uxbridge, all round this spot the First Dragoons and Second Life Guards slaughtered the hapless infantrymen of the division of Quiot without mercy. Meanwhile, the

La Haye Sainte from the east with the Butte du Lion beyond. Famously, Wellington complained that the mound had ruined his battlefield. (Author's collection)

area is an excellent spot from which to appreciate the Anglo-Dutch position from the point of view of Drouet's corps.

Louis Canler, corporal, Twenty-Eighth Regiment of Line Infantry:
   Still with our arms at the shoulder, we climbed the hill as far the cannons . . . but hardly had we reached the plateau than . . . the Queen's Dragoons [*sic:* actually the First, or Royal, Regiment of Dragoons] hurled themselves upon us to the accompaniment of the most savage cries. Not having had time to form square, the first division could not sustain such a charge and was immediately broken, whereupon a real slaughter was unleashed. Separated from their comrades, each man could only make head on his own account, whilst sabres and bayonets were the order of the day when it came to cleaving the palpitating flesh of an opponent, the two sides being too mixed up with one another to make use of firearms. However, fight though they might, foot soldiers fighting on their own in the midst of a crowd of horsemen could not hope to maintain their positions, and so I soon found myself disarmed and taken prisoner. Yet hardly had this occurred than the command 'At the trot' rang out. This coming from some lancers and cuirassiers who had come to our aid, the dragoons who had seized me had no option but to abandon me to my own devices so that they could repel the charge, and I therefore lost not a moment in throwing myself into a patch of rye that was growing nearby. The French cavalrymen attacked their opponents with the utmost fury and made such good use of their swords and lances that the latter ended up being put to flight, and not just that but leaving a good few of their number strewn on the battlefield. All this allowed me to start making my way back to my unit.[31]

32. Return to the crossroads, where the visitor may also care to patronise one of the various restaurants clustered in its north-western angle: whilst the presence of the buildings is lamentable, the food that they offer is not to be despised! Alternatively, there are plenty of restaurants in Waterloo itself.

TOUR 2: THE FRENCH POSITIONS

Time: five hours (breaks excluded). Going: mostly well-maintained tracks, though some patches may be waterlogged in wet weather; moderate slopes with occasional steeper stretches.

1. Begin just south of the motorway junction at the southern end of Braine l'Alleud (there is some space to park along the lane leading south-eastwards from the junction).

Hougoumont viewed from Jerome Bonaparte's front line on the track from Lasne to Braine l'Alleud. Note the manner in which the complex sits in a hollow. That said, in 1815 as today, the fact that it represented a substantial complex of buildings should have been obvious to anyone positioned in this area, and it is therefore odd that no-one in the French army appears to have realized the existence of the chateau. (Author's collection)

A. Wellington's Right Flank

Thanks to the construction of the motorway, not to mention the expansion of Braine l'Alleud, this is the most altered section of the battlefield, yet another issue being the extensive tree cover that masks the slope behind Hougoumont. However, even to the naked eye, it is apparent from the lie of the land that the ridge which Wellington chose as his main fighting ground turned northwards in the vicinity of the motorway junction, thereby providing him with an excellent position from which he could stave off any attempt to move around his right flank. That this might be precisely the move that the emperor would try was something that deeply concerned the British commander and so he placed most of his reserves in positions where they could block such an attack. Thus, Mitchell's brigade was on the ridge where it turned north, thereby blocking the Nivelles road (this still exists, though it is now cut off from the battlefield by the motorway), whilst Chassé's Third Netherlands Infantry Division was holding Braine l'Alleud. Directly supporting Mitchell was Grant's light cavalry brigade and further back still Sir Henry Clinton's Sixth Division and the Brunswick contingent. In the event, however, Wellington was proved wrong: although the cavalry division attached to II Corps was sent to occupy the area where the visitor is now standing, Napoleon never showed any interest in such a move, believing that he would do better to strike the eastern end of the Army of the Netherland's line. However, so close together were the two armies in this area that skirmishing broke out very early in the battle.

William Wheeler, private, Fifty-First Regiment of Foot:
   Our brigade went into position on the right of the line on high ground that commanded the farm of Hougoumont . . . Major Keyt commanded the light troops in advance, consisting of Captain Phelps' company . . . [and] the light companies of the Twenty-Third and Fourteenth Regiments. About [eleven] o'clock . . . Captain McRoss' company was ordered down to reinforce the advance, who were warmly engaged. A quarter of an hour had not elapsed before four more of our companies were ordered to the front, [of which] the company I belong to was one. We soon saw what was up: our advance was nearly

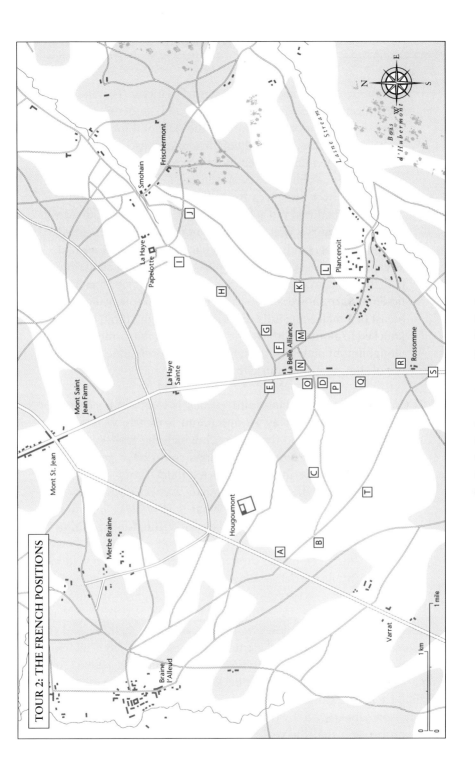

TOUR 2: THE FRENCH POSITIONS

surrounded by a body of the enemy's lancers. Fortunately
the Fifteenth Hussars were at hand and rendered willing
assistance. Our appearance altered the state of things and, ere
we could make them a present of three rounds each, the lancers
were glad to get off. We were now exposed to a heavy fire of
grape and were obliged to push across a large space of fallow
ground to cover ourselves from their fire. Here we found a
deep cross road that ran across our front, on the opposite side
of [which] the rye was as high as our heads. We remained
here some time, [and] then retired back to the ground we had
advanced from . . . Grape and shells were dropping about like
hail: this was devilish annoying . . . and we advanced again . . .
under a sharp shower of shells: one of the shells pitched on the
breast of a man some little distance on my right, [and] he was
knocked to atoms. A little to the . . . left stood the farmhouse of
Hougoumont on which the enemy was pouring a destructive
fire of shot, shell and musketry.[1]

2. Continue along the lane until a track is reached breaching off
to the left. The whole way Hougoumont is clearly visible across
the fields to the left, and the ease with which the artillery batteries
attached to Piré and Jérôme's divisions could have pounded the
position had anyone thought to order them to do so is all too
apparent, screened though the chateau was on its western side
in 1815 by a line of poplar trees. What is very clear, meanwhile,
is that Hougoumont was not the key to Wellington's position in
the slightest. Thus, too far away to block a move by Napoleon on
Braine l'Alleud even by the direct route along which the visitor is
walking, let alone the deep valley which runs parallel to it some 400
yards to the west, its loss would not have endangered Wellington's
main position either, given that the slope behind it is very steep,
the whole area commanded by the Anglo-Dutch artillery and the
Hougoumont complex little suited to act as a base from which to
launch an attack. Given that Hougoumont could be masked very
easily by driving the garrison back from its outer perimeter and
that La Haye Sainte lacked adequate firing positions due to the
garrison's inability to fortify it properly the night before the battle,
it can be seen that the real importance of the outlying positions

occupied by Wellington was that they broke up French attacks and greatly restricted the area available for manoeuvre.

B. Jérôme Bonaparte's Position

The spot where the visitor is standing marks the left flank of the infantry division commanded by Jérôme Bonaparte, this forming one of the three divisions belonging to General Reille's II Corps that was present on the battlefield (a fourth, that of the mortally-wounded General Girard, had been so badly hit at Ligny that it had been attached to Grouchy's command). The only one of the Bonaparte brothers to attempt to make a name for himself as a commander, Jérôme in fact possessed little military talent, and had been sent back to his puppet kingdom of Westphalia in disgrace in the early stages of the campaign in Russia. At Waterloo, he was not to distinguish himself, becoming bogged down in repeated attempts to storm Hougoumont that sucked in more and more French troops, but the fault was not entirely his in that Napoleon never made it plain to his subordinates that all that was needed in the Hougoumont sector was a holding attack designed to ensure that Wellington could not use it as a base from which to launch a counter-attack.

Jean-Baptiste Jolyet, major, First Regiment of Light Infantry:
Hardly had we arrived . . . than we were ordered to move forward and deploy on the left of the Fifth Division [i.e. that of Bachelu: this suggests that at this moment the division of General Foy had not yet arrived from the rear]. Before we had occupied the ground in question, I dispatched my *voltigeur* company to check out the little wood called Hougoumont on which it was planned to anchor the left of the army [note the absence of any reference to a chateau here: the manner in which the chief map used by the French rendered the terrain was extremely vague, and a number of French accounts make it abundantly clear that nobody knew the chateau was there – from the French lines, after all, it was almost entirely hidden]. Meanwhile, I deployed the rest of my battalion to the left of the Sixty-Ninth Regiment [*sic*: the regiment concerned was actually the Sixty-First]. A fold of the terrain hid all sight of the English and also served to place our Second Battalion in cover,

but, as he was getting the latter unit into position, our brigade commander (who was killed shortly afterwards) ordered it to move forward and place itself in advance of the sunken road in which it was stationed. This put it in view of the enemy, and ... the English batteries, stationed, as they were, in front of their line, opened a very heavy fire upon it that laid low some twenty of its men, the balls following one another with such rapidity that the battalion was forced to withdraw to the sunken road.[2]

3. Continue along the lane noting how the view of Hougoumont changes, the manner in which it sits in a hollow becoming far more noticeable. Very soon, however, the chateau starts to disappear, and that despite the fact that the wood that masked it in 1815 is no longer extant apart from the three dead trees that stand in front of the south gate and serve as a useful reminder of the height that they and their long-gone companions once attained (so dreadful was the damage that it suffered that the wood was cut down in its entirety in 1817). Carry on till the lane becomes sunken and then ascend the bank on the right-hand side: from here there is an excellent view of the whole of the

Flooding along the track from Lasne to Braine l'Alleud looking east towards the Charleroi highway. On 18 June 1815 conditions would have been much the same. (Author's collection)

western half of Wellington's position as it appeared to his opponents, even if the northern skyline is inevitably dominated by the Butte du Lion. Note, though, not just that it is impossible to see anything beyond the crest of Mont Saint Jean, but also that the precise configuration of the ground is not apparent, it being particularly difficult to spot the significance of the watershed linking the rival positions.

C. Foy's Position

The visitor is now standing roughly in the centre of the position taken up by Reille's II Corps: to the left was the division of Jérôme Bonaparte; in front, that of General Foy and to the right that of General Bachelu, all these formations being arrayed on a line roughly parallel with the track, together with their attached foot artillery batteries, in a position that was protected from direct fire by the intermediate ridge. Immediately to the rear, meanwhile, was the III Reserve Cavalry Corps of General Milhaud with one division of dragoons and cuirassiers and another of cuirassiers and carabineers, and, still further back, the Guard Heavy Cavalry Division of General Guyot.

Sylvain Larréguy de Civrieux, cadet, Ninety-Third Regiment of Line Infantry:
   Along with that of Prince Jérôme, my division was deployed opposite Hougoumont . . . The opening scene of the duel between 200,000 men that was about to take place, and which history was going to baptise as the battle of Waterloo was an impressive spectacle. I was barely nineteen years old, but I had been through so many different tests and taken part in so many terrible combats that it seemed to me that I had every right to number myself among the army's old soldiers. Would I survive this memorable day? I spared an affectionate thought for my mother, for each one of my loved ones.[3]

4. Continue along the lane in the direction of the Charleroi highroad, noting that the copse of trees to the north is a post 1815 addition to the scenery. At the highroad, pause by the 'Wounded Eagle' monument.

The lane from Lasne to Braine l'Alleud looking west from the vicinity of the Charleroi highway. The cobbles post-date the battle. (Author's collection)

D. Bachelu's Position

The area immediately to the left of the Charleroi highroad looking north from the Wounded Eagle was that occupied by the division of General Bachelu. Immediately to the rear were the two divisions that made up the infantry of the Old and Middle Guard, these being stationed in the hollow that may be clearly seen from the southern side of the lane, which in this section is quite deeply sunken.

Philippe Doulcet de Pontécoulant, lieutenant, Horse Artillery of the Guard:

About nine o'clock the sky began to clear and a number of artillery officers arrived with the news . . . that in a hour or so it would be possible to move guns without the slightest difficulty. At this the emperor mounted his horse with the intention of carrying out a complete reconnaissance . . . Having ridden to our outposts opposite the farm of La Haye Sainte . . . he studied the whole of the enemy line with the most profound attention . . . This done to his satisfaction from several different viewpoints, he then ordered General Haxo . . . to check whether any field works had been erected to cover the enemy's wings . . . the latter soon reporting that he had perceived nothing of the sort . . . Although Napoleon paused in thought for a moment, the plan of attack must have already been firmly fixed in his head, for he lost no hesitation in giving the necessary instructions, these being taken down by two generals sitting on the ground. Very soon, then *aides de camp* were dashing about in all directions so as to give every unit its orders . . . Finally, having first ridden along the full length of his line to ensure that his orders were being carried out, Napoleon stationed himself on a small knoll on the left of the highroad a few yards along from the farm of Rossomme . . . and remained there for a large part of the rest of the day: not only was it in the very midst of his reserves, but it was so high that it gave a good view of the whole field of battle.[4]

5. Walk northwards along the highroad to La Belle Alliance and cross the road by the crossing: the utmost care is needed in this operation: although visibility is reasonably good in both directions, the traffic is both very heavy and extremely fast.

La Belle Alliance viewed from the track from Lasne to Braine l'Alleud. In 1815 only the right-hand portion of the building was in existence. (Author's collection)

E. La Belle Alliance

In 1815 La Belle Alliance was a tavern, the name of which commemorated the marriage of the widow of the original owner to the man who had taken over the business in the wake of the death of her first husband. Though in essence the same building as the one which existed at the time of the battle, its appearance has been much altered: for example, a Denis Dighton watercolour painted shortly after the battle shows that the whitewash and plaster of today should be discarded in favour of faded brickwork, while the large block at the northern end of the building was added at some point in the nineteenth century. Traditionally, it is the scene of the much-pictured meeting that took place between Wellington and Blücher at the close of the battle but it is probable that the encounter actually took place some distance to the south. Be that as it may, delighted with the symbolism of the name, Blücher wanted the battle to be named after the inn, but Wellington rather insisted on following his usual practice and calling it after the place where he had spent the previous night, i.e. Waterloo. During the battle, the building was used as a hospital while the area provided an ideal position from which heavy artillery – specifically, the three 12-pounder batteries attached to I, II and VI Corps – could batter the Anglo-Dutch lines. Note, however, that the reverse slope on the further side of Wellington's position cannot be observed at all: whatever the reason for the French cavalry charges, it was certainly not that Ney spotted masses of troops heading for the rear. As maintained in the account of the battle offered by this guide, though still initiated by Ney, the charges were rather intended to keep Wellington pinned down until a fresh assault could be launched on his left.

Hyppolyte Mauduit, sergeant, First Regiment of Foot Grenadiers of the Imperial Guard:

The ground on which we had to operate was boggy and slippery, and so our artillery experienced a thousand difficulties in establishing their batteries in the places where they needed to be, whereas the enemy's infantry and artillery had been at their posts for more than twelve hours. This stroke of good fortune was incontestably in favour of our adversaries and contributed not a little to preventing their defeat at our hands, just as it also played a major part in rendering our downfall complete, the extraordinary difficulties experienced by the artillery . . . being felt still more severely at the moment when it had to undertake a fighting retreat across muddy ground, and all the more so after all the fatigues of the day. However, the gauntlet had been picked up, and there was now nothing for it but to draw our swords.[5]

6. Cross the Charleroi highway and take the road to Plancenoit. A short walk will then bring the visitor to a knoll marked by a hedged enclosure from where Napoleon is reputed to have spent much of the latter part of the battle (the signage at the site, indeed, specifically claims that he was there from four o'clock onwards).

F. Napoleon's Command Post
Whether Napoleon actually used the spot where the visitor is standing as his command post is a moot point: for one thing, the view of Wellington's positions is more complete from the vicinity of La Belle

NAPOLEON ON THE FIELD OF WATERLOO.
From the Painting by L. Royer.

Napoleon astride his favourite horse, Marengo, on the battlefield at Waterloo. Seemingly abandoned after the emperor fled the battlefield, Marengo was captured by a British officer and lived out his days in exile in Britain, where he survived until 1831. (Wikimedia Commons)

Alliance. However, the knoll does command a good view of the area from which the Prussians were attacking Plancenoit, so it is certainly plausible that the emperor was there at some point. Also important to note is the fact that the position offers a view of a small portion of the heights on the far bank of the river Lasne that Bulöw's corps had to cross on its way to the battlefield (this is discernable as a tree-crowned mound on the far horizon). That said, whether the very small area of ground in question could actually be seen on the rather murky day that was 18 June 1815, or even that the road that the Prussians were following actually crossed it is another matter. Also in doubt is the question of Napoleon's whereabouts at the decisive moment: in so far as is known, he was at Rossomme and from there there is no such view. On balance, then, the story that Napoleon spotted the oncoming Prussians before they reached the battlefield seems most unlikely.

Jean de Crabbé, aide de camp to Marshal Ney:
Marshal Soult . . . summoned me. He told me that the emperor had confided his ultimate reserve, all that remained of the Guard, to Marshal Ney to make a decisive attack on the English lines. He had asked for an experienced officer of his headquarters to carry supplementary orders. I reached the rise near the farm [*sic*] of La Belle Alliance where the emperor was located. He was surrounded by a squadron of the Guard *Chasseurs à Cheval*, jackets and trousers green trimmed with red, and shabraques of the same . . . From this position one could see the whole of the battlefield . . . The emperor was on a chair in front of a table on which some maps were spread . . . General Count Drouot and two *aides de camp* were at his side. He wore his usual grey riding coat over his uniform of a colonel of *chasseurs* and on his head his legendary hat. Slumped in his chair, he appeared to me both exhausted and angry.[6]

7. Retracing his steps to La Belle Alliance, the visitor should next take a dirt-track angling to the right between the Plancenoit road and the Charleroi highway. Just past a small copse, this brings the visitor out onto a broad spur jutting forward from the French ridge which offers an excellent view of the whole of the eastern half of the battlefield. Immediately in front lies La Haye Sainte, though only its

roof may be seen, together with a second intermediate ridge akin to that on the other side of the Charleroi highway: in the course of Drouet's assault, this last was occupied by the six batteries belonging to I Corps, these having advanced alongside the infantry and then deployed to give them covering fire (it was these guns that were overrun by the Union Brigade in its famous charge across the valley). To the right, meanwhile, can be seen the high ground known as the Heights of Agiers: completely covering, as these did, the movements of the Prussian army, the latter would have remained invisible to the French troops deployed against Wellington, and, for that matter, the men opposing them, until Bülow's corps attacked Mouton south of Frischermont after it had got through the Bois de Paris. Finally, looking to the left, it will be seen that the western horizon is constituted by the cross-ridge leading to Mont Saint Jean: as a result, French troops stationed in the eastern half of the battlefield could not possibly have seen, or even been aware of, either the advance or the retreat of the Imperial Guard, what produced the collapse of Napoleon's forces in this sector rather being the eruption of Ziethen's corps from the direction of Papelotte.

Wellington's centre-left viewed from La Belle Alliance. The distance is such that even the heaviest French guns would have been firing at extreme range. Note, too, how the view is obscured by the intermediate ridge. (Author's collection)

G. Quiot's Position

The track which the visitor has followed to reach this spot marks the original front line of Napoleon's forces, and, more particularly, the position from which Drouet's corps set off to attack Wellington's centre-left, the troops stationed in this particular sector being the division of General Quiot. To its rear there is an extensive area of dead ground, but, seemingly intent on over-awing the Anglo-Dutch army with his massed ranks, the emperor made no attempt to make use of the reversed slope with which he was thus presented in the same fashion as Wellington, the result being that his men suffered significant losses from artillery fire before they had advanced even a single step in the direction of the enemy. All the more was this the case given the defective nature of the formation adopted by Drouet, the battalions of his two centre divisions being formed in line one behind the other with little or no distance between them: not only were such targets hard to miss, but each Allied cannonball struck down as many as a dozen men. On the other hand, the ridge did offer a perfect position for the French artillery and one can only surmise that the decision to move so much of the latter forward to the intermediate ridge reflected the fact that the batteries concerned were all armed with 6-pounder guns and were therefore essentially all but out of range. That said, this ensured that Drouet's men had little artillery support for much of their advance, whilst, being somewhat lower than its predecessor, the new position offered even less chance of hitting troops hidden behind the reversed slope.

Louis Canler, corporal, Twenty-Eighth Regiment of Line Infantry:
    Towards noon we took up our positions on the plateau of [La Belle Alliance], where a battery of eighty guns was deployed [*sic*: Canler is mistaken here: the only guns in position at La Belle Alliance as this point were the three 12-pounder batteries that constituted the corps artillery reserves of I, II and VI Corps], and next they had us descend into the ravine of the same name, where we were sheltered from a formidable battery the English had established during the night . . . which fired continuously . . . Pretty soon, our guns fired back and the result was a terrifying duel between

some 200 guns, the balls and shells of both sides shrieking by just over our heads.[7]

8. Continue along the track in the same direction as before, thereby passing through the positions initially occupied by the division of François-Xavier Donzelot, a sometime private in the old French regular army who had risen to the rank of brigadier by 1794 and thereafter seen service in Egypt, Italy and the Ionian islands. After several hundred yards a substantial wood is passed: ahead and to the right can be seen the slopes where VI Corps tried to delay Bülow, whilst, straight on, the horizon is dominated by the Heights of Agiers (a substantial ridge that made it almost impossible for the French to spot the advance of the Prussians); note, meanwhile, that, like so many of their fellows, the various copses that dot the area were not there in 1815.

The track from La Belle Alliance to Papelotte looking west in the area occupied by Donzelot's division. Note how the watershed blocks all visibility in respect of the western half of the battlefield. (Author's collection)

H. Marcognet's Position

The copse where the visitor is now standing marks the approximate position of the division of General Pierre Binet de Marcognet. A good example of an officer of the old regular army – he had enlisted as an officer cadet in 1781 – who had stayed on to fight for the Revolution rather than emigrating as so many of his erstwhile colleagues did, Marcognet was a veteran of many battles in the Revolutionary and Napoleonic Wars and had seen action against Wellington at the battles of Busaco and Fuentes de Oñoro. Like Donzelot's division, his eight battalions were deployed in line one behind the other with very little space between them, the idea being that this would give the attackers the best of both worlds in terms of both firepower and shock.

Jacques Martin, lieutenant, Forty-Fifth Regiment of Line Infantry:
    The army was soon drawn up in battle order . . . In the course of the morning the weather had got a lot better, and now a splendid sun illuminated the lines of combatants and made their weapons shine in the brightest of fashions. It was a most magnificent spectacle: bayonets, helmets and cuirasses gleamed in the sunlight; flags, guidons and pennants . . . fluttered in the breeze; drums beat; trumpets sounded; the bands of every regiment played 'Watch over the Safety of the Empire'. And in the midst of it all Napoleon was reviewing his army before battle for the last time. Never could he have heard the cry of 'Long live the emperor!' being uttered with more enthusiasm; never had such absolute devotion been painted on the faces of his soldiers or for that matter reflected in their gestures or voices. It was like a dream.[8]

9. Continue along the track in the same direction, noting the view of the farm of Papelotte that soon appears on the left. Very shortly, the track drops steeply downhill between high banks on each side.

I. Durutte's Position

The son of a merchant from Douai, Pierre Durutte enlisted in one of the numerous battalions of volunteers formed to augment the French army in 1791 and 1792. As devoted as he was brave, he distinguished himself in battle after battle and by 1812 had reached the rank of

The track from La Belle Alliance to Papelotte looking east in the area occupied by Durutte's division. (Author's collection)

divisional commander. At Waterloo the commander of the right-hand-most division of I Corps, he participated in the general advance mounted by that formation around one o'clock, but did not make use of the same massive columns employed by many of the other troops involved in the attack: instead, his men were formed in eight small battalion columns which were much more adapted to the broken terrain, and therefore made considerable progress, occupying Frischermont, Smohain and part of La Haye and possibly even effecting a lodgement in Papelotte. However, such was the broken nature of the terrain and the nature of the defenders – veteran troops from the Second and Third Battalions of the Regiment of Nassau who had seen much service in the Peninsular War – that he could get no further, despite the fact that the charge of the Household and Union Brigades had only affected one of his battalions. In this area, then, the battle for some time descended into a stalemate that was only ended by the advance of Ziethen's corps at about half-past seven. By this time reduced to half-strength by Durutte's dispatch of one of his two brigades to support operations in the centre, the French at first put up some resistance but were quickly overwhelmed.

Joseph Rullière, major, Ninety-Fifth Regiment of Line Infantry:
  From three to four o'clock [*sic:* the time referred to by Rullière is likely to have been at least two hours later], one began to see the movements of the Prussians on the right of our army. Some time later we came under musket fire from their skirmishers. My battalion was set to stop them in which it succeeded. The firefight had raged for half an hour, when General de Labedoyère, *aide-de-camp* to the emperor . . . came to announce it was Marshal Grouchy who was debouching on our right. I remarked to him that . . . it was the Prussians . . . we had opposite to us, and that they had already killed and wounded many men . . . At the same moment, the captain of the *voltigeurs* of my battalion fell wounded with a musket-ball in his thigh. As the Prussians were beginning to show in force, I made him mount my horse, and sent him to the army's hospital.[9]

10. Continue downhill between banks that become increasingly high. At the bottom of the slope, turn right into another sunken lane and head back uphill, pausing at the crest of the ridge.

Jacquinot and Durutte's initial positions viewed from the valley beneath Wellington's front line near the Frischermont convent. The area in the foreground witnessed fierce fighting during the latter stages of the charge of the British heavy cavalry. (Author's collection)

J. Jacquinot's Position

The spot where the visitor is now standing marks the extreme right flank of the original French position and was held by the light cavalry brigade attached to I Corps under the command of Charles Jacquinot: it was this force that launched the counter-charge that destroyed much of the Union Brigade in the wake of the latter's rout of the divisions of Donzelot and Marcognet. Straight ahead the ridge opposite is cloaked by a mass of trees. One of the few patches of woodland on the present-day battlefield to have existed in 1815, this was the site of the Chateau of Frischermont, a substantial structure that was occupied at the start of the battle by troops from the brigade of Prince Bernhard of Saxe-Weimar, but was quickly evacuated as being too far forward to defend. The ridge running from left to right, meanwhile, marks the line of advance of Bülow's advance on Plancenoit.

Octave Levavasseur, aide-de-camp to Marshal Ney:
    At daybreak, the marshal [i.e. Ney] gave me the job of reconnoitring . . . the movements of the enemy. This task I began over on the extreme left, and at first, despite the conversations that I had with every single picket that I came to, I could discover very little. However, when I arrived at the extreme right-hand end of the line, a scout told me that detachments of the enemy could be seen coming and going the whole time, and that various officers had been seen riding off in various directions. I therefore stayed put for an hour to verify the veracity of these reports, and, having done so, rode off to find the marshal, convinced that the enemy was manoeuvring against our right. In the interim Ney had joined the emperor, but, as soon as I reached him, I told him of . . . my conjectures. At this, he spoke to Napoleon, saying, 'Sire: my *aide-de-camp* has just conducted a reconnaissance, and he tells me that the enemy are trying to turn our right.' 'Not to worry', the emperor replied. 'Our plan will still do.'[10]

11. Drop down the slope to a T-junction and turn right. The main route from Papelotte and Smohain to Plancenoit, the track the visitor is now following marked the axis of the advance of Ziethen's corps

The track from Smohain to Plancenoit looking west. Mouton's final position was constituted by the ridge in the distance. At the end of the battle part of Ziethen's corps advanced along this valley in the direction of La Belle Alliance. (Author's collection)

at the end of the battle. Note the open nature of the terrain: almost unchanged since 1815, this ensured that the French retreat was continually harried by Prussian cavalry. After approximately one kilometre the track angles sharply to the south just to the west of a substantial modern property standing in a grove of trees.

K. Mouton's Second Position

On the high ground ahead and to the right will be observed a line of modern houses. This marks the left wing of the position adopted by Mouton's VI Corps after it was driven back from the vicinity of Frischermont and continued to be manned even as Ziethen's corps flooded across the low ground where the visitor is now standing. Heavily outnumbered from the start, the two divisions of VI Corps had been fighting continually for over three hours against ever increasing numbers of enemy by the time the new arrivals came in sight, and yet they managed to win a little more time for Napoleon even now. As such, they are far more worthy of the respect usually paid to the largely fictitious 'last stand of the Old Guard'; to paraphrase the emperor himself, however, history is on the side of the big battalions. With the appearance of Ziethen's corps in the area north of Plancenoit, meanwhile, all French resistance in the eastern half of the battlefield came to an end.

Pierre Durutte, GOC, Fourth Division, Army of the North:
All of a sudden . . . I noticed that the main road was covered with a large crowd of soldiers in full flight. Members of the Middle Guard, some of these fugitives got as far as the four twelve-pounders which General [Drouet] had placed at my disposition, and infected the gunners . . . with the same terror which had taken hold of them, and in a moment the whole battery was taking itself off at the gallop. Having formed up the brigade of General Brue, I led it towards the main road in an attempt to check the rout and give the fugitives the chance to rally behind a unit which was still in perfect order and ready to do its duty, but my efforts were in vain: in front of us we saw the whole of the left wing of the army retiring at full speed. As we were now forming the most advanced point of the line, I realised that we would soon be surrounded if I did not order a retreat. That being the case, I fell back across the main road in an attempt to reach the brigade of General Pégot . . . but found that the way was blocked . . . Much alarmed . . . I set off to find an alternative route . . . but, when I returned, to my astonishment the brigade was no longer where I had left it.[11]

12. Continue along the track. This now runs uphill to the crest of the ridge followed by Bülow. Just at the edge of the built-up area that forms the northern outskirts of Plancenoit (a village which is today much bigger than it was in 1815), the visitor will encounter the Prussian monument.

L. The Prussian Monument
Erected in 1819 and unmistakably Germanic in design, this bears the inscription, 'To our fallen heroes in gratitude from king and country: may they rest in peace. La Belle Alliance, 1815' (thanks to its obvious symbolism, 'La Belle Alliance' was the name for the

battle that was preferred in Germany throughout the nineteenth century). Completely treeless in 1815, the knoll on which it stands is supposed to mark the spot from which Prussian guns bombarded the area round La Belle Alliance at the end of the battle, though it is far too small to have afforded enough space for a full battery. What is more conceivable is that it was from here that General Mouton directed the struggle to hold back the oncoming Prussians: driven from their original positions east of Plancenoit, it was more-or-less on the line running north from the monument that three of his four brigades took their stand (the fourth had rather retired into Plancenoit itself).

Friedrich Bülow von Dennewitz, GOC, IV Corps, Army of the Lower Rhine:
   Continuously the target of the enemy musketry, the skirmishers of the Fifteenth Brigade had to be relieved several times and our fire began to slacken on this part of the line. The foe seemed to have obtained a momentary advantage there and his intention was perhaps to act offensively against our right wing, while the fight increased in violence at Plancenoit, so as to penetrate between our right wing and the English left. Indeed, strong masses of his infantry and cavalry could be seen opposite Fifteenth Brigade.[12]

13. At the road beyond the monument turn right and head uphill. With the possible exception of a walled farm on the left called Sainte Catherine, in 1815 there were no buildings in this area: inexplicably, it was excluded from the protected zone established by the Belgian government in 1914. Continue uphill to a junction with a road coming from the left.

M. Milhaud's Position

As a small monument at the road junction reminds the visitor, this spot marks the position which Eduard Milhaud's IV Reserve Cavalry Corps occupied at the start of the battle, though in fact Milhaud's troops stretched a long way to the east from this point. Meanwhile, it was from this area that *aides de camp* dispatched from the left wing first caught a glimpse of the oncoming Prussians.

Jean-Baptiste Lemonnier-Delafosse, aide de camp to General Foy:
Masses of troops began to appear from the direction of Saint Lambert . . . As was announced by their cannon, it was the Prussians . . . In response, the emperor cried, 'It is Grouchy: victory is ours!', and sent out his *aide de camp*, Labedoyère, to announce the latter's arrival. On all sides cries went up of 'En avant! En avant!', but orders were lacking, and nothing came for us . . . Much perturbed at this, I wanted to learn the truth of what was going on, and asked General Foy for permission to go and find out. The latter being equally concerned, I rode across the whole width of the battlefield and eventually . . . found the VI Corps of General Mouton and the Young Guard drawn up at right angles to our position and Bülow and his Prussians heading straight for them in such a way that, if they were not stopped, they could not but reach the main road before our centre and left had had a chance to get away. Coming across an adjutant-major . . . named Servatius, I asked him whether Grouchy had really come. 'Grouchy?' he said. 'Does it look like Grouchy?' I now saw dark masses of troops debouching on to the battlefield from the direction of Ohain. It was General Ziethen, who, thinking that they were French, had just attacked the troops of the Prince of Saxe-Weimar and, after a very sharp combat, driven them from a village which they had been defending. Returning at once to General Foy, I gave him the news . . . 'Dreadful! Dreadful', he exclaimed. 'But not a word!'[13]

14. Carry on along the road to La Belle Alliance. Shortly before Napoleon's observatory, take a track to the left (this is a continuation of the track followed in the first part of the tour and at the time of the battle formed part of the road from Braine l'Alleud to Plancenoit). After a short distance, the visitor will arrive at the Charleroi highway opposite the Wounded Eagle monument. Turn right and proceed a few yards northwards to the Victor Hugo monument.

N. Victor Hugo Monument
A gigantic column whose design was much influenced by masonic beliefs, the Hugo monument commemorates not so much the battle

itself as Hugo's endeavours to romanticise the story of the French defeat through, for example, his invention of the image of the French cavalry being defeated not by the unshakeable resistance of Wellington's infantry but rather the accident of the sunken lane. In thus misrepresenting reality, however, Hugo was but following the precedent set by Napoleon.

Marie de Baudus, aide de camp to Marshal Soult:
    I cannot find the words to express the emotions that I felt when, returning from taking orders to our right wing, where I had seen the shot and shell of the corps of Bülow slicing through VI Corps . . . the emperor announced that the firing that could be hard from that direction was that of Marshal Grouchy. The object of this monstrous lie was to get the army to make a last effort to support the attack of a part of the Guard against the centre of the English army, and this certainly had an effect not only on the men who were still capable of putting up a fight, but also on the wounded: quite extraordinarily, all of the latter who could still walk got to their feet and advanced on the enemy amidst cries of 'Vive l'empereur!' Indeed, the emperor . . . even made dupes of the officers of his general staff, for I heard one such courtier . . . say, 'It is Marengo all over again: the arrival of Marshal Grouchy is for us what the arrival of General Desaix was for the Army of Reserve.' However, the illusion could not last for very long and in the end the result was but to aggravate our situation. Thus, whipped up by a man who in his heart knew that he could not flatter himself with hopes of success, the enthusiasm which the hope of victory had unleashed amongst the troops in the end inspired nothing but enormous rage: however vigorously it was pressed, the attack did not have the slightest chance of success in the situation in which we were placed.[14]

15. Cross the road and walk back to the Wounded Eagle Monument. Visitors wishing to end the tour here may now head back to the start of the tour along the tracks that were followed in the first part of the itinerary. Having walked a few yards down the slope, however, they may wish to avail themselves of the handrail that will be found on

The hill alongside the Charleroi highway on which the left wing of the last of Napoleon's reserves attempted to block the Allied onrush at the close of the battle. (Author's collection)

the left-hand side of the track to pull themselves up to the level of the field above: this will be found to afford a good view of the hill on which part of the Guard made a stand in the closing moments of the battle.

O. The Wounded Eagle Monument
Built to commemorate the last combatants of the Army of the North, the Wounded Eagle rather marks the spot from which the Old and Middle Guard launched the final assault on Wellington's positions.

Hyppolyte Mauduit, sergeant, First Regiment of Foot Grenadiers of the Imperial Guard:
    Following the advance of the troops of Generals Domon and [Mouton] . . . we left our position at Rossomme . . . Very soon we were saluted by the artillery drawn up in serried ranks in the vicinity of Hougoumont. Several of the balls concerned falling . . . in the midst of our ranks, one of them killed a *cantiniére* attached

to the company next to mine . . . The unfortunate *cantiniere*, the first casualty which our battalion suffered that day, had come from Elba with a grenadier with whom she had decided to share her fate. As she was marching directly behind him when she was struck, her blood coated his bearskin and knapsack . . . whilst such was the impact that the little barrel of liquor which she had been carrying was split apart . . . Given that we had just halted, we were able to help the old grenadier pay his last respects to a companion whose devotion merited an end that, if not less glorious, should have been much more gentle. We dug a grave for her beside the highroad, and her lover stood beside it with his hands pressed to his heart, while several grenadiers took the girl by the arms and lowered her into her last resting place . . . A cross improvised from a couple of branches . . . was placed on the grave and an inscription fastened to it with a pin, this running as follows: 'Here lies Maria, *cantiniére* of the First Regiment of Grenadiers of the Old Guard, dead on the field of honour at half-past two in the afternoon on 18th June 1815. Passer-by, whoever you may be, render Maria a salute of honour!'[15]

16. Continue southwards along the main road. After a short distance a turning is passed to Plancenoit. Just beyond it there is a rather nondescript brick house with a tiled roof: in 1815 this was a tavern belonging to Jean Decoster, the local man who achieved fame on account of the fact that he was pressed into serving Napoleon as a guide, a role that he does not seem to have performed especially well. Immediately after this, the road cuts through a pronounced knoll. Depending on the state of the ground and/or crops, it may be possible to leave the road and walk the few yards to the summit. Clearly a dominant position, this is the spot which witnessed – or rather did not witness! – the famous episode of the so-called *mot Cambronne.*

P. The Mot Cambronne

We come here to the capture of the commander of the First Regiment of Chasseurs, Pierre Cambronne. According to legend, summoned to surrender after he and his men were surrounded by Allied cavalry, Cambronne is supposed to have shouted either 'The Guard dies, but never surrender', or the more prosaic 'Merde!', a word that ever

The area in which Cambronne was captured by Halkett looking north towards the Victor Hugo monument. The troops the former was with neither died nor surrendered, but beat a hasty retreat which eventually took most of them to safety. (Author's collection)

since has been referred to as the *mot Cambronne*. Throughout his life, however, Cambronne denied that he said anything of the sort, while, rather than going down fighting in the midst of a storm of shot and shell, it is clear that his story was actually distinctly inglorious, and, not just that, but that it took place to the accompaniment not of a heroic last stand, but an ever-more hasty retreat. At all events, whatever the truth of the story, it was acted out somewhere in this vicinity as Cambronne's unit, the First Regiment of Foot Chasseurs of the Imperial Guard, fell back in haste from the rear-guard position it had initially taken up at La Belle Alliance in the wake of the repulse of the Guard towards Rossomme:

> *Hugh Halkett, GOC, Third Hanoverian Brigade*:
> The moment General Adam's brigade advanced, I lost no time to follow with the Osnabruck battalion . . . During the advance we were much annoyed by the enemy's artillery. The first company . . . broke into platoons, and, supported by the sharpshooters of the battalion, made a dash at the artillery on our right and captured six guns with their horses. Some hundred yards to our right were

some troops of hussars (I believe the Tenth). I rode up to them and got them to charge a column of infantry which was drawing to their left in rear of the French Guards. The charge succeeded admirably and the column dispersed behind some enclosures . . . During our advance we were in constant contact with the French Guards and I often called to them to surrender. For some time I had my eye upon, as I supposed, the general officer in command of the Guards [i.e. Cambronne] . . . trying to animate his men to stand. After having received our fire with much effect, the column left their general with two officers behind, when . . . I made a dash for the general. When [I was] about cutting him down, he called out he would surrender, upon which he preceded me [to the rear], but I had not gone many paces before my horse got a shot through his body and fell to the ground. In a few seconds I got him on his legs again, and found my friend, Cambronne, had taken French leave in the direction from where he came. I instantly overtook him, laid hold of him by the aiguillette, and . . . gave him in charge to a sergeant to take to the Duke.[16]

17. If necessary, return to the highway, and continue in the direction of Charleroi. After approximately 300 yards a restaurant is reached called 'Kai-Yu'. Turn right here along a track that runs along the northern edge of the property. This peters out on reaching the fields behind the restaurant, but from the end of the track an excellent view may be obtained both of the shallow valley occupied by the Old and Middle Guard in the first part of the battle and the area across which the French left wing fled in the wake of defeat.

Q. Position of the Old and Middle Guard
Having spent the night bivouacked in fields in the area of the farm known as Le Caillou which Napoleon had requisitioned as his headquarters, early in the morning of 18 June the Old and Middle Guards advanced to a position in the shallow valley running from left to right.

Hyppolyte Mauduit, sergeant, First Regiment of Foot Grenadiers of the Imperial Guard:
    General Friant formed us into closed column of divisions to the right and left . . . of the knoll of Rossomme, the same place,

The shallow valley west of the Charleroi highway in which the infantry of the Guard waited in reserve for much of the battle. (Author's collection)

indeed, where Napoleon spent the first hours of the battle. My regiment was placed just on the left-hand side of the highroad . . . Placed as we were, we dominated the whole of the plain in front of us and to our left: the terrain was rather broken up with undulations running in different directions, but . . . tended to rise steadily in the direction of the position occupied by the Anglo-Dutch army . . . We could see the whole of its right and centre, and even pick out the batteries stationed in its front line, but its left was beyond our view as the ground on the right of the road rose up in a broad plateau that ran on without a break until it was a mere cannon-shot from the enemy line . . . To our left and a little in our rear, there rose a wooden tower that had been erected in connection with a geographical survey . . . Comrades who had been attracted to visit it . . . told us that affixed to it was a placard written in large letters with the strange inscription, 'This place will be the grave of the French!' Although the tower was situated no more than a few hundred yards from our position, none of us ever got the chance to go and view this death sentence for ourselves. . ... The slopes of the valley that separated the two armies were fairly gentle with the exception of a spot a few yards beyond La Haye Sainte: here they attained all the aspects of a rampart.[17]

18. Return to the highway and turn right. After another 300 yards an isolated house is passed: the property opposite stands on the site of the farm of Rossomme which was burned down in 1895.

R. Rossomme

The knoll to the south of Rossomme saw some of the last resistance to the oncoming allies. At the heart of the defence were the two battalions of the First Regiment of Foot Grenadiers. Meanwhile, the site is best visited from the lay-by mentioned below. That said, the affair was not the heroic scene of legend. Once the safety of Napoleon had been assured, the two battalions simply turned and forced their way off the field.

The site of the supposed last stand of the Old Guard looking north towards the site of the long-gone farm of Rossomme. (Author's collection)

Hyppolyte Mauduit, sergeant, First Regiment of Foot Grenadiers of the Imperial Guard:

The two battalions of my regiment . . . grew ever more angry at the terrible confusion that marked the battlefield. On all sides our view was obstructed by hundreds of soldiers of every rank . . . searching frantically for some . . . refuge. The drummers had been ordered to beat the grenadier march in the hope that this might offer the army something around which to rally, and at this sound . . . our unfortunate comrades had come surging towards us . . . However, with the interior of our two squares already encumbered with generals and other officers whose men had been killed or run away, we were very soon reduced to the cruel necessity of denying access to anyone who sought to enter so as to ensure that we did not become the victims of our generosity . . . As for the battery of twelve-pounder guns belonging to the artillery of the Guard that had for the past two hours been flaying Bülow's corps with canister fire . . . it was completely wiped out before our very eyes, all of the gunners choosing a glorious death rather than . . . take shelter in our square, thereby letting the English cavalrymen in with them. 'No quarter! No quarter!' That was what those savages were crying, but . . . their ranks shattered on our bayonets, and for fifty paces around the ground was soon covered with their corpses . . . Subjected to a hail of fire from three sides though we were, we were therefore able to begin our retreat in the midst of the general disorder.[18]

19. Continue south along the Charleroi highway. After a slight ascent it swings to the left. To the right of the road is a lay-by (actually the route of the road of 1815: this would have run through a deep cutting at this point). More energetic visitors may wish to cross the road here and scramble up the bank on the far side: the field beyond the tree-line gives a good impression of the view that Napoleon would have had of Plancenoit and the heights beyond from the spot where his headquarters was situated for the first part of the day. Meanwhile, the field immediately beside the road marks the site of the famous 'last stand of the Old Guard', such as it was. Otherwise take the more southerly of the two tracks leading off to the east (i.e. the one marked

Napoleon's position at Rossomme looking north. In 1815 the terrain would have been empty of trees, but, even so, it is clear that the emperor's view of Wellington's positions would have been extremely limited. (Author's collection)

'No Entry'), and climb the slope out of the lay-by. Almost immediately turn left on to a farm track, climb a short ascent and then turn left again onto the area of field immediately above the Charleroi highway. Traditionally, this is the spot from which Napoleon watched the battle from about eleven o'clock until he rode forward to La Belle Alliance at perhaps four o'clock in the afternoon: note, however, that, even from the elevated position occupied by the visitor, it is impossible to see beyond the crest of Mont Saint Jean. Meanwhile, the woods on the skyline to the west mark the site of the observation tower that is depicted in so many paintings and engravings of the battle: contrary to stories widespread at the time, this was neither constructed by the French nor (so far as is known) made use of by them.

S. Napoleon's Headquarters

Napoleon's personal conduct at the battle of Waterloo has been the subject of much debate, with some authorities portraying him as being very fatigued and lethargic and others as being far more dynamic. What is very clear, however, is that his command style was very different from that of Wellington: whereas the latter was constantly very much in the front line and therefore able to animate his troops, judge the constantly-changing situation for himself and personally superintend every crisis, the emperor rather remained far behind the lines and relied on such information as was brought to him. This represented a direct clash between two models of generalship of which the first was typical of the battles of the seventeenth and eighteenth centuries and the latter those of the nineteenth and twentieth. In the context of Waterloo, both are perfectly defensible, but it has to be said that the French paid a heavy price for Napoleon's decision. Possibly the fruit of illness and fatigue – another subject about which there has been much debate – this led directly to such errors as the prolongation of the futile struggle at Hougoumont and the loss of the French cavalry as a fighting force, as well as depriving the emperor's forces of the personal inspiration that might have been derived from his presence.

Marie de Baudus, aide de camp to Marshal Soult:
   The rain having stopped and a stiff wind got up that bid fair to dry out the ground fairly quickly, around nine o'clock in the morning the army began to form its line of battle. As for the emperor, he stationed himself on a knoll which dominated the whole battlefield. A small table was brought him for him to lay out his maps, and he stayed there virtually the whole time that the battle lasted in a state of apathy pretty similar to the one for which he has been reproached with respect to the day of the battle of the Moscowa: he was not seen to approach any of the troops who were engaged until the moment that he sent a part of the reserve into action in so unfortunate a manner.[19]

20. Return to the lay-by and take the other track. Once the nursery plantation is passed on the right hand side, this takes the visitor across the position occupied at the start of the battle by the Guard heavy-cavalry division of Claude Guyot. After several hundred yards a turning to the left is reached.

T. The Flight of the French Left
On the western half of the battlefield, the French collapse was precipitated by the repulse of the Imperial Guard. With various

units of Wellington's army in hot pursuit, the remains of II Corps disintegrated. Whilst some of the survivors headed instinctively for the Charleroi highway, others had enough sense to flee due south and avoid the chaos that developed between La Belle Alliance and Le Caillou.

Pierre Robinaux, captain, Second Regiment of Line Infantry:
Accompanied by . . . another captain by the name of Wanroo, I left the regiment for a moment to see if we could get any orders. Hardly had we gone . . . 300 paces, when what did we see? Our troops in full retreat at every point. At the same time we happened to encounter the general in command, the latter having just given the command to retreat in column. Seeing us, he . . . ordered us return to our unit and implement his orders, while keeping what we had seen a secret and maintaining the very best order. At first all was well, but this did not last for very long . . . Looking behind them, some of the increasingly frightened soldiers saw some of our Polish lancers. Taking these last for English cavalry, they began to cry 'We are lost!' The word quickly spreading through the entire column, in a moment we were in complete disorder: nobody thought of anything but his own safety and it proved impossible to rally the ever more scattered soldiers. As for the cavalry, meanwhile, it followed the example of the infantry: I saw dragoons riding down men on foot at full gallop . . . and in fact almost myself fell prone to such a fate. Outraged at the disorder . . . I did not cease to bellow, 'Halt! Rally, for God's sake: there is no-one pursuing us!' However, my efforts were useless, and at length I armed myself with a musket and confronted two or three dragoons . . . telling them in a firm voice that nobody was chasing us and that I would shoot dead the first man who tried to pass me.[20]

21. Continue along the track. After perhaps half a mile, this passes the turning for the Wounded Eagle and Plancenoit, and may now be followed directly to the starting point of the tour.

TOUR 3: THE DEFENCE OF HOUGOUMONT

Time: three hours. Going: generally good, though a mixture of metaled roads, unmade tracks, field paths, grass and cobbles; one short ascent.

1. Although built on the site of a much older manor, the Chateau of Hougoumont that witnessed the Battle of Waterloo dated from the seventeenth century and was a substantial complex of solid brick buildings ranged around two interconnected courtyards situated beside a country lane that ran from Braine l'Alleud to La Belle Alliance. Roughly rectangular and constructed on an axis of west-north-west to east-south-east, it was centred on the chateau itself, a substantial three-storeyed building with a tower and single-storey farmhouse projecting from the eastern face and a family chapel projecting from the southern one. Around most of the perimeter of both the northern and the southern courtyards were a series of barns, cow-sheds and stables, whilst the few gaps between the buildings were blocked by substantial brick walls. As for access, this could be obtained at four points only: a gate in the northern wall between a stable on the one hand and a barn on the other, a gate from the southern courtyard into the formal garden on the eastern side of the complex; an archway through the range of buildings on the southern side of the southern courtyard, and a small door that gave access to the barn on the western side of the self-same courtyard, the northern, eastern and southern entrances all being blocked by stout wooden gates, and the southern one surmounted by an apartment that in 1815 was occupied by the gardener. Nor was this all: to the east was a large formal garden shut in on two sides by a high brick wall strengthened on the inside by substantial buttresses and garnished with ready-made loopholes, this being enclosed on its northern and eastern sides by orchards of apple trees and on its southern one by a thick wood that was roughly square in shape and ran several hundred yards in the direction of the French positions. Wood and orchards alike were surrounded by thick hedges whilst the complex was completed by

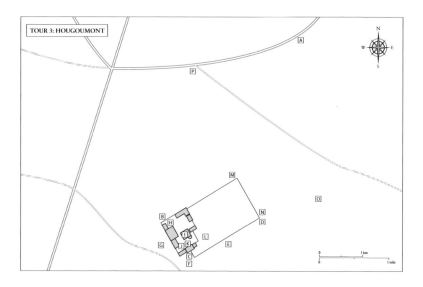

a kitchen garden on the western side of the buildings and a number of enclosed pastures on the periphery of the property. Begin the tour in the Hameau du Lion and walk along the Ohain road as far as the monument to Mercer's battery.

A. The Key to Mont Saint Jean?

In many British accounts of Waterloo, Hougoumont is regarded as the key to the entire Anglo-Dutch position and its successful defence by extension the most important factor in Wellington's victory. A mere glance at the situation of the chateau from the ridge suggests that this is anything but the case, however. Not the least is this the case because, with its walls, hedges, buildings, woods and orchards, it was scarcely an area in which large numbers of troops could be assembled for an assault, whilst, even if it fell, it was completely dominated by the steep slopes immediately behind it: devoid of trees in 1815, these were lined by cannon capable of subjecting the whole complex to a rain of shrapnel, not to mention decimating any columns that advanced up the slope with canister. Nor, meanwhile, was the loss of Hougoumont likely to be of much importance in terms of the cover it provided to Wellington's positions in terms of flanking fire: although troops posted in the outermost hedges of the estate would enjoy a wide view of the field, no sooner had they been driven from their positions than the post would have effectively been blinded and completely neutralized. All this being the case, it is difficult to see why so much effort was put into its fortification: as we shall see from a consideration of the garrison, it seems likely that the initial intention was limited to a rearguard action at the very most.

Edward Cotton, sergeant-major, Seventh Regiment of Light Dragoons:
The important farm of Hougoumont . . . was then a gentleman's seat with farm, out-buildings, walled garden, orchard and wood. The latter has been since cleared in consequence of the injury the trees sustained in the battle . . . The hedges were all banked up, and, with the ditches on the inner side, formed excellent breast works. A ravine, or hollow-way, [which] runs along the northern boundary of the premises . . . during the battle frequently served as a covered communication with the walled enclosures and the buildings, as also for a rallying point and cover . . . The chateau, farm, walls, etc., were at the time of the battle of a substantial nature. The garden, or park, was walled on the east and south sides, where our troops made . . . loop-holes, and, in the inside of the front, or south, wall, they cut down a portion of the buttresses for the purpose of erecting a scaffolding to enable them to fire over the top of the wall to bayonet intruders. At the east wall an embankment, with the loop-holes and scaffolds erected with some farming utensils, enabled the Coldstreams . . . to throw such a fire upon the enemy's left flank when in the large orchard that Colonel Hepburn, who commanded there from about two o'clock, considered the east wall as the strength of his position. Loop-holes were also made in the stables joining the south gate, and a scaffold was erected against the west wall that ran from the stables to the barn. The flooring over the south gateway was partly torn up to enable our men to fire down upon the enemy should they force the gate, which had been blocked.[1]

2. Continue downhill along the Ohain road. Beyond the patch of woodland (to repeat, a feature of the landscape that was not present

The ruins of Hougoumont after the battle. To the left can be seen the archway that separated the two courtyards and to the right the gate that gave access to the garden. (Wikimedia Commons)

in 1815), turn left and walk along the lane leading to the chateau (at the time of the battle this was the most direct route from Braine l'Alleud to La Belle Alliance), pausing outside the northern gate.

B. The Defenders

Although its defence is always associated with the British Foot Guards, at the beginning of the battle Hougoumont was largely in the charge of German troops. On the evening of the seventeenth the light companies of the four Foot Guard battalions that made up the First Division were sent to occupy the complex, but the next morning, seemingly on the initiative of not Wellington but the Prince of Orange, the light companies of the Luneburg and Grubenhagen militia battalions and a further company of riflemen turned up from Baron von Kielmansegg's First Hanoverian Brigade. These 300 men soon having been joined by 800 men of the First Battalion of the green-clad Second Regiment of Nassau, two of the four companies of Guardsmen were withdrawn and the other two – those of the Second and Third Regiments – sent out to hold the pasture and kitchen garden on the western periphery of the complex. Why the Nassau battalion was called over from its post at the far extremity of the field is unclear, the only explanation that comes to mind being that the Prince of Orange had been impressed with its conduct at Quatre Bras in which it had performed with considerable courage.

> *Moritz Büsgen, major, Second Regiment of Nassau:*
> On the morning of 18 June, the Second Nassau Regiment was positioned on the left flank of the allied army. However, its First Battalion (800 men) under my command was ordered to march off immediately to the farm of Hougoumont, to our right-centre, and occupy it . . . On my arrival with the battalion, the farm and the garden were unoccupied. A company of Brunswick [*sic*] *jäger* stood on the furthest edge of the wood. A battalion [*sic*: in reality two companies only] . . . of the Coldstream Regiment [*sic*: actually two different regiments were represented, namely the Second Regiment of Foot Guards, or Coldstreams, and the Third Regiment of Foot Guards, this later becoming the Scots Guards] . . . was deployed partly behind the farm and partly in a sunken road behind the garden . . . I immediately undertook the necessary deployment for the defence. I had the grenadier company occupy the buildings and sent two companies to the . . . garden next to them. I placed one company behind the hedge of the orchard, moved the *voltigeurs* into line with the Brunswick *jäger* and placed one company in reserve a little to the rear.[2]

3. Walk along the western side of the complex: all the ground immediately to the right constituted the chateau's kitchen garden, whilst the modern entrance to the chateau will be found halfway along on the left. Just past the buildings, meanwhile, will be discovered a square of open ground which is seemingly used as a staff carpark.

C. South Gate of Hougoumont

The western side of the yard in which the visitor is standing was a hayfield in 1815. Along with the kitchen garden beside it, at the start of the battle this was held by the light companies of the Second Battalions of the Second and Third Regiments of Foot Guards. At the southern edge of the yard, meanwhile, will be observed three ancient sweet-chestnut trees: these are the only survivors of the wood that in 1815 completely covered the southern aspect of the chateau and stretched as far as the crest of the slope that can be seen beyond them; so badly damaged was said wood left that it was cut down in 1817.

Matthew Clay, private, Third Regiment of Foot Guards:
   Imagining that we should have to contend with the enemy on our present ground, [we] employed ourselves (the hedge being thick) in clearing away branches on our side and making clear openings through [which] . . . we could take a more correct aim at the enemy. Whilst thus employed, we were quietly instructed to turn to our right and march in the direction of . . . the farm house. Passing the gates and round the . . . corner of the building, our company led into a long and

The south wall of Hougoumont showing the monument to Pierre Bauduin, the commander of the first of the two brigades of Jerome Bonaparte's division. However, it is clear from eyewitness accounts that Bauduin did not die before the walls, but rather somewhere in the fields outside the complex. In 1815 a lane ran the length of the wall, this being separated from the wood that screened the complex by a thick hedge. A natural killing ground, every attempt to cross it was beaten back with terrible losses. (Author's collection)

narrow kitchen garden which was extended under cover of a close hedge next to a corn field.³

4. Turning to the left, walk to the far end of the garden wall noting *en route* the loopholes; though employed in the battle, these actually dated from at least a century before, having probably been inserted in the course of the War of the Spanish Succession. The night before the battle, many others were added, but none of these appear to have survived. The northern edge of the wood, meanwhile, is marked by the line of the wire fence.

D. The South Wall (1)
The time that the Battle of Waterloo began is generally agreed as having been approximately half past eleven, the Sixth Division of Jérôme Bonaparte advancing to the Anglo-German positions under the cover of a heavy artillery bombardment designed to suppress the fire of the British batteries on the ridge.

> *Jean-Baptiste Lemonnier-Delafosse, aide-de-camp to General Foy*:
> The division of Prince Jérôme Bonaparte . . . was the first unit to go into action, marching as it did, on the farm of Hougoumont . . . To its right was the division of General Foy. Deployed ready for battle, this had already advanced its batteries so as to respond to the fire of the English guns under whose fire it lay . . . To the rear and in reserve there stood the brigade of Carabiniers [of the Guard], and this took the brunt of the balls which overshot us: to avoid being hit any more, the unit made a move to the left, on seeing which General Foy burst out laughing. 'Ah-ha!' he said. 'It seems that the "Big Boots" don't like the rough stuff!' As for us, we stood firm in the face of the enemy cannon balls. They covered us with mud while, conserving, as it did, the marks of their trajectory, the boggy ground looked as if it had been ploughed up by the wheels of a carriage. The fact that the ground was so boggy was a piece of good fortune for our line for many of the projectiles were stripped of their energy or buried themselves altogether.⁴

5. Walk back along the line of the wall, pausing at approximately its middle point.

The south wall of Hougoumont. Mentioned in contemporary accounts as they are, the stone-faced loopholes long predate the battle and may have been inserted during the War of the Spanish Succession. (Author's collection)

E. The South Wall (2)

Between the wood and the south wall of the garden, meanwhile, there was a lane: recalled as one of the worst killing grounds on the entire field, this was lined on the side of the wood by a hedge so thick that it was described as being all but impenetrable. All trace of this last is now gone, but the line it followed is marked by the wire fence along the edge of the field. Plunging through the wood, Jérôme's troops drove back the Hanoverian and Nassauer light infantry facing them, and some of the latter eventually made a break for the ridge, thereby giving rise to many claims that all the German soldiers among the defenders abandoned their posts. This, however, is demonstrably untrue, for when the victorious French reached the northern edge of the wood, they were met by heavy fire, and, what is worse, confronted by a defensive position of whose existence even Napoleon had been completely unaware: not only was the chief map used in the course of the campaign extremely vague as to what the wood contained, but the chateau was situated in a hollow and was consequently all but invisible from the French front line, let alone La Belle Alliance or Rossomme.

> *Théobald Puvis, sub-lieutenant, Ninety-Third Regiment of Line Infantry:*
> We threw ourselves as skirmishers into a wood with tall trees that was on our left and arrived in front of . . . a vast construction (the Hougoumont farm), fortified at every point and defended to the utmost by tall hedges protected . . . by deep ditches . . . Traversing these cuts . . . we arrived at a hedge defended with the greatest vigour by the enemy. In vain we attempted to take this hedge . . . Our losses were enormous: the lieutenant of my company was killed near me. A musket ball hit the peak of my shako and struck my cheek, the shock to my head being so strong that I believed myself to be injured. However, there was no blood and I soon recovered from the shock.[5]

6. Return along the south wall to the yard outside the south gate.

F. The South Gate (Reprised)
The yard in which the visitor is standing was the scene of desperate fighting which saw French infantry make repeated attempts to smash their way in though the south gate, although this proved impossible, the archway beyond having been heavily barricaded. Despite the plaques dedicated to the memory of the Guards, throughout the battle the building enclosing it was held throughout the battle by three companies of the First Battalion of the green-coated Second Nassau Regiment. A well-known print shows bodies being buried beneath the very spot on which the visitor is now standing, while a plaque just round the corner on the garden wall recalls the death of the commander of the first brigade to assault the walls, Pierre Bauduin. Taking the chateau was clearly going to be a difficult task, for the French did not possess a single ladder and could not bring up artillery too close for fear that the batteries concerned would be subjected to a surprise attack from the flank (the only face of the chateau open to bombardment was that to the west and this was literally under the guns of the main Anglo-Dutch line). Yet merely by advancing to the walls the attackers had carried out the

The only trees of the wood at Hougoumont that survived the latter's clearance in 1817: examined close to, they will be found to be scarred with bullet holes. Laid waste by the howitzer fire to which it was subjected by the British batteries on the ridge above, the wood was the greatest environmental casualty of the battle. (Author's collection)

task expected of them, for, as some of the better informed among them later realized, all that they had needed to do was to mask the position while the rest of the army assaulted Wellington's centre and left wing.

> *Pierre Robinaux, captain, Second Regiment of Line Infantry:*
> Having been ordered by Count Reille . . . to take the position occupied by the English and hold it to the end of the battle without either advancing any further or ceding any ground, the corps of which I was a member marched on the farm of Hougoumont . . . Immediately the charge was ordered and we rushed upon the enemy and crossed bayonets with him . . . The position was well contested by both sides, but half an hour sufficed to give us control.[6]

7. Return along the west wall to the modern entrance to the chateau complex.

The site of the kitchen garden at Hougoumont looking north. It was from this area that French light infantry managed to surge around the north-western corner of the complex and enter the north gate. (Author's collection)

G. The Kitchen Garden

It will be recalled that the area outside the western walls of the chateau was held by two light companies of the Foot Guards. As the triumphant French infantry surged out of the woods, the men concerned now found themselves in a very difficult position.

> *Matthew Clay, private, Third Regiment of Foot Guards*:
> Our company . . . extended under cover of a close hedge next to a corn field through which the skirmishers of the enemy were advancing to the attack. We remained in a kneeling position under this cover, but [were] annoyed by a most galling fire from our opponents . . . The expected signal [being] given for us to retire from the garden: the front of the company was led by Lieutenant-Colonel Dashwood . . . into the [chateau]; I, being in the rear sub-division, on quitting the garden [was less fortunate, for, on our] reaching the road . . . Lieutenant Sandon . . . called our attention to join him and charge the enemy. We then went up the road towards the

wood. The enemy's skirmishers being under cover about the hedge to the right of the wood, our party took advantage of cover, myself and a man of the name of . . . Gann [taking] our position under cover of a circular . . . stack . . . from whence we fired on the enemy . . . Left to ourselves (as we imagined by not seeing anyone near us) and the enemy's skirmishers remaining under cover [and continuing to fire] at us, we likewise kept firing and [retired] down the road up which we had advanced . . . Supposing ourselves shut out from the farm, we were for a moment or two quite at a loss how to act, but, on turning my eyes towards the lower gates, I saw that they were still open . . . at the same time apprising my comrade of so favourable an opportunity, [and so] we hastened towards that way.[7]

8. Visitors with less time may wish to continue with the tour at this point. However, the extra hour spent visiting the interior of Hougoumont is certainly time well spent. There is an excellent

The 2015 monument to the soldiers of the Guards who closed the gates of Hougoumont, thereby trapping the party of troops who had managed to enter the courtyard. However, whether they really saved the day is a moot point. (Author's collection)

bookshop, a small museum, a very good video and, very importantly on a battlefield singularly devoid of such facilities, public toilets. Having watched the video and reflected on the fact that the building in which it is shown witnessed the death by fire of several dozen wounded who had been carried inside for shelter, only to be trapped in the flames when a large part of the complex was set alight by French artillery fire at some point in the afternoon, walk clockwise around the site, pausing first at the north gate.

H. The North Gate (Interior)

Kept open to admit messengers, reinforcements – most importantly, numerous detachments of the Second Battalions of the Second and Third Regiments of Foot Guards who were sent down in the course of the first part of the afternoon – and waggon-loads of ammunition, the north gate was the scene of one of the most dramatic episodes in the battle, this having been immortalized by the new monument set against the north wall of the barn. In brief, having advanced up the western face of the complex, a large group of French troops burst through the gates and charged into the courtyard. There followed a desperate fight, but the commander of the Foot Guards detachment, Lieutenant-Colonel James Macdonnell, eventually succeeded in shutting the gates in the rear of the intruders who were then shot or bayoneted with the exception, or so it is said, of a single drummer boy. Lamentably, however, there is no personal account of this episode, but it is well attested to, while Macdonnell and an Irish corporal who played a leading part in assisting him named James Graeme were much lionised after the battle, even being publically labelled by the Duke of Wellington as the bravest men in the whole battle.

> *Matthew Clay, private, Third Regiment of Footguards:*
> On entering the courtyard, I saw the ... gates were riddled with shot holes and [that] it was also very wet and dirty. In its entrance lay many dead bodies of the enemy: one I particularly noticed ... appeared to have been a French officer, but they were scarcely distinguishable, being ... very much trodden upon and covered with mud. On gaining the interior, I saw Lieutenant-Colonel Macdonnell carrying a large ... trunk of a tree in his arms ... with which he was hastening to secure the gates against the renewed attack of the enemy.[8]

The chapel at Hougoumont. In 1815 it abutted the south wall of the chateau proper. To the left, meanwhile, can be seen the remains of the tower that stood at the south-eastern corner of the house. (Author's collection)

9. From the north gate move round the enclosure to the site of the chateau, passing *en route* the complex's well (in 1815, this was surmounted by a large dovecote). All that is left of the building, which was completely engulfed in the fire, is a stub of tower and, beside it, the chateau's tiny chapel.

I. The Chapel
As is well known, the chapel was miraculously spared when the flames raging only feet away died away having done no more than singe the feet of the great fifteenth-century crucifix hanging over the door exactly as it does today, though, sadly, one of the lower legs of the Christ figure was sawn off by some nineteenth-century souvenir hunter (in a further miracle, the crucifix was stolen from the chapel in 2011, only to be recovered intact from a lock-up garage in Waterloo just in time for the bicentenary four years later). In the cramped space inside, as many as forty wounded men had taken refuge, and it is said that they all survived, though how the smoke did not asphyxiate them is unclear. Extraordinarily enough, meanwhile, a number of defenders continued to fight on inside the building even as it burned around their very ears.

Matthew Clay, private, Third Regiment of Foot Guards:

I, being now told off with others under Lieutenant Gough of the Coldstream Guards, was posted in an upper room of the chateau. [This] being situated higher than the surrounding buildings, we annoyed the enemy's skirmishers from the window, which, the enemy observing, [they] threw their shells amongst us and set the building on fire . . . Our officer, placing himself at the entrance of the apartment, would not permit anyone to quit his post until our position became hopeless and too perilous to remain . . . and in our escape several of us were more or less injured.[9]

10. Having left the chapel, turn left and then left again to enter the old south courtyard (in 1815 this was separated from its northern counterpart by a wall with a gate in it). The cobbles are believed to be original so this is one place where the visitor is quite literally following in the footsteps of the men of Waterloo.

The south courtyard at Hougoumont showing the chapel to the left. In 1815 the building with the archway was the residence of the chateau's gardener. During the battle, it was occupied by troops of the Second Regiment of Nassau, and it was largely from its windows that the French soldiers who managed to gain entrance to the courtyard at some point in the afternoon were shot down. (Author's collection)

J. The South Courtyard

The fight at the northern gate was not the only time the French succeeded in penetrating the walls. As noted above, the southern courtyard possessed two entrances from the outside world, namely the archway through the building that lined its southern face and a door in the outside wall of the barn on its eastern side. At some point in the afternoon, it seems that this door was forced, the result being something of a minor panic.

Andreas Buchsieb, sergeant, Second Regiment of Nassau:
Us four sergeants were each assigned a post by our officers. Together with eight men, I was stationed at a door in which there were four firing holes . . . Hardly had we occupied our position when the infantry division of Jérôme attacked with the greatest force . . . Due to the smoke and flames, his grenadiers pushed ahead through a small side door in the upper court . . . As they stormed into the court, we had to run into the house and give fire from the windows, the door and the roof . . . When we occupied the farm, we had placed our colour on . . . the roof, and, fearing that it would be lost in the current struggle, our First Lieutenant, Hardt, took it down and . . . gave it to me, whilst he himself sped back to the court. Hardly had he entered, then he received a shot in the head, and instantly fell dead on the spot. Having recovered ourselves, in the despair of our anger, we were fortunate enough to be able to chase the remainder of the enemy from the court, which was covered with dead and wounded.[10]

11. Proceed across the courtyard to the archway beneath the gardener's residence.

K. The Gardener's House

Probably wrongly, the range of buildings on the southern side of the south courtyard is referred to in its entirety as the gardener's house. For most of the battle, this was in the charge of men from the Second Regiment of Nassau, but late in the battle they seem to have been joined by a number of guardsmen.

The gardener's house at Hougoumont viewed from the outside. Note the light-coloured bricks to the right of the bricked-up windows. These represent repairs necessitated by bullet damage. (Author's collection)

Matthew Clay, private, Third Regiment of Foot Guards:
A man (killed in this action) of the name of Philpot and myself were posted . . . to defend a breach made in the wall of the building, it being upstairs and above the gateway; the shattered fragments of the wall [were] mixed up with the bodies of our dead countrymen . . . cut down defending their post. Being at this time under the command of Captain Elrington of my own company, I was then posted within a projecting portion of the ruin; on the opposite side of the breach was Sergeant Aston. We kept a watchful eye upon the enemy whose attacks now became less frequent. As it was drawing towards the close of the action and the approach of evening, the firing shortly after ceased, and, our complete victory being announced in our little garrison, we had a look around and saw the sad havoc the enemy had made of our fortress.[11]

The site of the formal garden at Hougoumont showing the south wall and the buttresses used to build firing platforms. (Author's collection)

12. From the gardener's house pass through the gap into the garden: in 1815, this would have been blocked by a wall pierced by another gateway.

L. The Garden

Today just a paddock, at the time of the battle the garden was laid out in a pattern of beautiful gravelled walks and rosebeds. For the visitor, however, other than the French memorial located at the far end and the graves of an officer of the Guards who died in the garden and the long-term guide to the battlefield, Edward Cotton, the chief interest is the wall. Much restored though this is, it still gives a very good impression of the original construction. Of particular note, meanwhile, are the substantial buttresses placed at regular intervals around the inner side: during the night before the battle, pioneers worked hard to knock away the upper levels of brickwork so as to provide footings for improvised firing platforms made of beams taken from the chateau's various outbuildings. In a corner near the gardener's house a platform has been erected to allow the visitor to attain the same viewpoint as the men posted on the wall and from this it is easy to imagine the hopeless task faced by the French troops who repeatedly tried to rush across the lane separating the garden from the wood.

Johann Leonhard, rifleman, First Nassau Flanker Company:
    The hail of musket balls we sent against the French was horrifying, so that soon the pastures were covered with . . . French bodies . . . We were attacked for the fourth time in the garden, but . . . the French were beaten back again . . . As for the row of hornbeams under which we stood, as well as the beautiful tall wood that adjoined the farm, everything had been completely shot and cut down by the tremendous cannon fire.[12]

13. Return to the entrance to the complex and turn right. At the north-west corner turn right again and walk eastwards along the perimeter wall. At the far end of the garden enter a shallow gully lined on one side by bushes: this is all that remains of the sunken lane or (to use the contemporary term) hollow road that connected Hougoumont with the track from the ridge to La Belle Alliance, and, with it, the hedge that enclosed the orchard.

An incident in the defence of Hougoumont. Sergeant Ralph Fraser of the Third Foot Guards engages the commander of the French First Light Infantry, Amedée Depans de Cubières, in single combat outside the north gate. Having thrown the Frenchman to the ground, Fraser leapt upon his horse and rode it into the chateau. (Wikimedia Commons)

M. The Hollow Road

The hollow road played an important part in the battle for Hougoumont. Protected only by hedges and, unlike most of the chateau complex, open to heavy fire from beyond the perimeter, the orchard was almost impossible for the garrison to defend, but the natural trench constituted by the road gave the defenders a place to rally and proved completely impervious to French assault, especially as the troops stationed in the garden were able to subject any men who tried to cross it to a hail of fire from the flank (once again, however, it should be noted that what they could not do was to fire at targets in the open ground beyond: not only did the apple trees exclude their view, but the effective range of their weapons was little further than the width of the orchard anyway). As a result the fighting surged to and fro incessantly, the orchard being taken and retaken many times. Unlike in the garden and, still more so, the chateau itself, meanwhile, in this sector the combatants all came from the Foot Guards.

Douglas Mercer, captain, Third Regiment of Foot Guards:
The battalion . . . was in extended order for the purpose of defending the whole length of the hedge, which, owing to our great loss, was much more than we could occupy in close order. Here it was that our chief loss in officers and men occurred. The hedge afforded small protection, the earth bank being but little raised above the general level of the ground . . . our [right was exposed] . . . to the fire of light troops who occasionally advanced through the wood [and] on our left . . . there were dense bodies of the enemy lying in the high grain which was only trodden completely down on the grand advance . . . the dead lay very thick on the whole length of the ground we occupied. After a time the enemy drove us back as far as the hedge in our rear . . . Here we remained for a short time when we made a rush and, driving the enemy back, re-occupied the hedge . . . from which we had been driven.[13]

14. Leave the hollow road and walk southwards along the outside of the garden wall, pausing at the far corner.

The main orchard at Hougoumont viewed from the lane that separated the formal garden from the wood. Though the defenders were not able to hold out in the orchard for any length of time, any French troops who entered it were exposed to fire from two sides and therefore quickly shot down. (Wikimedia Commons)

N. The Orchard

The visitor is now standing at what was the south-west corner of the orchard. From here a thick hedge ran along the latter's southern edge, whilst across the lane that ran from the chateau along the south edge of the garden towards the track to La Belle Alliance a further hedge bordered an open pasture that the French used as an assembly area for their numerous assaults. We here come to the great tragedy of Hougoumont as far as the French were concerned: taking the chateau was, first, all but impossible and, second, completely unnecessary (to repeat, all Napoleon wanted was for the position to be masked), and yet Reille allowed half his corps to be dragged into assault after assault when the men concerned were desperately needed elsewhere.

Sylvain Larréguy de Civrieux, cadet, Ninety-Third Regiment of Line Infantry:

The division of the erstwhile King of Westphalia having melted away in the face of the enemy fire, that of General Foy was sent forward to replace it beneath the batteries [*sic*] of Hougoumont. All round the place the ground was piled high with thousands of dead and wounded, and of these we quickly doubled the number, ripped apart in our turn as we were by the canister of the English . . . Soon our feet were bathed in blood: in less than half an hour, our ranks had been reduced by more than half. Everyone stoically awaited death or horrible wounds . . . and yet our courage remained at the highest possible degree of exaltation. Albeit in a voice that was becoming ever weaker, my captain, who had been struck by two musket balls and was losing a lot of blood, kept encouraging us until he succumbed in the midst of that immortal hecatomb.[14]

15. Walk along the edge of the field of crops in the direction of the track to La Belle Alliance: in 1815 the path marked the southern edge of the orchard, the field to the right then as now being open ground (the eastern edge of the wood extended no further than the line of the garden wall). After some 200 yards the path angles sharply to the left:

The Hougoumont area viewed from the lane from the Ohain Road to La Belle Alliance. The orchard occupied the area to the left of the scrub in the centre of the picture, whilst the attack described here crossed the open area in the foreground. (Author's collection)

at this point the visitor is standing at the site of south-western corner of the orchard, the eastern face of which ran straight across the field in parallel with the garden wall until it intersected with the sunken lane leading to the north gate of the chateau. Meanwhile, a gap in the hedge and ditch surrounding the orchard that gave access to the open ground to the left made this a particularly difficult spot to hold, many of the defenders being shot down by skirmishers hidden in the tall crops.

O. Foy and Bachelu

By the middle of the afternoon the French troops trying to assault Hougoumont had become so exhausted that the constant attacks died away. However, there was one last episode of the fighting in this sector. In brief, as the last of the French cavalry charges receded, so Reille at last thought of trying to do something other than trying to take a target that neither could be taken nor needed to be taken. Still in reasonable order were the Fifth Division of Gilbert Bachelu and half the Ninth Division of Maximilien Foy, and at around six o'clock these troops were ordered to form up in column and attack the ridge. The results, however, were disappointing even by the standards of a day full of disappointment.

Toussaint Trefcon, chief of staff, Fifth Division, Army of the North:
    At six o'clock . . . we were ordered to . . . second the efforts of our cavalry. Hardly had we . . . formed up in column . . . than we were struck by a hail of shot and canister. Right beside me General Bachelu was struck by several projectiles and his horse shot from under him. The commander of the leading brigade having also fallen, I provisionally assumed the command of the division. Despite the enemy's fire, we were carried away by emotion and were on the point of overwhelming them when they suddenly received substantial reinforcements: without these they would beyond doubt have been forced to retreat. Virtually at the point of crossing bayonets with them, we were then swamped by a fire so murderous that our men fell by the hundred, those that survived having no option but to retreat: had they not done so, not a man would have escaped. As for me, I took two massive blows to the chest, whilst my horse was killed under me by a piece of canister. In falling to the ground, meanwhile, I sprained my left wrist, the shock and pain that

I experienced being such that I lost consciousness. Luckily for me, I was not out for the count for very long and soon had my wits about me once again. Hidden behind the body of my horse, I let some English dragoons who were pursuing my unfortunate division pass by, and, as soon as they were out of the way, set about trying to reorientate myself.[15]

16. Continue along the path. In a short distance the track running downhill from the ridge above the chateau in the direction of La Belle Alliance is reached once more. Turn to the left and ascend the slope to the Ohain road.

P. Du Plat's Brigade
Among the various reserve formations brought forward to hold the ridge was the First Infantry Brigade of the King's German Legion under Lieutenant Colonel Georg du Plat. Having played a considerable part

Workmen clearing Hougoumont of dead after the battle. Archaeological explorations have suggested that pyres of the sort shown here were constructed at various places around the site. (Wikimedia Commons)

in the defeat of the attack by Foy and Bachelu, this now found itself under heavy fire from enemy skirmishers and artillery alike.

Heinrich Dehnel, lieutenant, Third Line Battalion, King's German Legion:

Both the fire from an enemy battery that had moved up on our left and the skirmish fire directed at us from the Hougoumont [orchards] all of a sudden became extremely deadly. Captain Heise, our battalion commander, was mortally wounded, and killed on the very same spot were Captains Von Holle and Diedel . . . The fourth captain of the battalion, Beurmann, received a glancing shot to the head through which he lost consciousness for a considerable time . . . At the same time, grape blew down a corner of the now small square . . . Since the enemy musketry . . . kept causing us losses, and remaining further in this position would completely annihilate our small group, I then . . . stepped before its front and led it against the nearest of our annoying enemies . . . The enemy did not wait for the clash of arms, however: they yielded and withdrew behind the next line of hedges. Soon thereafter swarms of enemy *tirailleurs* pushed ahead past the hedges and towards the main position, but were energetically thrown back . . . The attacks and advances of the French . . . until then of increasing vehemence, diminished at that moment, and . . . an English soldier approached us. His left arm had been smashed by a cannon ball so that his lower arm seemed to hang on by just a strip of flesh . . . He calmly asked us to cut off his injured arm or have somebody do it, since it was inconveniencing him very much . . . Without repeating his wish, the unfortunate man took a few steps, then . . . suddenly fell down and was dead.[16]

17. Return to the Hameau du Lion, reflecting perhaps on the horrors seen at Hougoumont by the first visitors to the battlefield:

Charlotte Eaton:

Never shall I forget the dreadful scene of death and devastation which it presented. The broken branches were strewed around, the green beech leaves, fallen before their time and stripped by the storm of war and not by the storm of nature, were scattered over the surface of the ground, emblematical of the fate of the thousands who had fallen on the same spot in the summer of their days . . . the trunks of the trees had been pierced in every direction with cannon balls . . . Among the long grass lay broken arms [i.e. weapons], shreds of gold lace, torn epaulettes, and pieces of cartridge boxes, and upon the tangled branches of the brambles fluttered many a tattered remnant of a soldier's coat. At the outskirts of the wood and around the walls of the chateau huge piles of human ashes were heaped up, some of which were still smoking. The countrymen told us that so great were the numbers of slain that it was impossible entirely to consume them. Pits had been dug into which they had been thrown, but they were obliged to be raised far above the surface of the ground. These dreadful heaps were covered with piles of wood which were set on fire so that underneath lay quantities of human bodies unconsumed. The chateau itself . . . presented a most melancholy spectacle, not merely . . . from its being a pile of ruins, but from the vestiges it presented of that tremendous . . . warfare by which those ruins had been caused . . . At the garden gate I found the holster of a British officer, entire but deluged with blood . . . All around were strewn torn epaulettes, broken scabbards and sabretaches stained and stiffened with blood: proofs how dreadfully the battle had raged.[17]

TOUR 4: DROUET'S ATTACK

Time: three hours. Going: mostly either metalled roads or well-maintained tracks, though some patches of the latter may be waterlogged in wet weather; moderate slopes with occasional steeper stretches; short stretches of field walking (see Map 3).

1. Begin the tour at La Belle Alliance. From the beginning of the campaign Napoleon had sought by every possible means to keep the Anglo-Dutch and Prussian armies apart, and his plan at Waterloo fitted in entirely with that idea. Thus, while the emperor's own left wing – Reille's II Corps – secured his forces from a flank attack by masking Hougoumont, his centre and right were to break through Wellington's left wing and roll him up from the right, thereby forcing

Napoleon is acclaimed by troops of Drouet's corps immediately before the attack on Wellington's left-centre. (Wikimedia Commons)

the Duke to retreat westwards and, by extension, away from the Prussians. With Blücher on the way, however, it was essential that this task was completed without delay. When the commander of I Corps, Jean-Baptiste Drouet, ordered his four divisions – those of Quiot, Donzelot, Marcognet and Durutte – to advance at about one o'clock in the afternoon, then, it is not too much to say that the fate of the battle hung in the balance.

A. La Belle Alliance

In 1815 La Belle Alliance was a tavern, the name of which commemorated the happy marriage of its owner. Though in essence the same building as the one which existed at the time of the battle, its appearance has been much altered. Traditionally, it is the scene of the much pictured meeting that took place between Wellington and Blücher at the close of the battle but it is probable that the encounter actually took place some way to the south. Be that as it may, delighted with the symbolism of the name, Blücher wanted the battle to be named after the inn, but Wellington instead insisted on following his usual practice and calling it after the place where he had spent the previous night, i.e. Waterloo. During the battle, the building was used as a hospital while the area provided an ideal position from which heavy artillery – specifically, the three 12-pounder batteries attached to I, II and VI Corps – could batter the Anglo-Dutch lines. Note, however, that the reversed slope on the further side of Wellington's position cannot be observed at all: as a result, even the very significant firepower represented by eighteen 12-pounder guns and six 8in howitzers could achieve very little in the way of preparing the way for Drouet: while the howitzer shells could certainly lob shells over the ridge, solid shot would generally fly straight over the heads of the defenders or bury itself in the soil of the crest: trying though the bombardment was, it is estimated that its initial phase only cost Wellington around 500 casualties.

Frederick Pattison, lieutenant, Thirty-Third Regiment of Foot:
Held in reserve, in complete inaction . . . [we were] yet exposed to the fire of destructive artillery which ever and anon sent showers of . . . shells and cannon balls into our ranks, occasioning heavy casualties. In order to shelter the men as

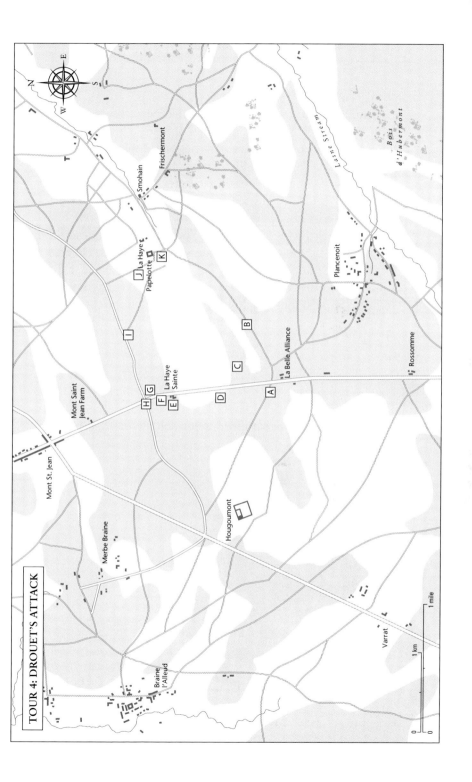

TOUR 4: DROUET'S ATTACK

much as possible in this hazardous situation, orders were given to them to lie down and thus to let the shells pass over them. This manoeuvre saved the lives of many a brave fellow. When in this prostrate position, it so happened that Lieutenant Pagan, Captain Trevor and Lieutenant Hart were lying on the ground close to one another in the centre of the square. I was standing up, much interested in what was going on on our left, when a missile, supposed to be the fragment of a shell, hit Hart so severely on the shoulder as to cause instant death, and, passing over Trevor, scooped out one of Pagan's ears. He got up, staggering and bleeding profusely, [whereupon] I, with others, placed him on a bearer [i.e. stretcher] to carry him to the rear. The men thus employed had hardly left the centre of a square when a cannon ball hit one of them and carried off his leg.[1]

2. From La Belle Alliance, the visitor should take a dirt track angling to right between the Plancenoit road and the Charleroi highway; in the latter stages of the battle a battery of 12-pounder guns of the artillery of the Imperial Guard was stationed in the field in the angle between

French Guard foot artillery manning a 6in howitzer. At this stage of the battle none of the Guard's artillery had been deployed, but the three batteries of Line artillery stationed at La Belle Alliance included six of these pieces. (Wikimedia Commons)

track and road so as to provide fire support for the troops defending Plancenoit. Just past a small copse, the track, which throughout its length marks the front line of Drouet's I Corps, brings the visitor out onto a broad spur jutting forward from the French ridge.

B. Donzelot's Position

The spur on which the visitor is standing marks the initial position of Donzelot's division and offers an excellent view of the whole of the eastern half of the battlefield. Immediately in front lies La Haye Sainte, though only its roof may be seen, together with the intermediate ridge: in the course of Drouet's assault, this last was occupied by the six batteries belonging to I Corps (it was these guns that were overrun by the Union Brigade in its famous charge across the valley). To the right, meanwhile, can be seen the high ground known as the Heights of Agiers that hid the advance of the Prussian army Finally, looking to the left, it will be seen that the western horizon is constituted by the cross-ridge leading to Mont Saint Jean: as a result, French troops stationed in this area could not possibly have seen, or even been aware of, either the advance or the retreat of the Imperial Guard, what produced the collapse of Napoleon's forces in this sector rather being the eruption of Ziethen's corps from the direction of Papelotte.

> *Jacques Martin, lieutenant, Forty-Fifth Regiment of Line Infantry:*
> The army was soon drawn up in battle order . . . In the course of the morning the weather had got a lot better, and now a splendid sun illuminated the lines of combatants and made their weapons shine in the brightest of fashions. It was a most magnificent spectacle: bayonets, helmets and cuirasses gleamed in the sunlight; flags, guidons and pennants . . . fluttered in the breeze; drums beat; trumpets sounded; the bands of every regiment played 'Watch over the Safety of the Empire'. And in the midst of it all Napoleon was reviewing his army before battle for the last time. Never could he have heard the cry of 'Long live the emperor!' being uttered with more enthusiasm; never had such absolute devotion been painted on the faces of his soldiers or for that matter reflected in their gestures or voices. It was like a dream.[2]

3. Return to La Belle Alliance and turn right along the Charleroi highway. Follow the pathway beside the road for perhaps 300 yards and then, the state of the crops permitting, just before the road enters something of a cutting marked by a line of scrub, bear off uphill at an angle to the right following a line of manholes. Pause at the third manhole: the visitor is now standing on the crest of the eastern half of the intermediate ridge. If there are standing crops or the ground is too waterlogged to proceed, continue along the road until a flight of steps is reached ascending the bank on the right-hand side: from the top of these it is possible to obtain much the same impression.

C. The Intermediate Ridge

For much of the battle, not least because it was close enough to the Anglo-Dutch positions to offer the 6-pounder guns that formed the bulk of Napoleon's artillery support a much better chance of doing damage, this was an important French artillery position, but, despite the claims of many writers, it was not occupied at the start of the

Wellington's centre-left viewed from the intermediate ridge showing the ground crossed by the divisions of Quiot and Donzelot. (Author's collection)

battle: to have occupied the position with artillery alone at this point would have been to risk disaster as the guns could easily have been overwhelmed by a massive cavalry charge. What actually occurred, then, is rather that the position was only occupied in the course of the advance of Drouet's infantry, the five 6-pounder batteries attached to his corps being dragged forwards in the wake of the foot soldiers and unlimbered so as to able to fire over their heads, not that they would have had time to get off many shots before their view was obscured by the advancing infantry. Only later in the battle, then, did the position come into its own. Lastly, there remains the much debated issue of the formation Drouet deployed his four infantry divisions in: according to tradition, all of them were arrayed in massive columns with each of their eight battalions arrayed in line one behind the other, but in reality only the two central divisions – those of Donzelot and Marcognet – were deployed in this fashion, the other two divisions – those of Quiot on the left and Durutte on the right – rather being deployed in more flexible brigade or even battalion columns. Beyond La Haye Sainte, meanwhile, the attack was supported by the cuirassier brigade of General Dubois.

Jacques Martin, lieutenant, Forty-Fifth Regiment of Line Infantry:
As soon as it was felt that the English had been sufficiently softened up by the fire of our pieces, the four divisions of [General Drouet] formed up in separate columns. Like the others, the third division, that of Marcognet, of which my regiment formed a part, was ordered to deploy all its battalions in line, one behind the other, with a distance of only four paces between them, a strange formation that would cost us very dear as we could not form square to defend ourselves against cavalry, and at the same time presented the enemy artillery with a target twenty ranks deep . . . To what did the First Corps owe this unfortunate formation that was one of the causes – indeed, perhaps, the principal cause – of its lack of success? Nobody knows . . . At last it was time. At the order to attack, there was a frenetic cry of 'Long live the emperor!', and, with their arms at the shoulder and their ranks well closed up, the four columns crossed the little ridge that separated us from the enemy army and began to ascend the slope on the other side . . . The distance

is by no means far – an ordinary pedestrian could do it in five or six minutes, but the ground was sodden and broken up, whilst the standing crops were so encumbering that they considerably slowed down our rate of march, the consequence being that the English artillery had all the time it wanted to exercise its work of destruction upon us. Nevertheless we did not lose heart and at length we reached a point from which it was possible to take the enemy position by assault.[3]

4. From the crest of the ridge, angle back to the Charleroi highway: this can be rejoined with ease at the northern end of the line of scrub at whose start the visitor took to the fields. Follow the main road until the far end of the line of cottages on the far side of the road (an addition to the battlefield dating from the middle of the nineteenth century). It was more-or-less in front of the furthest of these cottages that the British cavalry commander, Lord Uxbridge, lost his leg to a French cannonball in the last moments of the battle.

The knoll and the Hanoverian monument from immediately east of La Haye Sainte. The so-called sand-pit was beside the road immediately in front of the clump of trees. Held by two companies of the Ninety-Fifth Rifles, the area appears to have been evacuated amidst scenes of considerable disorder. (Author's collection)

D. Bourgeois' Advance

In returning to the road, the visitor has followed in the footsteps of the brigade of General Charles Bourgeois. Composed of the Twenty-Eighth and 105th Regiments of Infantry of the Line, each of which was made up of two battalions, this unit was expected both to assist in the capture of La Haye Sainte and advance on the positions occupied by elements of Sir James Kempt's brigade immediately to the east of the crossroads.

Pierre Duthilt, aide de camp to General Bourgeois, GOC, Second Brigade, First Division:

Having initially been stationed in a fold in the ground, the Second Brigade formed column of attack by battalion, and set off at the *pas de charge*, proceeded by its skirmishers and emitting cries of joy, but its very precipitation and enthusiasm soon proved a disadvantage in that, having a fair way to go before encountering the enemy, the soldiers soon became fatigued on account of the difficulty they found in manoeuvring across the sodden terrain, characterised, as this was, by a mixture of mud and trampled crops: so bad was the going that many of them ripped the straps of their gaiters and lost their very shoes, weighed down as these were by the quantity of clay that adhered to their soles and heels. Nor was this all, for the orders could no longer be heard, drowned out as these were by the constant cheering of thousands of voices and the beating of the drums. Very soon, then, there was some confusion in the ranks, and all the more so once the head of the column came within range of the enemy's fire . . . a terrible blast of musket balls, cannon balls and canister laying low one third of the brigade the instant that this was the case.[4]

5. Continue up the Charleroi highway in the direction of the crossroads. After a very short distance the farm of La Haye Sainte is reached. Whilst it is on the other side of the road, there is no need to cross over to view it close up, and all the more so as the traffic is such that attempting to do so renders any such attempt very dangerous. To the right an excellent view may be obtained of the slopes crossed by the divisions of Donzelot and Marcognet as they advanced to attack the Anglo-Dutch positions.

La Haye Sainte viewed from the site of the abatis that was erected to block the Charleroi highroad. The troops deployed in the orchard that masked the southern face of the complex had an excellent field of fire, but no easy means of retreat. (Author's collection)

E. La Haye Sainte

With the exception of the addition of some modern sheds on its further side, the farm of La Haye Sainte looks much the same as it did in 1815, and all the more so given the recent restoration of the south-eastern corner of the walls (for many years this was missing). However, in 1815, an orchard occupied the patch of ground immediately to the south of the barn while the highway, then of course much narrower, had been blocked at the south-east corner of the complex by a barricade constructed of fruit trees that had been cut down and dragged into the road with the bushy tops facing the French positions. As for the defenders, these consisted of the rifle-armed and green-uniformed Second Light Battalion of the King's German Legion commanded by Major Georg Baring: whilst some manned the roof of the pig-shed (the low structure protruding above the wall to the right of the gate) and a few loopholes that had been hacked in the walls, others lined the hedge that surrounded the orchard. Along the front wall may be observed plaques commemorating the forty-nine officers and men of the Second Light Battalion killed in the defence of the farm; the commander of the Second Brigade of the King's German Legion, Colonel Christian von Ompteda, who was killed in a desperate attempt to retake the farm after its capture by the French; and the French troops who eventually drove out the defenders.

Friedrich Lindenau, private, Fifth Line Battalion, King's German Legion:
About midday . . . two columns of enemy troops . . . marched forwards so quickly that we said to one another, 'The French are in such a hurry, it's as if they wanted to eat in Brussels today.' At first, as the enemy were packed in front of our hedge, we opened such murderous fire on the dense crowd that the ground was immediately covered with a mass of wounded and dead. For a moment the French halted, [but] then they fired causing major destruction . . . My friend, Harz, collapsed at my side with a bullet through his body, [and] Captain Schaumann fell too . . . When the columns on the right advanced as far as the barn door and threatened to cut off our withdrawal into its entrance, we . . . drove them back and went inside, admittedly with many casualties. Then we gave such unbroken fire in the barn behind towards the open entrance, in front of which the French were massed, that they did not attempt to enter. I stood here for perhaps half an hour, then, as the pressure of the French became weaker, I moved in front of a loophole near the closed gate that led to the highway. The French stood so close-packed here that several times I saw three or four enemy fall by one bullet.[5]

6. Continue up the track beside the Charleroi highway. Just at the further end of the farm a small parking area will be encountered.

F. The Sandpit
Referred to in accounts of the battle as a 'sandpit', in 1815 the area where the visitor is standing was a rectangular excavation 100 feet long by fifty wide that at the end furthest from the road was as much as twenty feet deep. Probably dug out in course of either farming or road-mending activities, as such it was employed by the First Battalion of the Ninety-Fifth Regiment of Foot (the so-called 'Ninety-

Troops of Charlet's brigade surge around the walls of La Haye Sainte while the defenders launch a desperate sortie. (Wikimedia Commons)

Fifth Rifles') – the unit holding the sector of Wellington's front line directly in rear of the feature – as an outpost, the garrison consisting of two companies under Captains Leach and Chawner. After the battle it was made use of as a ready-made mass grave in which men of many different units were buried, but the only monument is to an infantry regiment of Durutte's division that was brought over with the rest of the brigade to which it was attached to reinforce the last assaults on Wellington's position.

John Kincaid, captain, Ninety-Fifth Regiment of Foot:
> The column destined as our particular friends . . . seemed to consist of about 10,000 infantry . . . We saw Bonaparte himself take post on the side of the road, immediately in our front, surrounded by a numerous staff, and each regiment, as they passed him, rent the air with shouts of 'Vive l'empereur!' Nor did they cease after they had passed . . . Backed by the thunder of their artillery, and the . . . rub-dub of drums . . . it [rather] looked as if they had some hopes of scaring us off the ground, for it was a singular contrast to the stern silence reigning on

our side, where nothing as yet, but the voices of our great guns, told we had mouths to open when we chose to use them. Our rifles were, however, in a very few seconds required to play their parts and opened such a fire on the advancing skirmishers as quickly brought them to a standstill, but their columns advanced steadily through them, although our incessant *tiraillade* was telling . . . with fearful exactness, and our post was quickly turned in both flanks, which compelled us to fall back and join our colleagues, though not before some of our officers and theirs had been engaged in personal combat.[6]

7. A short walk along the verge of the highway will take the visitor to a broad flight of steps leading up to the so-called Hanoverian memorial, this commemorating the numerous members of the King's German Legion killed in the course of the battle: together with the Gordon monument across the highway, it gives a very good idea of the depth of the cutting by which the latter ascended Wellington's position. Having returned to the area of the sandpit, the track turns to the right and then to the left whereupon it immediately cuts through

The view south-east from the knoll looking towards the French front line. Drouet's assault spanned the entire width of the photograph. (Author's collection)

the raised area of land on which the Hanoverian memorial is sited. Immediately after the second bend climb up the bank to the right and walk along the edge of the field keeping as close as possible to the bushes lining the track.

G. The Knoll

Together with the somewhat loftier area that constitutes the site of the Hanoverian monument, the mound on which the visitor is standing offers an excellent view of the western half of the battlefield and is all that is left of a knoll which at the beginning of the battle was held by Captain Johnston's company of the Ninety-Fifth, this unit being reinforced in the face of Drouet's attack by the First Light Battalion of the King's German Legion. This garrison quickly being forced to withdraw in disorder, the two companies in the sandpit were left no option but to flee up the high-road in the direction of the crossroads.

> *George Simmons, lieutenant, Ninety-Firth Regiment of Foot*:
> Under cover of their guns, four columns . . . made their appearance . . . They moved steadily towards us. We formed a sort of line and commenced a terrible fire upon them which was returned very spiritedly, they at the same time advancing [to] within a few yards. I had an impression I would not be touched, and was laughing and joking with a young officer . . . [when] I . . . received a ball which broke two of my ribs, went through my liver, and lodged in my breast. I fell senseless in the mud, and some minutes after found our fellows and the enemy hotly engaged near me. Their skirmishers were beaten back and the column stopped . . . Most of the men with me were killed, so it was some time before any officer noticed me and not until I had been trampled over many times.[7]

8. Return to the track by walking northwards along the edge of the bank and follow it past the picnic area to the Ohain road. Note that the grove of trees to the left was not present in 1815.

H. The Picton Monument

A few yards from the junction of the track the visitor has followed from La Belle Alliance and the Ohain road will be found a small monument marking the spot where the commander of the Allied Fifth Division, Sir Thomas Picton, a notoriously redoubtable commander who fought at both Quatre Bras and Waterloo in civilian clothes on account of his baggage having gone astray, was shot down at the climax of Drouet's assault. What happened is not entirely clear, but Bourgeois' brigade appears to have been forced to the right and therefore hit Wellington's front line virtually side-by-side with the division of Donzelot. In consequence, then, the main impact of the French attack fell on not British troops but rather the five battalions of Bylandt's brigade of the Second Netherlands Division. Already badly hit at Quatre Bras, this fell back with only limited resistance, whereupon, shouting 'Charge! Charge!', Picton ordered Kempt's brigade to assault the French from the front and left flank alike.

Unknown British officer, Kempt's brigade:
   After having tried the right and found it strong, Bonaparte manoeuvred until he got forty pieces of artillery to play on the left where the Fifth Division . . . [was] posted. Our lines were formed behind a hedge with two companies of the Ninety-Fifth extended in front to annoy the enemy's approach. For some time we saw that Bonaparte intended to attack us, yet as nothing but cavalry were visible, no-one could imagine what were his plans, It was generally supposed he would endeavour to turn our flank, but all on a sudden . . . large masses of infantry . . . advanced . . . in the most gallant style to cries of 'Vive l'empereur!' while a most tremendous cannonade was opened to cover their approach. They had arrived at the very hedge behind which we were – the muskets were almost muzzle to muzzle and a French mounted officer had seized the colours of the Thirty-Second Regiment – when . . . Picton ordered the charge of our brigade, commanded by Sir James Kempt. When the French saw us rushing through the hedge and heard the tremendous hurrahs which we gave, they turned . . . and allowed themselves to be butchered without any material resistance . . . Poor Picton was killed at the head of our division while advancing.[8]

9. Proceed to the end of the track and, noting the monuments to the Twenty-Seventh Foot and the Belgian dead of both sides, turn to the right along the Ohain road. In 1815 this was both sunken (though not nearly to the same extent as on the other side of the crossroads) and lined on both sides with a stout thorn hedge. Carry on for perhaps 500 yards to a fork in the road. The large building ahead and to the left is the convent of Frischermont (not to be confused with the chateau of Frischermont) which was erected in 1929 in defiance of the regulations protecting the battlefield from development, but the course of the lane is unchanged, while beyond the road junction it is in much the same condition as it was at the time of the battle and offers excellent views over the western half of the battlefield. On the other hand the two cottages on the south side of the Ohain road in front of the convent are also a lamentable twentieth-century intrusion.

I. Monument to Marcognet's Division
Situated at the left-hand side of the Ohain road just prior to the fork in the road, the monument to Marcognet's division marks the high-water mark of French fortunes at Waterloo in that the moment that that unit

The view north from the knoll looking towards the Frischermont convent. Note that guns posted here could fire into areas normally protected by the reverse slope. (Author's collection)

reached the further side of the Ohain road was probably also the moment when Wellington came closest to defeat at Waterloo. Unhindered by the fire of the riflemen placed in and around La Haye Sainte, Marcognet's 4,200 men were initially faced by no more than two battalions of Dutch militia, and the latter fled broke and fled, although not without firing several volleys at the oncoming French and, according to one British account, even attempting a bayonet charge. Posted behind the Dutch troops were the four battalions of Sir Denis Pack's British brigade, but even they were hard pressed to save the day.

James Hope, lieutenant, Ninety-Second Regiment of Foot:
With their drums beating [and] colours flying . . . the enemy advanced in solid column . . . As they ascended the ridge, the Belgians poured on them a very destructive fire of musketry . . . The French having almost gained the ridge, the Belgians partially retired from the hedge. These troops were induced to return again . . . but . . . at length the whole corps ran as fast as their feet could carry them . . . The post abandoned by the Belgians was ordered to be occupied by the Third Battalion, Royals [i.e. the First Regiment of Foot or Royal Scots], and the second battalion, Forty-Fourth. These two corps retarded the advance of the French, who, although they saw themselves opposed by fresh adversaries, still pressed forward . . . The two British battalions retired on the approach of the enemy who, no doubt, imagined that they would meet with no further opposition . . . but they were soon undeceived . . . Sir Denis Pack . . . perceiving the urgent state of affairs, galloped up to the Ninety-Second, and . . . said, 'Ninety-Second! You must charge! All the troops in your front have given way.' The regiment . . . formed in line . . . moved forward, and, with cheers, approached their veteran enemy.[9]

10. From the road junction take the fork to the right and follow the road (known as the Chemin du Dimont) diagonally across the slope of the ridge, noting in the process that the final slope ascended by the French is much steeper that at first appears, the consequence being that, already disordered by having to struggle through a mixture of ankle-deep mud and trampled crops, the troops would have been quite blown by the

Papelotte viewed from the east. The enclosures greatly aided the defenders in their attempts to hold the area. (Author's collection)

time they reached the Ohain Road. On reaching a thick hedge at the left-hand side of the road turn left on a farm-track. By following this through two right-hand bends, the visitor will reach the farm of Papelotte.

J. Papelotte

The farm of Papelotte was the third of the strongpoints established by Wellington in advance of his line in an attempt to break up and disrupt French advances, and during the battle was held by Prince Bernhard of Saxe-Weimar's brigade of Nassau troops, many of whom had fought for the French in Spain and Portugal in the Peninsular War. Having already fought extremely hard at Quatre Bras, they distinguished themselves once more at Waterloo: driven from the nearby hamlet of Smohain and farm of La Haye though they were, they clung on to Papelotte in the face of a sustained attempt to take it on the part of Durutte's division (many accounts claim that Durutte took the farm, but this does not seem to have been the case; it is, however, just possible that some French troops did gain access to the southern-most end of the complex). Badly damaged during the battle, the buildings remained derelict for fifty years, but were then rebuilt in more-or-less the same form which they had taken in 1815, the only major change being the addition of the ornamental tower above the main gate.

Carl von Rettberg, captain, Second Nassau Regiment:
    Between three and four o'clock the reinforced enemy skirmish line advanced once more, and in support followed considerable infantry columns. Forced to vacate my position, I was thrown back upon Papelotte, which I now quickly turned into a redoubt. On receiving a request for reinforcements, Captain Frensdorff gave me the command of the Tenth, Eleventh and Twelfth Companies, these being joined by the flanker company of the Second Battalion of our regiment. The enemy column was checked by the fire from Papelotte and the small houses [La Haye?], where the occupants bravely resisted, and was now thrown back by a swift bayonet attack and pursued as far as the . . . outer [hedges]. Here an enemy battery welcomed us at barely 500 paces with canister. Although our losses were considerable – the third Flanker Company lost two officers . . . and melted away to half strength by the end of the battle – the enemy nevertheless did not attempt another serious attack, but instead limited himself to a lively skirmish fire from behind a [hedge] at the other side of the meadow at the foot of his position.[10]

11. From Papelotte take the lane down the hill. To the left can be seen the farm of La Haye, which was also occupied by the Nassauers but wrested from them after a fierce struggle. According to some accounts, this is completely different from the structures that existed at the time of the battle, and it is certainly probable that the main house dates from after 1815. However, the imposing barn at the near end of the complex looks as if it could well be a survival of the period, exhibiting signs, as it does, of what appears to be battle damage. Pause at the crossroads at the foot of the hill by the small wayside chapel (like the houses and farm-buildings to the right a post-1815 addition to the scene).

The farm of La Haye. Set ablaze in the course of the battle, the barn beside the track affords clear evidence of the extent of the reconstruction that had to be undertaken after 1815. (Author's collection)

K. Chemin des Cosaques

Curiously enough the road running to right and left at the foot of the hill is called the 'Chemin des Cosaques'. There were, of course, no Cossacks at the battle of Waterloo, but the Prussian corps commanded by Ziethen included a number of units of both lancers and militia cavalry, and it may be that the name is a reference to them: certainly it was in part along this lane that Ziethen's men erupted onto the battlefield at around half-past seven in the evening, whilst so poorly mounted and uniformed was much of the Prussian cavalry that the local inhabitants can be forgiven if they remembered them in such a guise. Prior to Ziethen's arrival, meanwhile, the hedges that line the northern side of the road provided a reasonably secure defensive line for Saxe-Weimar's men, though it has to be said that Durutte's men were much more thinly spread than their comrades to the west and therefore able to mount much less of an assault.

Johann Doring, sergeant, Twenty-Eighth (Orange-Nassau) Regiment:

The battle now began to rage with . . . a steady, thunderous and earth-shaking rumble. The powder smoke . . . blew towards us and was so dense at times that the enemy opposing us could only be recognised by the . . . flashes from their guns and muskets . . . Because of the terrible noise, the officers' orders could no longer be understood and the necessary commands were largely communicated by the [drummers], buglers and . . . hornists. Our battalion was posted . . . at the chateau and farm of Frischermont, which was surrounded by a three-to-four foot high wall. We were able to defend this fairly important position for quite some time against the attacks of a regiment of *voltigeurs*. They attempted several times to force the wall, albeit without success until they were reinforced by the arrival of a corps of some 4,000 men. We then had to retire from this position in a hurry, and we continued our defence further back at a hamlet [i.e. Smohain] . . . For us this was the day's most critical and dangerous moment as the French moved against us with ever more powerful columns. We were separated from the enemy by a distance of not more than half the range of a musket shot . . . The turmoil became more general by the minute, and there could no thought of some sort of order. Without interruption, we loaded and fired into the enemy's ranks: [there was] no use in aiming at a particular target.[11]

13. Turn left along the lane and proceed along the Chemin des Cosaques in the direction of La Haye. Just before the buildings take the turning to the left and go up the lane a little way to inspect the barn of the farm of La Haye and get a good view of the eastern walls of Plancenoit, whose aspect is much less altered than on the other side of the complex. Return to the lane, turn left and follow the road to the road junction just past the 'Trois Canards' restaurant. Turn right and follow the road round into Smohain. After 100 yards a lane leads uphill: following this a short distance leads to a spot where a low wall at the top of the bank above the road is one of the few visible remains of the chateau of Frischermont. Little damaged by

the battle, it was nevertheless demolished in 1857 and replaced by a more modern structure that was pulled down in its turn a century later. Whether Wellington knew that in 1705 it had briefly been the headquarters of the Duke of Marlborough during the Ramillies campaign is unknown. Returning to the centre of Smohain, follow the same lane as before. This soon runs steeply uphill. At a crossroads turn right and ascend the track to the crest of the hill. From here an excellent view may be obtained of Papelotte from the point of view of the French forces attacking the area. Follow the track straight on down the hill, and at the bottom turn left and ascend the sunken lane to the crest of the hill. To return to La Belle Alliance follow the track straight on, noting the views of the ridge followed by Bülow's corps in its advance on Plancenoit on the one hand and of Wellington's centre-left on the other.

TOUR 5: UXBRIDGE'S COUNTER-ATTACK

Time: three hours. Going: metalled roads or mostly well-maintained tracks, though some patches of the latter may be waterlogged in wet weather; moderate slopes with occasional steeper stretches; some stretches of field walking (optional). See Map 4

1. If there was a moment when the Duke of Wellington came within an ace of losing the battle of Waterloo, it was the point when the leading divisions of Drouet's corps struck the line of the Ohain road. The front line of the defenders was constituted by Bylandt's Dutch-Belgian brigade, a force that had suffered heavy losses at the battle of Quatre Bras, and this broke and ran after a brief resistance. Also driven from their positions were the companies of the First Battalion of the Ninety-Fifth holding the sandpit and knoll just up the road from La Haye Sainte, whilst the King's German Legion and Hanoverian troops holding the line immediately to the west of the crossroads were threatened by a large force of cuirassiers that had circumvented the farm and ascended the ridge. Reaching the line of the road, the French then confronted the British infantry brigades of Kempt and Pack. Despite the fact that the divisional commander, Sir Thomas Picton, had hardly given the order to charge before he was shot dead, the former were able to check the single French brigade facing them, but, to their left, Pack's four battalions were confronting two entire divisions and they were pushed back and in some cases possibly even broken. This being a moment of great crisis, it is arguable that Wellington's army was only saved by the quick thinking of the commander of the Anglo-Dutch cavalry, Lord Uxbridge. Immediately in the rear of the sector of the line threatened by the French attack were Wellington's only two brigades of heavy cavalry. Known as the Household and Union brigades, at Uxbridge's command these now swept forward in a great counter-attack.

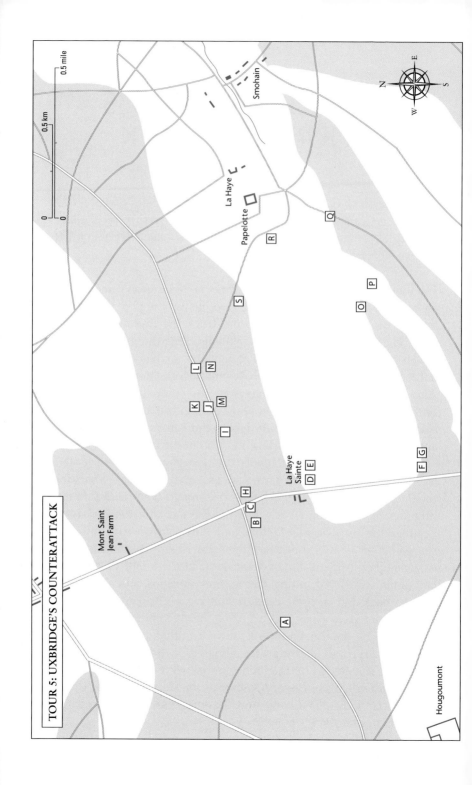

TOUR 5: UXBRIDGE'S COUNTERATTACK

0.5 km
0.5 mile

N
E
W
S

Mont Saint
Jean Farm

La Haye

Papelotte

Smohain

R

S

Q

P

O

L

N

K

J

M

I

H

C

B

D

E

La Haye
Sainte

F

G

A

Hougoumont

The initial position of the Household Brigade viewed from the lane to Merbe Braine looking towards Mont Saint Jean. Though out of sight of the French, the area was still at risk from howitzer shells and roundshot that had overshot the crest. (Author's collection)

A. The Household Brigade (1)

Begin the tour on the Ohain road at the eastern edge of the Hameau du Lion. If the visitor stands on the bank overlooking the road and looks in the direction of the farm of Mont Saint Jean, they will have a good view of the position of the so-called Household Brigade of Lord Edward Somerset, this running parallel to the Anglo-Dutch front line and roughly 300 yards to its north. Thus positioned, the four regiments concerned – the Royal Horse Guards, the First Regiment of Life Guards, the Second Regiment of Life Guards, and the First Regiment of Dragoon Guards – were completely out of sight of the French and therefore able to launch a surprise attack.

Thomas Playford, sergeant-major, Second Regiment of Life Guards:
   The word 'Mount' was given and the trumpet sounded 'Draw swords' . . . This done, the advance was given . . . We saw no enemy, yet there was a strange medley of shouts, musket shots and the roar of cannon beyond the rising ground in front

of us. Presently we met a number of English foot-soldiers running for their lives . . . and I supposed they were very young soldiers for no veterans would have done so [NB. the troops seen by Playford were almost certainly either Hanoverians of Kielmansegg's brigade or members of the King's German Legion: in both cases the troops concerned wore British-style uniforms]. The Earl of Uxbridge . . . approached us; he took off his hat, waved it . . . and then passed [it] forward over his horse's head. It was a signal and the trumpets sounded 'Charge!' 'Hurrah!' shouted the soldiers . . . At that moment a line of French horsemen appeared in front of us: they were shouting, waving their swords and sabreing the English infantry and artillery men who had not got out of their way. Our shouts had arrested their attention and, looking up, they saw fearful ranks of red-coated horsemen coming galloping forward, shouting and brandishing their swords . . . They met us in mid-onset near the brow of the hill as men confident of victory, but the shock of battle overthrew many of them, for the weight and power of our horses was too great for their less powerful men and weaker horses . . . Many fell; others fled and were pursued towards their own lines.[1]

2. Walk along the Ohain Road in the direction of the Charleroi highway. The slopes to the right saw fierce fighting between the First Life Guards and the First Dragoon Guards and the cuirassiers who had advanced to support Drouet. Note the height of the bank beside the road: this is such as to constitute a major barrier for cavalry, whilst it would originally been paralleled by a similar bank on the French side of the road as well; at best, then, the British riders would have been moving at a trot. Pause at the track leading down the slope to La Haye Sainte.

B. The Household Brigade (2)
En route to attack the French, the Household Brigade had to pass through the positions held by the infantry brigades of Kielmansegg and Ompteda. This, however, was not too problematic as both had formed all their battalions in square so as to be able to resist the oncoming French cuirassiers.

The Life Guards rout Dubois' cuirassier brigade in the fields west of La Haye Sainte. (War Heritage Institute, Brussels)

Eberhard von Brandis, lieutenant, Fifth Line Battalion, King's German Legion:

The powder smoke was so dense that nothing could be seen. After a few minutes Colonel von Ompteda sent me . . . to determine whether it was infantry or cavalry that was approaching. I soon found myself in front of a line of enemy cuirassiers, which was advancing at walking pace. I therefore quickly turned my horse around in order to notify the brigade, but at the same moment a brigade of English heavy dragoons came towards me at the trot in line about to attack the cuirassiers. It being impossible for me to pass through that line, much against my will I had to turn round again and, to avoid being overrun, charge against the cuirassiers. Having to make the best of this awkward game did not appeal to me at all. Still, I flourished my sabre . . . in front of the dragoons . . . [and] tried to enhance their fighting spirit by shouting some . . . encouraging words at them. However, I steered my ride in such a way that, while still some twenty paces away from the enemy, I happened to end up in a squadron interval . . . Letting them pass, I now hurriedly went back to Ompteda in fulfilment of my last assignment.[2]

3. Continue along the Ohain road to the crossroads.

C. The Household Brigade (3)

Having crossed the Ohain road, the left wing of the Household Brigade found itself confronted by La Haye Sainte and therefore swung to the left, thereupon wither galloping straight down the Charleroi highway or veering still further to the left so as to attack the brigade of Charles Bourgeois. Seemingly, the troops concerned – the First Dragoons and the Second Life Guards – were moving at a much slower rate than the units further to the right, and this enabled a number of Dubois' cuirassiers to seek shelter by riding across the north face of the farm and rallying on the high road, only to be swept away in their turn.

> *Thomas Marten, cornet, Second Regiment of Life Guards*:
> It was about one o'clock when we were called to advance from our position in rear of the right-centre to charge a body of cuirassiers, but I never saw them till we had crossed the road

Soldiers of the Life Guards in action against the remnants of Dubois' cuirassiers near La Haye Sainte. (Wikimedia Commons)

near La Haye Sainte and just beyond where the Rifles were, and there it was that our first collision took place, and not on the crest of the ridge as you suppose. It is not impossible, however, that the other regiments of the brigade might have there met the French cavalry, but we, having the farm in front of us, were obliged . . . to bring up our right shoulders and descend the hill by the left of it, and in doing so . . . we met with many obstacles . . . Just after we had crossed the road (as I have said before), we came in contact with a line of cavalry, either cuirassiers or carabiniers: I cannot remember which, but they all had cuirasses. A pause here took place and I then beheld plenty of single combats around me. We then progressed onwards . . . and it was either just before or about this period that we were in the midst of French infantry who appeared widely dispersed all around, many of whom had thrown themselves flat on the ground and were apparently dead, but these gents [*sic*] I afterwards saw get up and fire after us. From this scene we pursued our broken course a little further on, but still in the low ground . . . and, there finding no force to oppose, our people . . . thought it best to take the shortest way back, over to the left of our position, and, in doing this, got behind our infantry who rose and cheered us.[3]

4. Cross the road via the pedestrian crossing, turn right and take the track leading southwards parallel to the Charleroi highway to a point opposite the main gate of La Haye Sainte. Just before the farm is reached the track skirts a small lay-by. This marks the site of the sandpit originally held by two companies of the Ninety-Fifth. During the fighting, many wounded men had been laid there and most were now trampled to death as the Life Guards poured across in pursuit of the French. One casualty of the charge whose last resting place is known is Lieutenant James Carruthers of the Second Dragoons or Royal Scots Greys. Badly wounded, he lay on the battlefield all night and was not discovered until mid-morning of the next day when he was picked up by a small party of men led by Sergeant William Clarke. Barely conscious, he was revived by a little spirits, only to expire a few minutes later as he was being carried to safety, his body then being laid to rest in a shallow grave directly opposite the main gate of the farm.

One of two regiments in Bourgeois' brigade, the 105th Line, loses its eagle to the First Dragoons in the fields west of La Haye Sainte. Of the French unit's forty-two officers, thirty-two were killed or wounded, the vast majority falling victim to the swords of Uxbridge's cavalry. (Wikimedia Commons)

D. La Haye Sainte

Taken completely by surprise, the French infantry attacking La Haye Sainte suffered heavy casualties, whilst the defenders were, by the same token, much encouraged.

Friedrich Lindenau, private, Fifth Line Battalion, King's German Legion:

Suddenly English hussars [*sic*] appeared at our side, hacking into the enemy so furiously that a great crowd of them turned back to us without their weapons and asked for quarter . . .I was glad to see heaps of dead enemy lying more than a foot high near the *abatis*. By the wall I saw a grenadier lying with a bullet through his body: he wanted to run himself through the breast with a sabre, but no longer had the necessary strength to do it. I seized the hilt of the sword to throw it away, [and] the Frenchman let go immediately, no doubt fearing that I might wound his hands by pulling it away. Near the *abatis* a wounded man with a bullet through the leg lay in a pool of water: he cried out loudly in pain and tried to roll out of the water, [so] I seized him by the arms and another took hold of his legs, and . . . we laid him by the wall with his head on a comrade who had been shot.[4]

5. Take the stub of track leading east from La Haye Sainte to its end in the middle of the field.

E. Bourgeois' Brigade

The charge of the Household Brigade revealed a disadvantage with regard to La Haye Sainte that does not appear to have been anticipated. Thus, in brief, in the event of a counter-attack, as now, it was as much an obstacle to the defenders as it was to the attackers. Thus, hardly had it crossed the Ohain Road than the Household Brigade was split

The intermediate ridge from the Charleroi highway. Relatively steep, the slope would have quickly exhausted the already blown horses of the British cavalry. (Author's collection)

into two, thereby losing much of its cohesion. On the right-hand side of the farm, the presence of Lord Uxbridge appears to have preserved a measure of unity, but on the left-hand side this was far from the case: splitting into ever smaller groups, the First Dragoons and Second Life Guards simply galloped ever deeper into the French positions, sabreing all who stood in their way. For the French infantry caught beneath their hooves, however, it was still a terrifying experience.

Louis Canler, corporal, Twenty-Eighth Regiment of Line Infantry:
Still with our arms at the shoulder, we climbed the hill as far the cannons . . . but hardly had we reached the plateau than . . . the Queen's Dragoons [*sic*: actually the First, or Royal, Regiment of Dragoons] hurled themselves upon us to the accompaniment of the most savage cries. Not having had time to form square, the first division could not sustain such a charge and was immediately broken, whereupon a real slaughter was unleashed. Separated from their comrades, each man could only make head on his own account, whilst sabres and bayonets were the order of the day when it came to cleaving the palpitating flesh of an opponent, the two sides being too mixed up with one another to make use of firearms. However, struggle though they might, foot soldiers fighting on their own in the midst of a crowd of horsemen could not hope to maintain their positions, and so I soon found myself disarmed and taken prisoner.[5]

6. Return to the Charleroi highway and turn left in the direction of La Belle Alliance. After a short distance a row of cottages will be encountered on the right; it was in the vicinity of the first of these houses – the Casa Victoria – that Uxbridge lost his leg at the end of the battle. Having vanquished the cavalry that had remained on the western side of La Haye Sainte, the remainder of the Union Brigade wheeled left around the farm and drove their fleeing opponents back to the Brussels road in this area. Now moving uphill, continue along the high road until a flight of steps is reached leading up the bank on the left-hand side.

F. The Cutting
The visitor is now standing in the cutting whereby the Charleroi highway makes its way through the intermediate ridge before

In a famous painting of an incident that never happened, French cuirassiers crash into the sunken section of the Ohain road during the cavalry charges that marked the afternoon. However, it is possible that something of the sort happened in the course of the fighting in and around the cutting whereby the Charleroi highroad passes through the intermediate ridge. (Wikimedia Commons)

climbing up to La Belle Alliance. In 1815 this was much narrower that it is today – a veritable defile, even – and it is just possible that scenes which were witnessed here gave rise to the myth of the sunken lane (i.e. the idea that the later French cavalry charges were wrecked by the leading riders coming to grief in the Ohain road). Thus, galloping over from the position to which it had advanced in support of Dubois to deal with the British breakthrough, the other brigade of the division concerned - namely that of Etienne Travers - would certainly have had to cross the cutting and may well have got into difficulty in the process. What is certainly true, meanwhile, is that the area witnessed serious congestion.

Octave Levavasseur, aide de camp to Marshal Soult:
A mass of horsemen appeared heading straight for us at the gallop. At this I tried to wheel my horse, but . . . he baulked, and I could not get him to move. Luckily for me, however, a nearby cuirassier seized his bridle, and, by digging in my spurs, I was able to catch up with the rearmost ranks of our own riders . . . but at that same instant a column of cavalry that had been sent to succour us rode down the very road that

we were trying to escape by and thereby blocked our way. In an instant . . . the enemy cavalry were on our rear, whilst we ourselves were so jammed together that not a man could make a movement to defend himself. All I could hear was the clanging of the enemy's swords as they cut through the men's cuirasses; the carnage was dreadful. However, the commander of the cavalry who had ridden to our aid, General Colbert, managed to disengage those of his squadrons that had not yet entered the defile, and, having led them around the banks that shut us in, fell on the horsemen who had attacked us: themselves just as shut up in the defile as we were, they were cut to pieces in their turn.[6]

7. Climb the steps to the top of the bank.

G. The Intermediate Ridge

The visitor is now standing on the ridge where Drouet positioned his divisional artillery. The five batteries involved opened a heavy fire on the oncoming British cavalry, but they were far the most part overrun and the gunners either sabred or forced to flee for their lives. This was, however, an empty victory: like their French counterparts later in the

Carried away by adrenalin and blood-lust, British cavalry overrun the 6-pounder guns positioned on the intermediate ridge. (Wikimedia Commons)

day, the British horsemen had no means of removing captured guns, whilst they were now badly blown and completely out of formation, the result being that they were vulnerable to counter-attack.

George de Lacy Evans, aide de camp to Sir William Ponsonby:
Our men were out of hand. The general . . . his staff and every officer within hearing, exerted themselves to the utmost . . . but the helplessness of the enemy offered too great a temptation to the dragoons and our efforts were abortive. It was evident that the enemy's reserves of cavalry would soon take advantage of our disorder. Anticipating this, I went back for a moment to where Sir James Kempt was to ask him to advance to cover our retreat . . . He told me he would advance a couple of hundred yards, but that he could not quit the position altogether without orders . . . I galloped back to Sir William Ponsonby. The dragoons were still in the same disorder, cutting up the remnant of the dispersed infantry. We ascended the first ridge occupied by the enemy, and passed several cannon on our right hand . . . French lancers . . . [advanced] on our left. If we could have formed 100 men, we could have made a respectable retreat and saved many, but we could effect no formation, and were as helpless against their attack as their infantry had been against ours. Everyone saw what must happen. Those whose horses were best, or least blown, got away. Some attempted to escape by going round to the left of the French lancers: Sir William Ponsonby was of that number; all of these fell into the hands of the enemy. Others went straight back – among whom myself – receiving a little fire from some infantry towards the road . . . as we retired. It was in this part of the transaction that almost the whole of the loss of the brigade took place.[7]

8. Having descended the stairs, turn right and return to the main Anglo-Dutch position, pausing at the Picton Memorial.

H. The Picton Memorial
The Picton Memorial marks the spot where Sir Thomas Picton was shot dead leading forward two battalions of the brigade of Sir James Kempt in an attempt to drive back Bourgeois' brigade

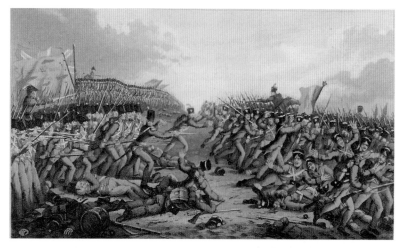

British infantry defeat a French attack in the same style as Kempt's brigade overcame the troops of Charlet and Donzelot. In the face of French columns, the standard tactic was to fire a single volley at close range and then launch a bayonet charge. (War Heritage Institute, Brussels)

of Quiot's division (the third battalion in the brigade, namely the First Battalion of the Ninety-Fifth, had retired in the face of the French advance in some disorder and was reforming a little distance to the rear). In the first instance, Picton's attack appears to have had some success, but whether it would have been sufficient to check the French onrush is at best a moot point: there are strong suggestions that the divisions of Donzelot and Marcognet broke into the Anglo-Dutch position and pushed past the left flank of Kempt's brigade, the latter therefore being in serious danger of being outflanked.

> *Henry Ross-Lewin, captain, Thirty-Second Regiment of Foot:*
> A strong body of French infantry advanced . . . and pressed on the lane. Sir Thomas Picton instantly placed himself at the head of his division to meet the attack . . . and charged the French, who, firing a volley, faced about and retired . . . The attack cost us a gallant leader, for Sir Thomas . . . received a ball through his right temple and fell dead from his horse: his body was borne off . . . by two grenadiers of the Thirty-Second Regiment . . . During the charge a French

officer seized a stand of colours belonging to the above-mentioned corps, but he was instantly run through the body by a sergeant's pike . . . Our troops pursued the retiring column down the hill and would inevitably have closed with them had they not begun to fire and thereby retarded their advance. However, a good account was given of this column shortly after, for Sir William Ponsonby's brigade, consisting of the Royals, the Scots Greys and the Enniskillen Dragoons, galloped in at the corner of the field, and took more than 2,000 of them prisoners . . . The prisoners were at once marched off to Brussels where their appearance served to convince the inhabitants of the falsehood of the reports spread by . . . runaway Belgians . . . that the battle was lost, our army nearly cut to pieces and the speedy entry of the victorious French inevitable. After the repulse of our opponents we resumed our former position and Sir James Kempt took the command of the division.[8]

10. Turn right along the Ohain Road in the direction of the Frischermont convent and proceed for a short distance to the east.

A general view of the charge of the Union Brigade which reproduces both the terrain and the general situation reasonably well. Napoleon can be discerned in the far distance near La Belle Alliance, whilst on the right Uxbridge observes the havoc he had just unleashed. Just in front of him, meanwhile, two French soldiers who had somehow escaped the first onrush of the British cavalry may be observed shooting their adversaries in the back, this being something that was much complained of by British veterans of the charge. (Wikimedia Commons)

I. Donzelot's Division

At the time of the battle the Ohain road had a very different appearance than it does today in that it that it was lined by banks on both sides rather than just the one, whilst the banks themselves were topped by stout thorn hedges that, though passable, represented a considerable obstacle. In the vicinity of the spot in which the visitor is now standing the leading brigade of the division of General Donzelot was struck by the First Dragoons, this unit constituting the right-hand regiment of Sir William Ponsonby's Union brigade (so-called because it had one unit that was primarily English, one unit that was primarily Scottish and one unit that was primarily Irish).

Alexander Clark Kennedy, captain, First Regiment of Dragoons:
The Marquis of Anglesey [i.e. Lord Uxbridge] came up at speed (apparently from the Household Brigade on the right), wheeled the Royals and Inniskillings into line, and ordered them to charge, the Greys forming a second line in support. . . . The infantry that . . . had previously lined the hedges . . . were firing on the left flank of the French column, the head of which had at this time passed both hedges unchecked, as far as I could perceive, and were advancing rapidly . . . We did not see each other till we were very close, perhaps eighty or ninety yards. The head of the column appeared to be seized with a panic, gave us a fire which brought down about twenty men, went instantly about and endeavoured to regain the opposite side of the hedges, but we were . . . amongst them before this could be effected, the whole column getting into one dense mass, the men between the advancing and retiring part getting so jammed together that the men could not bring down their arms or use them effectively, and we had nothing to do but to continue to press them the slope . . . The French on this occasion behaved very ill, many of our soldiers falling from the fire of men who had surrendered and whose lives had been spared only a few minutes before. I had a narrow escape myself. One of these men put his musket close to my head and fired, a sudden turn of my head saving my life, the ball taking off the tip of

my nose instead of passing through the head as was kindly intended.[9]

11. Continue along the road to the Marcognet Memorial.

J. Marcognet's Division

Like Donzelot's division to its left, Marcognet's division was deployed with its eight battalions arrayed one behind the other in line, a formation that was designed to maximise firepower without at the same time sacrificing speed and impetus. Thus arrayed, it achieved much success: in the face of the French advance, Bylandt's brigade, a unit that had been very hard hit at Quatre Bras, fell back in disorder after having put up only limited resistance, whilst a counter-attack by a part of Kempt's brigade was repelled with heavy losses. In short, the French had broken through, it being very clear that the key factor in turning the tide was the charge of the Union Brigade. With much of the area shrouded in smoke, the French infantry did not see the oncoming cavalry until they were almost on them and had little chance of putting up an effective defence.

Jacques Martin, lieutenant, Forty-Fifth Regiment of Line Infantry:
It is difficult, not to say impossible, for the best cavalry to force infantry formed in square who defend themselves with *sang froid* and intrepidity, but once horsemen have got in amongst troops who have been broken, resistance is useless, and the riders are confronted by little more than a slaughterhouse in which they can go on killing with little risk to themselves. That is what happened next. No matter how much our poor soldiers stood to their full height and stretched out their arms as far as they could reach, their bayonets had little effect on horsemen mounted on powerful chargers, while in the confusion such few musket shots as they managed to get off were as dangerous to our own side as they were to the English. In short, we found ourselves without any defence against a ferocious enemy who in the fury of combat went so far as to cut down our drummers and fifers. It was at this moment that our eagle was taken, and at this moment, too,

that death came close to me for all around me my best friends were going down . . . Seeing that we were no longer able to put up much resistance, the majority of the enemy riders decided to push on for the ridge between the two armies . . . and, as they did so a horse knocked me flying . . . As the enemy were not bothering to search for anybody who might still be alive . . . I got to my feet and set out to cross that fatal valley once again with all its mud, tangled crops, and, now, dead bodies lying in pools of blood.[10]

12. Walk a few yards back toward the crossroads. At the western boundary of the convent grounds turn right and follow the boundary northwards until it turns back to the east. From this spot an excellent view may be obtained of the line from which the Union Brigade commenced its advance and the slopes up which it advanced to reach the French.

The initial position of the Second Dragoons viewed from the vicinity of the Frischermont convent. Officially titled 'The Royal North British Dragoons', the regiment was popularly known as 'The Royal Scots Greys'. (Author's collection)

K. The Union Brigade

Consisting of approximately 1,000 men, the Union Brigade advanced from its starting point with its three regiments in line abreast, the consequence being that there was no reserve, a matter that was going to be of great importance later. Facing the ground occupied by the Frischermont convent was the Second, or Royal North British, Dragoons, a unit that is better known to history by its nickname of the Royal Scots Greys (a reference to the fact that it was entirely mounted on grey horses). Having been kept in garrison at home for the whole length of the Revolutionary and Napoleonic Wars, Waterloo was its first taste of battle and officers and men alike were therefore eager to prove their mettle.

> *George de Lacy Evans, aide de camp to Sir William Ponsonby:*
> The brigade was in a hollow in order to screen them from cannon fire . . . As the enemy advanced up to the crest of the position on their side, the . . . brigade was also moved up on ours. Our brigade came up to 100 yards in rear of the little sunken road and hedge . . . We waited there for a few minutes till the head of the enemy's column had just crossed the sunken road . . . to allow our infantry to pass round the flanks of the squadrons, and also that the enemy should be a little deranged in passing the road, instead of our being so had we charged across the road. The enemy's column . . . on arriving at the crest of the position, seemed very helpless: [it] had very little fire to give from its front or flanks, was incapable of deploying, must have already lost many of its officers in coming up [and] was fired into, close, with impunity, by stragglers of our infantry who [had] remained behind. As we approached at a moderate pace, the front and flanks began to turn their backs inwards [while] the rear of the columns had already begun to run away.[11]

13. Turning to the right follow the boundary of the convent to the east and at the further corner turn right and return to the Ohain Road.

L. Scotland for Ever!

In this area the Ohain Road is more-or-less in its original condition with thick hedges and steep banks on each side. As such, it would

The Ohain road east of the Frischermont convent. A substantial obstacle for cavalry, it could only have been negotiated at a walk. (Author's collection)

have offered a significant obstacle to cavalry travelling at speed, but it is probable the Scots Greys were moving at little more than a trot and were therefore able to negotiate it without much difficulty: certainly, no account mentions it as having been a problem. Meanwhile, the fact that the regiment was moving at such a slow speed helps to explain how, as is well known, a number of the soldiers of the Ninety-Second Foot (a Highland unit) were able to seize hold of the stirrup leathers of various riders and in this fashion have themselves carried forward into the *mêlée* which followed. However, whilst this episode is often portrayed as the result of a combination of high spirits, excessive valour and national feeling, it seems more likely that the men concerned were simply caught out of formation and endeavouring to do no more than save themselves from being trampled underfoot.

> *Robertson, sergeant, Second Regiment of Dragoons*:
> The shot and shell were playing very hard upon us [when] an *aide de camp* . . . came at full speed to Sir W. Ponsonby and said 'Your heavy brigade must be brought forward and charge the enemy immediately: they can no longer be wanted.' Our brave commander immediately complied with the order, and . . . we marched, cocksure of victory, cheering and waving our

glittering swords, to meet the chosen troops of France as they rapidly advanced to meet us . . . As we advanced, we came up with the Highland Brigade [*sic*] . . . who on our advance wheeled into open column to enable us to pass through their lines. [Once] our brigade had passed through the intervals, they were ordered to wheel into line and await further orders, but all entreaty on this hand was in vain, for . . . they were so overjoyed to see us that they pulled off their bonnets and gave us three . . . cheers and called out 'Scotland for ever!', and, instead of remaining in the position, mingled themselves among us, some holding our stirrups while others ran like bucks down the hill, and in this manner penetrated into the first French line.[12]

14. Follow the Ohain Road back to the Marcognet Monument.

Frischermont convent viewed from the valley showing the ground charged over by the Second Dragoons. It was somewhere in this area that Sergeant Ewart took his eagle. (Author's collection)

M. Sergeant Ewart

Erected to commemorate French military success, the Marcognet Monument rather marks the spot where the French may truly be said to have lost the Battle of Waterloo. Had Drouet broken through, Wellington would beyond doubt have been forced to retreat, leaving Napoleon at the very least master of the field. That, however, did not happen, Drouet's troops rather being ridden down and cut to pieces. Meanwhile, it was approximately at this spot that Sergeant Charles Ewart captured the eagle of the Forty-Fifth Regiment of Line Infantry. Born in 1769 near Kilmarnock, Ewart, a veritable giant of a man noted for his herculean strength, enlisted in the army in 1789 and by 1815 had reached the rank of sergeant and with it the position of regimental fencing master. As for the eagle taken by Ewart, it is on display in the Scots Greys' regimental museum at Edinburgh castle.

Charles Ewart, sergeant, Second Regiment of Dragoons:
It was in the charge I took the eagle from the enemy: he and I had a hard contest for it. He made a thrust at my groin; I parried it off and cut him down through the head. After this a lancer came at me: I threw the lance off by my right side, and cut him through the chin and upwards through the teeth. Next, a foot soldier fired at me and then charged me with his bayonet, which I also had the good luck to parry, and then I cut him down through the head. Thus ended the contest.[13]

15. At the road junction, take the road leading downhill and pause in front of the cottage occupying the space between the two roads (like the Frischermont convent, this was not present in 1815). From here a good view may be obtained of the route which the Second Dragoons followed as they pursued the fleeing French into the valley and up the slope on the further side.

N. The Pursuit

In the Peninsular War, British cavalry had developed a bad reputation for, as Wellington famously put it, 'galloping at everything', and the British commander had therefore taken care to employ them extremely sparingly (only at Talavera, Salamanca and Vitoria can one find even brigade-level actions). At Waterloo, this caution was

The intermediate ridge looking south-west from the valley beneath convent of Frischermont. The Union Brigade swept upwards across these slopes towards the French guns. (Author's collection)

shown to be well-founded. Like almost all the other regiments involved in the counter-attack, the Second Dragoons got completely out of control and, picking up speed, charged across the valley, only suddenly to find themselves in serious trouble.

Robertson, sergeant, Second Regiment of Dragoons:
The whole [front] line . . . was either killed or taken prisoner. We continued to charge until we broke through the second line, which we dispersed in the same manner. In this affair we suffered greatly in both men and horses owing to a battery placed on an eminence a little to our left . . . which battery was [then] silenced and taken. After the battery was silenced, there was nothing to be heard but the clashing of swords and bayonets and the cries of the dying and the wounded: here the carnage was dreadful beyond human conception. Many of our brigade after dispersing the second line advanced as far as the third, which was chiefly composed of lancers and cuirassiers whose horses were quite fresh and which our brigade could not penetrate, being few in numbers [on account of] the great losses sustained in the advance. At this time we were obliged to form our retreat, [but this] was discovered by the

aforementioned . . . lancers who made an oblique movement and got . . . between us and the British lines, by which a severe contest ensued . . . from which few indeed of the Greys returned to give an account of what happened.[14]

15. The state of the crops permitting, leave the road and walk southwards into the valley. On the far side ascend the slope and head for the eastern end of the rectangular copse that will be noted on the further crest (in both cases the gradient will be found to be much steeper than might at first have been expected). Failing this, continue along the road to a sharp-right bend and pick up the tour at No. 18.

O. The French Counter-Attack (1)
In advancing as far as they did and at such speed, the British cavalry were risking disaster in that the horses became ever more blown and the riders ever more scattered. Galloping along the ridge from the left to right, Jacquinot's brigade, in particular, was able to sweep all before it. In part composed of lancers, it was much better able to cope with the boggy terrain than the more heavily mounted British

The area crossed by Jacquinot's charge viewed from the western end of the intermediate ridge. (Author's collection)

dragoons and exerted a heavy toll. Amongst those who fell was Sir William Ponsonby although he was not simply ridden down, but taken prisoner and then killed in cold blood by a lance thrust when it looked likely that he might be rescued by a group of British cavalry who had contrived to remain in fighting trim.

> *Unknown sergeant, Second Regiment of Dragoons*:
> There we were . . . with sword in hand, every one killing another; so awful was the sight that it could be compared to nothing but the Day of Judgement . . . I was the orderly sergeant so I was covering my captain and, while he was engaged with a lancer, [another] came up to run him through. I struck the man and wounded him and saved my captain's life. He immediately made a push at me, but I struck at him again and just as the spear was entering my breast, I cut his arm off. When I was galloping off, a rifleman shot my poor horse in the head which killed him on the spot. He fell (poor fellow) and me under him. There I was, prisoner, but the Frenchman, thinking it too much trouble to draw me from under the horse, or perhaps [that] I had no money, left me, so I made the best of my way into a wood and came to Brussels that night.[15]

16. Walk southwards a few yards to the south-eastern corner of the copse.

P. The Cavalry Mêlée
The area in which the visitor is standing was the scene of fierce fighting as various French cavalry units overran the hopelessly over-extended Union Brigade. Among the troops caught up in the latter stages of the action was at least some part of the Guard Light Cavalry Division commanded by Charles Lefebvre-Desnouettes.

> *Jean Chevalier, lieutenant, Regiment of Chasseurs à Cheval of the Guard*:
> Executing a vigorous charge, a strong force of enemy cavalry threw back our infantry and captured sixteen cannons . . . Putting our heads down, we charged the English cavalry in turn, sabreing all those who sought to oppose us and taking back all our cannon . . . The mêlée that ensured was truly

Elements of the Second Dragoons clash with French cuirassiers on the slopes of the intermediate ridge. Blown and disordered, the British cavalry were quickly overwhelmed and suffered terrible losses. (War Heritage Institute, Brussels)

horrible: the carnage was appalling – the ground was strewn with dead or dying men and horses – and the sense of terror overwhelming. In the midst of this dreadful fight . . . we saw a regiment of English cavalry riding towards us, and making as if to charge: as we were in closed column of squadrons, they probably did not realise how strong we were. Seeing them, the general commanding us shouted, 'Let them come, but, when they get here, none of your sabreing: give them the point and that good and proper!' Very soon, drunk on brandy and dressed in their red coats, they were on us, slashing right and left with their poor-quality blades. Opening our ranks a little, we let them in, but then just swallowed them up, the result being that in less than ten minutes, not a single redcoat was left on horseback.[16]

17. Carry straight on across the fields until a track is reached running from right to left. Having reached this track, turn left, noting the view of Papelotte farm across the valley. Very shortly the track begins to run steeply downhill whilst before long it also becomes deeply sunken.

The lane from La Belle Alliance to Papelotte near the junction with the lane from Papelotte to Plancenoit. (Author's collection)

Q. The Lane to Papelotte

The lane which the visitor has now reached runs from La Belle Alliance and at the start of the battle its more westerly stretches marked the French front line. In the wake of Drouet's assault its more sheltered sections provided a refuge for the hundreds of soldiers who were too shocked and exhausted to fight any more. So numerous were these men that I Corps' losses could well have amounted to 50 per cent of its strength.

Jacques Martin, lieutenant, Forty-Fifth Regiment of Line Infantry:
All around me were scattered groups of English cavalry which our guns were subjecting to a rain of canister . . . As I was but a short distance from the nearest horsemen, I expected to see some of them break off to come and ride me down any minute, but, in the end my fears proved groundless, for it seemed they had other things to do than come and pick an individual fight with me. Like me, then, they made for our batteries, and we arrived amongst them more or less at the same time. However, while they set about fighting the

gunners, I slipped away and managed to reach the shelter of a ravine a couple of hundred paces to the rear. Throwing myself on the ground, I tried to catch my breath. That others of my units had managed to save themselves, I had no doubt, but, if they had done so, I had not seen any of them . . . In any case . . . whereas my strength had kept me going while the danger was pressing, now that it was past it abandoned me I simply could not move. Extreme fatigue, the pain of two wounds – a foot crushed by a horseshoe in the *mêlée* and a bayonet thrust not in my knee . . . but just above it – and astonishment at a deliverance so totally unexpected left me in the grip of an emotion of a sort I had never experienced while I was in peril.[17]

18. Carry on down the lane until it emerges at a metalled road opposite the farm of Papelotte. Turn left on to the metalled road and follow it first along the bottom of the valley and then uphill to the

The site of Vandeleur's charge looking north-east from the valley beneath Wellington's positions. (Author's collection)

right until it emerges into the open just past a clump of trees. Whilst the cavalry action was taking place this road was the scene of bitter fighting between the right-hand brigade of Durutte's division of I Corps and the Dutch and Nassauer infantry of the brigade of Prince Bernhard of Saxe-Weimar: indeed, for much of the time it appears to have formed a species of no man's land.

R. Vandeleur's Brigade (1)

Wellington's extreme left wing was held by two brigades of light cavalry, namely those of Sir John Vandeleur and Sir Richard Vivian. Seeing the increasing difficulties which the Union Brigade was experiencing, the former (which consisted of the Eleventh, Twelfth and Sixteenth Light Dragoons) was now sent into action to help bring off the fugitives, with which object in view it advanced from right to left diagonally across the slope directly in front of where the visitor is now standing.

> *William Tomkinson, captain, Sixteenth Regiment of Light Dragoons*:
>   We were ordered to mount and moved in front of the position to check the enemy's cavalry in pursuit of the Second Brigade [i.e. the Union Brigade] which had charged in advance of the position and was on its return to our line . . . in parties of twenty and thirty followed by the enemy, whose horses were not blown, and suffering greatly from [their own horses] being barely able to move. On moving to support them, we had to cross a deep lane which broke us and occasioned some confusion; we, however, got forward as quickly as possible, charged, and repulsed a body of lancers in pursuit of a party of the Scottish [*sic*] Greys. Lieutenant-Colonel Hay . . . was shot through the body: the shot entered his back coming out in front . . . I think he was shot by our own infantry firing to check the enemy, and not perceiving our advance . . . The Twelfth on our left attacked and dispersed a considerable body of the enemy, and by being . . . not so much delayed by the lane, got in advance. We supported them, having formed immediately after our charge, and by forming line with the Eleventh presented a front which enabled the Twelfth to retire with safety, as likewise all the men of the Second Brigade that had retreated on this point. We had

some difficulty in preventing the men of the Sixteenth from attacking in small bodies after the charge those parties of the enemy which had pursued the Second Brigade. Had they done this, we should have got into the same scrape.[18]

19. Continue up the hill until the road takes a sharp turn to the left.

S. Vandeleur's Brigade (2)

In the course of the charge of Vandeleur's brigade, the Twelfth Light Dragoons got badly out of hand, matters not being helped by the fact that the horse carrying its commander, Frederick Ponsonby (cousin to the Union Brigade's William Ponsonby) bolted and carried its badly-wounded rider deep into the French position. Famously, Ponsonby survived despite eventually falling from his horse and being for some time used for cover by a French skirmisher. It was, then, only with some difficulty that some of its men escaped to the safety of the Anglo-Dutch line.

British light dragoons of the sort commanded by Vandeleur move forward to engage the enemy. (Wikimedia Commons)

William Hay, captain, Twelfth Regiment of Light Dragoons:

Having made good our charge, the colonel said to me, 'Hang it! What can [be detaining] our centre squadron? I must get back and see. Lead the men out of this and tell off [i.e. re-form] the squadron behind the infantry.' These were the last words, poor fellow, he uttered that day . . . According to his directions, I communicated with the officer commanding the squadron, and he led the remaining part of it out of action. I stopped to see the last man down the sloping and deep banks of the lane [and] out of danger, and, while my attention was quite absorbed in the duty . . . a shell . . . burst under my horse and hurt his leg so severely that he sat down as a dog would do. At [that] moment I did not know the cause and used my spurs, but it was to no purpose, [and] I had therefore to let myself slide over his tail . . . When trying to kick him up, some men in the hollow shouted, telling me to take care of myself. On glancing round I saw two lancers coming full tilt at me. One instant more and both their lances would have been in the small of my back, [but] one spring into the hollow deprived them of their prey . . . No sooner had I got down into the road than several . . . brave hands were held out to pull me up, amongst them [those of] a little stout sergeant who congratulated me on my narrow escape and placed me in safety among his men.[19]

20. Conclude the tour by returning to the Hameau du Lion via the Ohain road and the crossroads. The Household and Union Brigades had suffered appalling casualties and were only able to play a limited part in the rest of the battle, but they had undoubtedly saved Wellington from immediate defeat and gone a long way towards ensuring that Napoleon could not but lose the day.

TOUR 6: THE FRENCH CAVALRY CHARGES

Time: three hours (up to six if the opportunity is taken to visit the Panorama and the Mémorial 1815). Going: mostly metalled roads or well-maintained tracks, though some patches of the latter may be waterlogged in wet weather; moderate slopes with occasional steeper stretches; some stretches of field walking (optional).

1. The great French cavalry charges that dominated the middle part of the Battle of Waterloo form one of the latter's most famous episodes. In brief, the story is well-known: starting at four o'clock, for two hours wave upon wave of French cavalry assailed the section of Wellington's line between Hougoumont and La Belle Alliance. In all, 9,000 cavalrymen took part in the charges and that on a front of scarcely 900 yards. How the attack originated is a matter of dispute, but the usual explanations – either that, seeing large numbers of stragglers and wounded making their way to the rear, Ney believed the Anglo-Dutch army was on the brink of collapse, or that what was originally intended as a mere probe got completely out of control as more and more units surged forward unbidden – are for various reasons distinctly implausible. What seems much more likely is that the attack began as an attempt on the part of Napoleon simply to hold Wellington's forces in place until matters had been put in hand for a fresh assault on the Anglo-Dutch left, and was then propelled by the sudden arrival of the Prussians into a desperate attempt to win the day before Blücher got all his men into action (hence the successive commitment of more and more troops). As to whether this last was ever a realistic aspiration is a moot point. At Eylau, Marshal Murat had led an even greater number of cavalry in a charge that won Napoleon sufficient time to plug a dangerous hole in his line, while the feat had been repeated on a smaller scale by Marshal Bessières at Aspern-Essling, but maintaining sufficient momentum to break an entire enemy army was quite another matter, and all the more so as the horse artillery normally attached to French cavalry divisions had in many cases been taken away from the units involved and

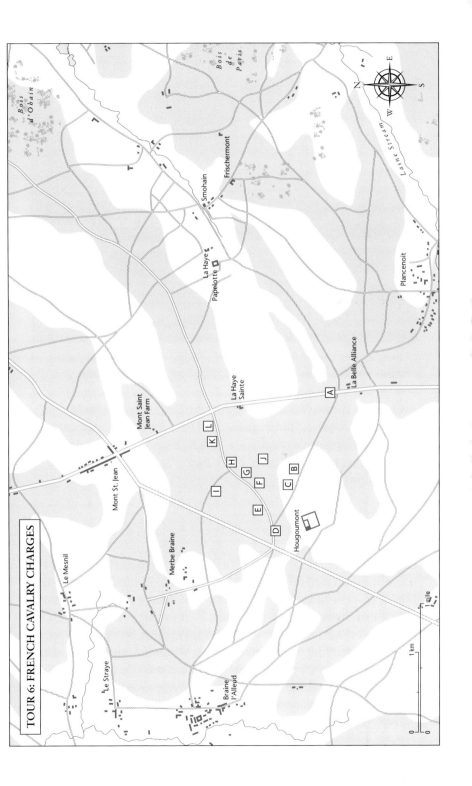

TOUR 6: FRENCH CAVALRY CHARGES

La Belle Alliance viewed from the intermediate ridge: the French cavalry advanced directly towards the camera along the axis of the track. (Author's collection)

given other duties. Yet it was already clear that many of Wellington's troops were anything but veterans, and so it was not unreasonable to hope that Napoleon's cavalry – a superb force superior to anything possessed by the Allies – could break their resistance. Begin the tour at La Belle Alliance.

A. La Belle Alliance

As one of the few buildings in the French sector of the battlefield, the inn of La Belle Alliance had quickly been designated as a hospital, and was now crammed with wounded who were being cared for by a hard-pressed staff of surgeons and medical orderlies headed by the famed pioneer of military medicine, Dominique Larrey. That said, whilst there was no deliberate intent of firing on a hospital as such, the more-or-less random fire of the Anglo-Dutch artillery had left it heavily scarred and pock-marked. Other wounded, meanwhile, were trying to make their way to the rear along the Charleroi highway, which was also thronged with men who were slinking away or had simply become lost or disorientated in the chaos. Having spent much of the first part of the day further back at Rossomme, the emperor had at some time come forward to the vicinity of La Belle Alliance, a small knoll just to the right of the road to Plancenoit being signposted as the spot from which he watched the last part of the battle. However, whilst the story is certainly not impossible, it is more likely that he took post somewhere in the vicinity of the road junction as this offered a wider view than the knoll. At all events the lines of sight are such that it was almost certainly from here that he watched, and, just possibly, ordered, the first cavalry attacks.

> *Pierre Fleury du Chaboulon, private secretary to Napoleon:*
> Carried away by his burning ardour, Marshal Ney . . . charged the enemy at the head of the cuirassiers of Milhaud and the light cavalry of the Guard, and, to the applause of the whole army, succeeded in establishing himself on the heights of Mont Saint Jean, which had hitherto been inaccessible. This tempestuous and hazardous movement did not escape the Duke of Wellington, the latter ordering his infantry to advance and hurling all his cavalry upon us. On the spot the emperor ordered General Kellermann to take his cuirassiers to disengage our first line. Whether spontaneously or on account of some error on the part of Marshal Ney, the dragoons and horse-grenadiers of the Guard . . . followed the cuirassiers without anyone being able to stop them.[1]

2. Follow the track from La Belle Alliance to Hougoumont to the point where it begins to dip down from the watershed ridge.

B. The Artillery of II Corps

The crest on which the visitor is standing is in all probability the spot occupied by Marshal Ney when he ordered the first cavalry attacks, if, indeed, he did so at all (in this respect take care to note the very limited view which he possessed of Wellington's positions: hence the implausibility of the story that he saw large numbers of Allied troops retiring in disorder). More importantly, the hillside had earlier provided a convenient position for the 6-pounder batteries attached to the divisions of Foy and Bachelu, the sixteen pieces which they could muster therefore being well placed to pound the hillsides above Hougoumont (the only spot where the defenders were seriously exposed). That said, however, they could no more observe the dead

The main axis of the cavalry's advance looking towards Wellington's position. (Author's collection)

ground in the rear of the crest of Mont Saint Jean than Marshal Ney, the consequence being that the artillery support available to support the cavalry charges was at best inadequate.

William Leeke, ensign, Fifty-Second Regiment of Foot:
    About three o'clock or a little after, the whole regiment . . . advanced up to and over the British position . . . Immediately on descending the slope . . .the regiment . . . formed two squares. I remember that, when we formed these two squares, we were not far from the north-eastern corner of the Hougoumont enclosure and on the narrow white road which . . . crosses the interval between the British and French positions in the direction of La Belle Alliance. The squares of Adam's brigade advanced until the Seventy-First were nearly half-way down the Hougoumont enclosure . . . [and] the right square of the Fifty-Second nearly 150 yards down the line of the enclosure . . . the left square of the Fifty-Second being on its left and more up the British position; whilst the square of the Second Battalion of the Ninety-Fifth . . . was the left square of the whole brigade and was still further up the position. The old officers who had

served during the whole of the Peninsular War stated that they were never exposed to such a cannonade as that which the Fifty-Second squares had to undergo on this occasion.[2]

3. Follow the track down into the low ground until a path is reached leading off to the left in the direction of Hougoumont.

Part of Guyot's heavy cavalry division, the Horse Grenadiers of the Guard, thunder up the slope towards a British square. Amongst the unit's many losses was its commander, Jean-Baptiste Jamin.

C. The Valley of Death

While perhaps half the cavalry followed the high ground to the right (by far the easiest route to the main Anglo-Dutch position), other units followed the axis of the track which the visitor has been following and assailed the four squares of Adam's brigade.

> *William Leeke, ensign, Fifty-Second Regiment of Foot*:
> I have a very vivid recollection of the charge of the French cavalry. Those who advanced on the right square of the Fifty-Second were cuirassiers, having not only a steel breast-plate bur the same covering for the back . . . They came on in very gallant style and in very steady order . . . till they were within forty yards of the front face of the square, when, one or two horses having been brought down, they got a somewhat new direction which carried them to either flank of . . . the square, which direction they one and all preferred to . . . charging home and riding on to our bayonets. Notwithstanding their armour, many of the men were laid low, [while] many horses also were brought down, and the men had . . . difficulty in disentangling themselves from them. The cuirassiers passed the square, receiving fire from all four faces, and proceeded up to the crest of the British position. They then reformed and came down the slope upon us in the same way, again avoiding to charge home . . . as they could scarcely hope to penetrate the squares.[3]

4. Ascend the track to the ridge-line ahead, noting in the process the absolute impossibility of seeing anything beyond the crest, and pause at its junction with the Ohain road.

D. The Ohain Road

For almost the whole length of the line attacked by the French cavalry, the Ohain road was only the most minimal obstacle, the story that it stopped the horsemen in their tracks, bringing many to grief in the process, being a figment of Victor Hugo's overly romantic imagination. In the immediate vicinity of the crossroads, certainly, the lane did enter a cutting of considerable depth, but the axis of the charge ensured that few, if any, of the oncoming cavalry crossed it on

An illustration typical of the erroneous manner in which Waterloo has been remembered. Given its position, the Highland square shown in the picture is clearly meant to depict one of Adam's battalions, but none of his men wore kilts and that despite the presence in their ranks of the Seventy-First Foot (i.e. the Highland Light Infantry). Indeed, none of Wellington's three Highland units ever had to contend with French cavalry at Waterloo. (Wikimedia Commons)

their way to attack Wellington's line. At best, a few men would have been inconvenienced by the cutting as they tried to make their way back, but that was about all. What defeated the French was rather a mixture of great courage and the clever use of ground. Thus, arrayed in a double line of squares a little way beyond the crest, the British and German infantry holding the front line were hidden from view until the very last moment and now presented the horsemen with an insuperable obstacle. Four ranks deep and devoid of vulnerable flanks, squares that stood firm could not normally be broken, and despite French claims to the contrary, in the course of the afternoon only one or two were even shaken, and then only temporarily.

Anonymous British officer:
 The day growing far advanced ... a succession of charges were executed along the centre by regiments or brigades of cavalry without combination ... The whole army then formed squares of battalions, reserving their fire with admirable steadiness till

the enemy approached close. The batteries along the brow were repeatedly carried by the enemy, but at each retreat reoccupied by our artillery, while soldiers in square, exposed at once to the furious but unavailing assaults of the enemy's cavalry and the dreadful havoc of their artillery, were seen closing their ranks over dead bodies and suffering no other effect than a gradual diminution of front. So dense was the smoke that the noise of arms was often heard before the enemy showed themselves . . . Dragoons, lancers . . . came on in masses with unequalled boldness threatening to overwhelm everything at once . . . again carrying the batteries; rushing with invincible force on the immovable squares; pouring through the vacancies of our line even beyond the rear, receiving as they passed volleys of musketry; then, halting in range of our fire confounded by repulse, suffering whole ranks to be mown down by our close unerring discharge . . . at other times anxiously wheeling round our battalions to find an opening, while small parties, urged on by a blind fury, often pressed forward to seize an unfurled standard and were hewn to pieces at the muzzles of our guns. In this manner the battle was carried out until nearly the whole of the French cavalry was annihilated.[4]

5. Follow the Ohain Road to the right. A little further on an isolated tree will be found on the left-hand side.

E. The Ninety-Fifth Regiment

At the time of writing, the tree mentioned in the directions shades an informal shrine to the Ninety-Fifth Regiment. Perhaps the most revered of all the British units that fought at Waterloo, this saw out the action in two separate areas as the First Battalion served under Sir James Kempt in the defence of Wellington's centre, whilst the Second Battalion and two companies of the Third Battalion served alongside the Fifty-Second Foot in Sir Frederick Adams' Third Infantry Brigade and took part in the advance into the valley described by William Leeke.

John Lewis, private, Ninety-Fifth Regiment of Foot:
My front-rank man was wounded by a part of a shell through the foot and he dropped as we were advancing.

I covered the next man I saw and had not walked twenty steps before a musket shot came sideways and took his nose clean off . . . Just after that the man that stood next to me on my left hand had his left arm shot off by a nine-pound shot just above his elbow and he turned round and caught hold of me with his right hand and his blood ran all over my trousers . . . Our large guns were firing over our heads and the enemy's . . . guns and small arms were firing at the British lines in our rear, and I declare to God . . . my pen cannot explain anything like it . . . Boney's Imperial Horse Guards [*sic*] all clothed in armour made a charge at us, [but] we saw them coming and . . . all closed in and made a square just as they came within ten yards of us. [Finding] they could do no good with us, they fired with their carbines . . . and came to the right-about directly . . . At that moment the man on my right hand was shot through the body and the blood ran out of his belly and back like a pig stuck in the throat. He dropped on his side . . . and died directly . . . Just at this time . . . a nine-pound ball came and cut the sergeant of our company right in two: he was not above three files from me.[5]

6. Continue along the Ohain road as far as the monument to Captain Mercer's battery of the Royal Horse Artillery.

F. Mercer's Position
Composed of five 9-pounder guns and one 5.5in howitzer, Mercer's troop was moved to the position the visitor is currently occupying in the course of the afternoon, and distinguished itself during the cavalry charges by (literally) sticking to its guns throughout and flaying the oncoming horsemen with discharge after discharge of canister (the usual practice was for the gunners to abandon their pieces and take shelter in the nearest square). A gifted writer, its commander later published one of the most detailed British accounts of the battle, albeit one marred by a considerable degree of embellishment and inaccuracy. One problem, for example, is his insistence that his battery was flanked by squares of Brunswickers, there being no such formations in the vicinity of his position.

Henry Paget, Lord Uxbridge. Commander of Wellington's cavalry and in addition his second-in-command, Uxbridge is usually remembered for his role in launching the charge of the Household and Union Brigades. However, he also played a major part in beating off the French cavalry charges. (War Heritage Institute, Brussels)

Alexander Mercer, captain, Royal Horse Artillery:

About three p.m. . .. Sir Alexander Fraser galloped up crying out, 'Left limber up, and as fast as you can . . . At a gallop, march!' And away we flew, as steadily and compactly as if at a review . . . So thick was the hail of balls . . . that it seemed dangerous to extend the left arm lest it should be torn off . . . Amidst this storm we gained the summit of the ridge . . . between two squares of Brunswick infantry . . . The Brunswickers were falling fast, the shot every moment making great gaps in their ranks which the officers and sergeants were actively employed in filling up by pushing their men together . . . To have sought refuge amongst men in such a state was madness: the very moment our men ran from their guns I was convinced would be the moment for their disbanding . . . Our first gun had scarcely gained the interval between the squares when I saw . . . the leading squadrons . . . coming on at a brisk trot, and already not more than one hundred yards distant . . . The very first round, I saw, brought down several men and horses . . . and I resolved to . . . take our chance, a resolve that was strengthened by the effect of the remaining guns as they rapidly succeeded in coming to action, making terrible slaughter and in an instant covering the ground with men and horses. Still they persevered in approaching us, though slowly ... but, in a twinkling, at the instant I thought it was all over us, they turned to either flank and filed away rapidly to the rear.[6]

7. Continue along the Ohain road to the De Mulder memorial.

G. De Mulder Memorial

An officer of the Fifth Cuirassiers wounded at Eylau, Aspern-Essling and Hanau who stayed on in the French army after the fall of Napoleon in 1814, De Mulder was of Belgian origins, and, not just that, but a native of nearby Braine l'Alleud. However, the presence of De Mulder, and not just him but a number of other Belgian officers, in the ranks of the French forces, should not be taken as evidence that the Belgians were unreliable in 1815. Whilst young men like De Mulder who had forged a career in the French army may have chosen to stay with their regiments in 1814 and rally to the emperor the next year, few Belgians serving in the Dutch army deserted to him, while Belgian units served with more distinction in the campaign than they have generally been credited with. Meanwhile, part of Milhaud's IV Reserve Cavalry Corps, the Fifth Cuirassiers lost fourteen of its thirty-nine officers.

A cuirassier officer. The gleaming breast and back-plates gave some protection against sword strokes, but were next to useless against musket-balls and canister, let alone shell fragments and roundshot. Still worse, the glutinous mud that coated the battlefield was so adhesive that many of those who were unhorsed had the greatest difficulty in getting to their feet. (War Heritage Institute, Brussels)

Michel Ordener, colonel, First Regiment of Cuirassiers:

Our first shock was irresistible. Despite a rain of iron that struck our helmets and cuirasses . . . we crowned the crest of the heights. Passing like a bolt of lightning through the guns, we approached the English infantry . . . However, the squares . . . held, the fire from their different faces causing heavy casualties in our ranks. It was absolutely necessary to resign ourselves to retreat or triumph in a final supreme effort against British tenacity.[7]

8. Continue along the road to the Hameau du Lion and pause outside the Rotunda.

H. Halkett's Position

During the cavalry charges, the area of the Hameau du Lion was held by the two composite battalions of the brigade of Sir Colin Halkett, of which the one consisted of the Thirtieth and Seventy-Third Regiments and the other of the Thirty-Third and the Sixty-Ninth

Carabineers of Albert Trip van Zoutland's Dutch heavy cavalry charge French cavalry who have succeeded in penetrating the double line of squares hidden just behind the crest of Mont Saint Jean. (War Heritage Institute, Brussels)

Regiments (very badly hit at Quatre Bras, they had lost so many men that they could no longer function as independent units). Nor was the effect of Quatre Bras limited to losses pure and simple: deployed in line in the open, at one point the brigade had been charged in the flank and overrun, the Sixty-Ninth having lost one of its two colours in the process. Finally, all four battalions were extremely inexperienced, not a single one of them having seen service in the Peninsula. As such, they were more susceptible to the French cavalry than any of the other British units on the field and the result was that the square composed of the Thirty-Third and Sixty-Ninth Regiments was temporarily broken.

Thomas Morris, private, Seventy-Third Regiment of Foot:
    A considerable number of French cuirassiers made their appearance on the rising ground just in our front . . .and came at a gallop down upon us. Their intrepid bearing was well calculated . . . to inspire a feeling of dread. None of them under six feet, defended by helmets and corselets made pigeon-breasted to throw off the balls . . . they looked so truly formidable that I thought we could not have the slightest chance with them. They came up rapidly until within about ten or twelve paces of the square when our rear ranks poured into them a well-directed fire which put them into confusion, and they retired: the two front ranks, kneeling, then discharged their pieces at them . . . The next square to us was charged at the same time, and, being unfortunately broken into, retired in confusion . . . but the Life Guards, coming up, the French in their turn were obliged to retrograde . . . At the next charge the cavalry made, they deliberately walked their horses up to the bayonet's point, and one of them . . . made a thrust at me . . . I could not avoid it, and involuntarily closed my eyes. When I opened them again, my enemy was lying just in front of me . . . In the act of thrusting at me, he had been wounded by one of my rear-rank men, and, whether it was the anguish of the wound or the chagrin of being defeated I know not, but . . . he took one of our bayonets which was lying on the ground . . . placed the point under his cuirass and fell on it.[8]

9. Such is the relevance of the great Panorama displayed in the Rotunda to this tour that it may be thought worth a visit, for it portrays the French cavalry charges and at the same time will always remain the most graphic depiction of the battle. Yet as a work of art it has many flaws: for example, a regiment of Highlanders is seen amongst the defenders and yet none of the Highland units were in the sector of the battlefield affected by the charges, while the French cavalry are seen approaching at full gallop when in fact the ground was so waterlogged that they could only approach at the trot, if that. Last but not least, the importance of the sunken lane is stressed, when in fact few French cavalrymen struck the Allied line at a spot where it was a serious obstacle. All this being the case, the visitor may care to press on, by taking the road opposite the Rotunda, namely the Route du Lion. Walk along this road to the car park at the far end, noting on the way the new underground museum known as the Mémorial 1815, and, more especially, the reverse slope which afforded so much shelter to Wellington's infantry.

The reverse slope in rear of Adam's brigade looking south from the Merbe Braine road. Hougoumont lies behind the wood to the left. Neither that, nor the thick line of trees to the right existed in 1815. (Author's collection)

I. The Allied Cavalry

In the course of the cavalry charges, Wellington deployed the bulk of his cavalry in an attempt both to cover the retreat of his army should this become necessary and to reassure his hard-pressed infantry. From the left the units concerned consisted of the remnants of the Household and Union Brigades, the British and/or King's German Legion brigades of Vivian, Vandeleur, Arentschildt and Grant, whilst the Dutch brigades of De Ghigny, Van Merlen and Trip constituted a final reserve. This substantial force did not just play a passive role in the fighting, however, launching charge after charge to drive the French cavalry back over the crest and down the hill.

Thomas Playford, sergeant-major, Second Regiment of Life Guards:
We again advanced, and I have a confused idea of lancers, cuirassiers and infantry retiring before us . . . There was, however, a solid mass of French horsemen, consisting of light cavalry and lancers in the centre and cuirassiers on the outside and for some time this body of men remained immoveable. I saw a corps of heavy horse belonging to the King of the Netherlands charge that mass without effect. Indeed, the Low-Country horsemen never came within some four or five yards of the French, but when they saw that the cuirassiers stood firm, the Hollanders faced about and retired. We were . . . directed to charge that mass in column. The First Life Guards, being at the head of the column, rode boldly up to . . . the French and made cuts . . . at the men . . . but the cuirassiers were in armour and stood their ground. This close combat producing no important consequences, we retired about fifty paces, and, facing about, confronted that formidable body of horse. Meanwhile, a troop of horse artillery had arrived and unlimbered behind us unseen by the French: the word 'open out' was quietly passed along, and we formed a lane along which cannon balls were fired . . . with terrible effect, men and horses falling in rapid succession. In an instant the whole column broke and fled.[9]

10. Return to the Hameau du Lion, cross the road and, the state of the ground permitting, proceed to the further end of the hedge surrounding the Butte du Lion (take care to do as little damage as possible to any crops that may be *in situ*).

The watershed looking towards La Belle Alliance from the foot of the Butte du Lion. A natural bridge between the rival positions, it somewhat eased the task of the French cavalry. (Author's collection)

J. The Watershed

The spot on which the visitor is standing is situated almost on the highest point of the watershed that crosses the battlefield from La Belle Alliance to the Hameau du Lion, this feature providing a natural bridge that led directly to the heart of Wellington's positions and avoided the steep gradients to be found elsewhere, particularly in the vicinity of La Haye Sainte. That being the case, as many French cavalry tried to follow it as possible: hence, perhaps, the disorder that was inflicted on Halkett's brigade.

> *Claude Guyot, GOC, Imperial Guard Heavy Cavalry Division:*
>
> Our two divisions charged this line of infantry alternately, seizing it each time, but always being obliged to retire quickly because we only had sabres to oppose to the fire of the squares and to the volleys of case-shot that we received as we approached. The enemy cavalry profited each time from the disorder that the musketry and case-shot caused in our ranks to instantly pursue our scattered squadrons, but we

did not allow him success for long, pushing him quickly back into his defence line. It was in the second charge that I was dismounted and obliged to retreat on foot. I did not get far, for I had not gone ten paces backwards, when I was knocked down and ridden over by cavalry that sabred me as it passed by. However, they were not able to grab hold of me, for I was immediately freed by a third charge executed by my division . . . A troop horse was quickly procured for me, but I was hardly in the saddle when I received a ball in the chest and a shell splinter in the left elbow.[10]

11. Return to the Hameau du Lion by circumventing the Butte du Lion. On reaching the Ohain road, turn right towards the Charleroi highway. After a very short distance ascend the bank on the further side of the road.

K. Kielmansegg's Position
The area between the point where the visitor is standing and the buildings clustered around the crossroads was held by Kielmansegg's Hanoverian brigade, the two (or, possibly, three) squares which it had formed being positioned on the upper part of the reverse slope stretching down to the left.

Lady Butler's classic study of a British square under attack from French cavalry. The expressions of the soldiers are especially interesting, ranging, as they do from wild excitement through determination and resignation to absolute terror (Wikimedia Commons)

Carl von Scriba, captain, Bremen Field Battalion:

The attacking force . . . were cuirassiers as before: I estimated their strength at 700 sabres. All the officers . . . made the greatest efforts to keep the men from prematurely firing single shots: the commander threatened to shoot with his pistol any violator . . . The cavalry came on at a trot and halted at seventy to eighty paces away as if to catch their breath. The temptation to shoot was great, but the entire square stood motionless with cocked weapons [and] I saw the square to our left doing the same. The French cavalrymen were . . . too slow. Instead of covering the short distance to us at the charge, they eventually trotted to the left corner of the square, wheeled left around it, passed the next side and finally the right flank. From all these sides they received a controlled fire and that at very close range . . . We soon regarded the cavalry attacks as a time of rest for us, because afterwards the devastating artillery fire began once more with increasing violence . . . Our brave commander lost his horse to a cannon ball . . . Less than a quarter of an hour later, the highly popular lieutenant-colonel had his right leg shattered by a cannon-ball . . . A short time later, at about five o'clock, Major von Schkopp was wounded and had to go to the rear.[11]

12. Continue along the bank as far as the '1815' hotel. En route it will be noted that the field on the left is in places as much as ten feet above the level of the road. Though later completely flattened by the need to gather up the earth needed for the Butte du Lion, at the time of the battle the ground on the other side would have risen just as high, and it is clear that the resulting ravine would undoubtedly have spelled disaster to any force of cavalry that sought to cross it at speed. However, at Waterloo, few horsemen were able to manoeuvre at anything more than a trot, and, as the Household Brigade had already shown, at that speed the obstacle was perfectly practicable even for horsemen in close order. Yet in reality the whole point is completely academic. Spilling over and along the crest from the point now obscured by the Butte du Lion the French would have been able to move along the northern side of the sunken road, thereby taking it in the rear. That said,

The Ohain Road looking towards the crossroads showing the height of the surviving bank. In this sector the sunken nature of the road would certainly have been an obstacle to cavalry travelling at speed, but it is clear from the experiences of the Union Brigade that the banks could be passed by horsemen moving at the walk or trot that was all the French cavalry could have managed on the crest of the ridge, so bad was the going. (Author's collection)

however, the fact that they were able to do so availed them very little, for they remained unable to inflict significant damage on the Allied infantry.

L. Ompteda's Position

From this spot to the crossroads the Allied line was held by Ompteda's brigade of the King's German Legion.

Edward Wheatley, ensign, Fifth Line Battalion, King's German Legion:

A black consolidated body was soon seen approaching, and we distinguished . . . the iron-cased cavalry of the enemy . . . No words can convey the sensation we felt on seeing these heavy armed bodies advancing at full gallop against us, flourishing their sabres in the air . . . But we dashed them back as coolly as the sturdy rock repels the ocean's foam . . . An ammunition cart blew up near us, smashing men and horses. I . . . felt shocked at the sight of broken armour, lifeless bodies, murdered horses, shattered wheels, caps, helmets, swords, muskets pistols . . . Here and there a frightened horse would rush across the plain trampling on the dying and the dead. [Near us] three or four poor wounded animals [were] standing on three legs [with] the other dangling before . . . The carnage was frightful . . . While [I was] busy in keeping the men firm in their ranks, closing up the vacuities . . . [and] inspecting the fallen to detect deception [or] subterfuge, a regiment of cuirassiers darted like a thunderbolt among us . . . In the confusion of the moment I made [for] the colours to defend them, and we succeeded with infinite difficulty in rallying the men again. I parried with great good fortune a back-stroke from a horseman as he flew by me, and Captain Sanders had a deep slice from the same blow on the head the instant after. The battalion once more formed into a solid square in which we remained the [whole] afternoon.[12]

13. By six o'clock in the evening, the French cavalry was a spent force and down to perhaps as little as half-strength. Continue to the crossroads, cross the main road at the lights and return to La Belle

Alliance via the track on the far side, reflecting *en route*, perhaps, on the horrors witnessed during the cavalry charges.

Herman Heuvingh, sergeant-major, Fourth (Dutch) Light Dragoons:
At last it was my turn. Suddenly I felt a dull thump on the right thigh. As I didn't feel any immediate pain, I suspected that it had been caused by a clod of clay . . . as the bullets that landed in the mud were continuously throwing up large lumps which splattered ourselves and our horses alike, but our captain had noticed differently: calling to me that I was wounded, he ordered me to ride to the rear . . . to see if the wound was dangerous. Now I saw myself that a thick stream of blood was gushing from my leg. Pressing my hand to the spot to stop the bleeding as much as possible, I told the captain that it probably didn't mean very much, [but] . . . my attempts did not help a lot . . . and I fell half lifeless from my horse . . . [Coming to my senses] I looked . . . around me. On all sides, as far as the eye could see nothing but bodies and more bodies, the roar of the artillery and the screams of the wounded, of which many lay close by . . . Near me lay a horse that judging by its harness belonged to the English cavalry. The poor animal tried to stand up, but each time, whinnying loudly, it fell to the ground . . . Each time the horse raised itself halfway, I feared it would crash on top of me.[13]

TOUR 7: BÜLOW, ZIETHEN AND MOUTON

Time: three hours (up to four if it is decided to include the diversion to Napoleon's headquarters). Going: mostly metalled roads or well-maintained tracks, though some patches of the latter may be waterlogged in wet weather; moderate slopes with occasional steeper stretches. See Maps 5 and 6.

1. This tour explores the terrain and events of the 'other' battle of Waterloo, in other words the advance of the Prussian forces onto the battlefield in fulfilment of Blücher's overnight promise to Wellington that he would march to support him from the temporary base to which he had withdrawn at Wavre following his defeat at Ligny. Thanks to Marshal Grouchy's lentitude in following up the retreating Prussians, in making this movement Blücher did not have

The Place du Plancenoit and the church of Saint Catherine. Note how the church completely dominates the rest of the village. (Author's collection)

to cope with fending off any French troops, and an early start ought therefore to have seen the Prussians reach the battlefield by midday at the latest, not least because the distance was no more than ten miles. However, due to a combination of mismanagement, ill-luck (namely, the outbreak of a severe fire in Wavre), a certain degree of obstructiveness on the part of the commander of the leading elements of the Prussian army, Bülow, and, finally, the wretched condition of the narrow country lanes which provided the only link with the climactic events taking place at Mont Saint Jean, it was well past four o'clock before the first Prussian troops debouched onto the battlefield. Begin the tour in front of the church of Saint Catherine in the Place du Plancenoit.

A. Plancenoit: Church of Saint Catherine

Situated on a prominent knoll and surrounded on three sides by a walled graveyard, the parish church of Plancenoit commands the whole of the centre of the village and was so heavily damaged in the course of the fighting that it had to be almost completely rebuilt: the only part of the exterior which is more-or-less original is the façade, though the relative absence of bullet holes suggests that even this was in large part refaced. Also largely rebuilt was the churchyard wall, although this probably has much the same aspect as it did in 1815. During the battle, the churchyard served the defenders of the village as a final redoubt, and a number of plaques commemorate their heroism, one of them being to an officer of Belgian origin named Louis. Initially the defenders consisted of the brigade of Antoine de Bellair – the Fifth and Eleventh Regiments of Line Infantry – but, already tired, they were overwhelmed and driven even from the churchyard. With Bellair's men now clinging only to the western fringes of the village, Napoleon was left no option but to send in the 5,000 men of the Young Guard of General Duhesme, these troops recovering the church and succeeding in stabilising the situation for some time, until they in turn were driven back by the arrival of a fresh wave of Prussian troops.

> *August Hiller von Gaertherin, GOC, Sixteenth Infantry Brigade*:
>   Overcoming all difficulties and with heavy losses from canister and musketry, the troops of the Fifteenth Infantry

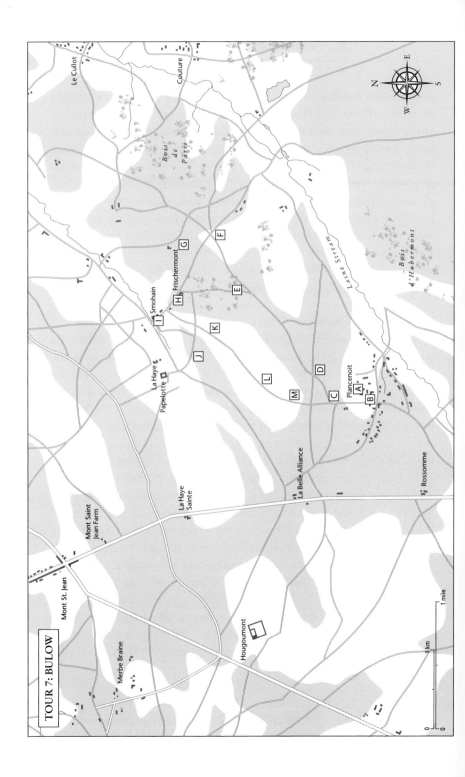

[Regiment] and of the First Silesian Landwehr penetrated to the high wall around the churchyard held by the French Young Guard. These two columns succeeded in capturing a howitzer, two cannons, several ammunition wagons and two staff officers, along with several hundred men. The main square around the churchyard was surrounded by houses from which the enemy could not be dislodged in spite of our brave attempts . . . Had I, at this moment, the support of only one fresh battalion at hand, this attack would certainly have been successful.[1]

2. Having explored the churchyard and noted the excellent field of fire it offered to the defenders, walk diagonally across the square to the Gros Vélo restaurant (of the various places to eat on the battlefield, this is by far the nicest).

B. Plancenoit: the Village

The village of Plancenoit was much smaller in 1815 than it is today, not least because the law that established the battlefield as a protected area failed to include it within its bounds. At the time of the battle,

The Place du Plancenoit looking east. By sunset the village was choked with dead and wounded and burning from end to end. (Author's collection)

then, it consisted of little more than the two streets parallel with one another to the south of the church, together with the buildings fringing the northern and eastern edges of the open space which surrounds it. Fought over continuously for several hours, virtually every building in the village was at the very least heavily damaged, if not set ablaze.

> *Jean-Jacques Pelet, GOC Second Regiment of Foot* Chasseurs *of the Imperial Guard*:
>   Entering [the village], I met poor General Duhesme, who was being carried away dead or dying on his horse, [and] then the *voltigeurs* [i.e. the Young Guard] running away; Chartran [second-in-command, Young Guard], who told me he could do nothing; [and] Colonel Hurel [CO, Third Regiment of Voltigeurs] . . . I promised them I would stop the enemy, and urged them to rally behind me. Indeed, I moved to the centre of the village and there . . . ordered Captain Peschot to advance with the First Company and attack the enemy who were coming down the street opposite the one we were on with the bayonet. His sergeant, Cranges . . . executed my order, but hardly had the enemy turned his back than the men began to skirmish and he lost control of them. The enemy sent new forces: Peschot was not able to concentrate his platoon and he was pushed back. I advanced another [platoon] . . . I led it myself and the enemy fled. However, this platoon dispersed too, and, with each charge I made, the same thing happened . . . In all these attacks we took many prisoners, but our soldiers were furious and cut their throats . . . Revolted and overcome with fury, I took several [of the former] under my protection.[2]

3. From the Gros Vélo walk eastwards along the Rue Saint Catherine, noting the rather atmospheric courtyard immediately beside the restaurant in the process. After a few yards turn right into a narrow lane and at the T-junction at the end turn left into the Rue de la Bachée: it was along this street and the turning from it that leads into the square that the two battalions of the Old Guard sent to stabilise the situation by Napoleon counter-attacked shortly before the emperor's

Prussian troops burst into Plancenoit. Embittered by years of impoverishment at the hands of France, Blücher's men showed little mercy towards their opponents. (Wikimedia Commons)

last attempt to break Wellington's army. After a few yards a close will be noted on the right with a large brick house at its further end: marked with the date 1789, in 1815 this was the house of the parish priest. At the road junction the truly committed may walk straight on along the aptly-named Rue Mouton to discover a memorial stone to the Fifth Regiment of Line Infantry, one of the units of Mouton's division that garrisoned the village, but, surrounded as it is by modern housing, this feels oddly misplaced. Most visitors will therefore wish to turn left and return to the centre of the village, once again noting the manner in which the church acts as a natural redoubt. On drawing level with the church take the road that runs diagonally across the village green and head uphill on the Chemin du Lanternier, noting in passing the large courtyard farm on the corner (another clear survival from the time of the battle): in 1815 this was no more than a country lane. After approximately 400 yards, the Chemin du Lanternier bends sharply to the left: at this point take the turning to the right (the Chemin du Camuselle). After a few yards, the visitor will come to the Prussian memorial.

C. Plancenoit: the Prussian Memorial

Erected in 1819 and unmistakeably Germanic in design, the Prussian memorial bears the inscription, 'To our fallen heroes in gratitude from king and country: may they rest in peace. La Belle Alliance, 1815' (thanks to its obvious symbolism, 'La Belle Alliance' was the name for the battle that was preferred in Germany throughout the nineteenth century and beyond). Completely treeless in 1815, the knoll on which it stands is supposed to mark the spot from which Prussian guns bombarded the area round La Belle Alliance at the end of the battle, though it is far too small to have afforded enough space for a full battery. What is more conceivable is that it was from here that General Mouton directed the struggle to hold back the oncoming Prussians: driven from their original positions east of Plancenoit (see below), it was more-or-less on the line of the Chemin du Lanternier that three of his four brigades took their stand (the fourth had rather retired into Plancenoit itself), and here again did much damage to the oncoming Prussians:

> *Friedrich Bülow von Dennewitz, GOC, IV Corps, Army of the Lower Rhine*:
> Continuously the target of the enemy musketry, the skirmishers of the Fifteenth Brigade had to be relieved several times and our fire began to slacken on this part of the line. The foe seemed to have obtained a momentary advantage there, and his intention was perhaps to act offensively against our right wing, while the fight increased in violence at Plancenoit, so as to penetrate between our right wing and the English left. Indeed, strong masses of his infantry and cavalry could be seen opposite Fifteenth Brigade.[3]

4. From the Prussian monument continue along the Chemin du Camuselle ignoring the track to the left: the fields to the right saw repeated Prussian attempts to envelop the defenders of Plancenoit and enter the village from the north, the absence of cover being such that their casualties were extremely heavy. Continue through the belt of trees and just beyond them you will reach another fork. In a moment we will follow the left-hand track, but first take the track leading diagonally downhill to the right for a little way, this being known as the Avenue des Pélérins.

The Avenue des Pélérins looking south-east towards the ground crossed by Bulow's left wing during its advance on Plancenoit. The houses all post-date the battle. (Author's collection)

D. Avenue des Pélérins

In the valley below will be observed an area of trees and houses extending across the track from right to left: it was through this area, and along the hillside traversed by the Avenue des Pélérins, that the Fourteenth and Sixteenth Brigades advanced to attack Plancenoit. Note that neither trees and houses existed in 1815, the only woodland in the area being that which fringed the River Lasne (the stream that rises just east of Plancenoit and at the village of Lasne constituted a major obstacle to the advance of the Prussian forces from Wavre, the only passage being a single narrow bridge). In the midst of the housing is a monument to the light cavalry of General Subervie, but, like the monument to the Fifth Line, this seems wildly misplaced.

Friedrich Bülow von Dennewitz, GOC, IV Corps, Army of the Lower Rhine:

The enemy disputed every foot of ground, but not with any great determination . . . Only in the village of Plancenoit and on the heights running up to our right flank did the enemy appear to want to show any serious resistance [NB. by 'the heights running up to our right flank' Bülow means the ridge on which the visitor is standing: obsessed with seizing

Plancenoit, Blücher deployed most of his cavalry and artillery support directly opposite the village, thereby enabling the men on the ridge to hold their ground far more easily]. Six battalions of the Sixteenth Brigade now came up to assault Plancenoit. They formed three attack columns next to each other with two battalions of the Fourteenth Brigade that had also reached the battlefield following up in support. Just as this brigade formed up behind the Sixteenth, the Thirteenth Brigade under Lieutenant-General Hake arrived and moved up behind the Fifteenth.[4]

5. Return to the Chemin du Camuselle and turn right (i.e. away from the Prussian monument). The broad ridge which the visitor is now following marks the line along which the Thirteenth and Fifteenth Brigades advanced to attack VI Corps, and, indeed, the axis of the latter's retreat; note, meanwhile, that for most of its length the crest is in full view of Wellington's position and that at least a part of Bülow's advance must have been visible to the troops holding his

The view of the battlefield that Bülow and Blücher obtained having occupied Mouton's first position. (Author's collection)

left wing (that said, the fact that progress along the ridge was much slower than it was in the lower ground in front of Plancenoit ensured that the Prussian attack probably seemed less impressive than was actually the case). Continue along the track until a turning is reached to the right.

E. Blücher's Command Post

It was approximately here that Blücher established his command post in the wake of the retreat of Mouton's troops, the view across the rest of the battlefield being absolutely outstanding: to the south-west can be seen the church spire of Plancenoit, to the west La Belle Alliance and to the north-west a very large part of Wellington's front line. As the Prussians advanced along the ridge, so they brought their artillery batteries along with them, and it was almost certainly from positions along the track just traversed by the visitor that the Charleroi highway and the troops waiting in reserve beside it came under fire in the latter part of the afternoon and early evening.

> *August von Thurn und Taxis, Bavarian liaison officer, Army of the Lower Rhine*:
> From a point to the right of the road . . . we could see . . . that part of the battlefield where the French right flank was attacking the English left. This attack was being made with great violence at La Haye Sainte in an attempt to force the English out of their position by bursting through their centre . . . Hard to believe as it may be, we could see into the rear of the enemy . . . and could even make out with our telescopes the wounded being carried back. The enemy was not gaining any ground and officers coming . . . from the Duke of Wellington brought us the news that the English were beating off all the attacks most brilliantly. However, the attacks were getting more forceful and a speedy diversion from us was needed.[5]

6. Continue along the track to a crossroads; beyond the line of modern houses can be seen the Bois de Paris through which the Prussian forces advanced on the last stage of their advance from Wavre. On each side of the track, there is a wood: both of these were in existence in 1815, the flank protection which they afforded Mouton's men undoubtedly

Mouton's battlefield looking east towards the Bois de Paris. Supported by the cavalry of Domon and Subervie, the two divisions of VI Corps were able to check the Prussians at this spot for an hour or more. (Author's collection)

enabling them to hold out longer than would otherwise have been the case. Indeed, although details are scarce, it seems likely that, after an initial stand in the vicinity of the crossroads, Mouton fell back to a line between the two.

F. Mouton's First Position

Though often overlooked, the area around the crossroads played an important part in Napoleon's conduct of the battle. Thus, any troops placed there could march northwards through Smohain and from there hit Wellington's left wing, and all the evidence suggests that, in the wake of the repulse of Drouet, Napoleon dispatched a large part of such reserves as he had available to the area for precisely this purpose, the troops concerned being the cavalry divisions of Domon and Subervie (both of them units which by rights should have been with Grouchy's command, but had somewhat arbitrarily been taken away from him by Napoleon) and Mouton's VI Corps, a force that thanks to various deductions amounted to just 6,000 men and twenty-eight guns. In short, the presence of French troops in the area had nothing whatsoever to do with holding off the oncoming Prussians, the fact being that Napoleon was completely unaware of the latter's approach. When the Prussians suddenly emerged from the Bois de Paris at about half past four, then, the French were taken completely by surprise. To his very great credit, however, Mouton maintained his composure, and formed up his troops along the lane running from right to left without delay, in which position he proceeded to stand his ground for a full hour. One of the first Prussians to fall was a certain Colonel Wilhelm von Schwerin. As the latter's grave (marked by a small monument) is on the slopes overlooking the River Lasne, this is often taken as confirmation of stories that French patrols pushed through the Bois de Paris and engaged in a skirmish on its far side, but this is not the case: in fact, Schwerin was carried to the rear by his grieving *aide de camp* and laid to rest in a spot where it seemed likely that his body would remain undisturbed.

> *Jacques Boudin de Tromelin, GOC, Twentieth Infantry Division, VI Corps*:
> The Prussian attack started towards half-past four. Our cavalry sabred the enemy squadrons. Then we formed in square by brigade and remained under fire of forty Prussian guns that caused us much damage . . . At half-past five the enemy were reinforced by infantry and cavalry, while the artillery fire became terrible. Maintaining a bold front, but suffering under the weight of shot, the four squares of the corps retired slowly in chequer-board formation in the direction of Plancenoit where we finally established ourselves . . . The débris of my three battalions occupied the gardens and orchards.[6]

7. At the crossroads head straight on and at the edge of the woods turn left: this road marks the initial Prussian front line (visitors wishing to visit Schwerin's grave may do so by heading straight on along the Rue Bois du Paris, but the detour involved will add at least half an hour to the tour). Follow the road along until it swings sharply to the right just after the first building to be encountered on the left-hand side of the road. Note, meanwhile, that the tree-line did not extend as far as the crossroads in 1815: Mouton would therefore have had a little more time to get ready for action than might at first sight seem to be the case.

The Bois de Paris viewed from the crossroads of the Plancenoit and Frischermont roads. The sudden eruption of Bulow's corps from cover came as a considerable shock to VI Corps, this having been sent to the area to support a second attack on Wellington's left flank. (Author's collection)

G. Domon and Subervie

While Mouton's infantry took up their positions on the line of the lane to Smohain, the light cavalry divisions of Domon and Subervie made heroic efforts to delay the Prussians. Among their officers was Marcellin de Marbot, a swaggering *beau sabreur* whose memoirs are both amongst the most entertaining and the most unreliable of the entire Napoleonic period. In said memoirs, he unfortunately says little about the Waterloo campaign, but in a separate letter one can find a claim that his regiment – the Seventh Regiment of Hussars – engaged the Prussians in the Bois de Paris and took the prisoner who is generally portrayed as having been brought to Napoleon at some point in the early afternoon. All the evidence, however, is that this was a fabrication, and that, although Marbot did indeed patrol the area to the east of the battlefield, he stuck to the roads further south along which Grouchy could be expected to appear. Certainly, there is no mention of any such skirmish in the Prussian accounts, or, for that matter, in the only account of the battle we have from Marbot's own regiment.

Victor Dupuy, major, Seventh Regiment of Hussars:

Until four o'clock we remained peaceable spectators of the action, and at about that point General Domon came by and told me that the English fire had all but ceased, that the day was won, that the enemy were in retreat, [and] that we ourselves were but waiting to make contact with Grouchy. Having closed by saying that we would all be in Brussels that evening, he rode off again, but, hardly had he gone, when, instead of greeting Grouchy, we found ourselves being attacked by a regiment of Prussian lancers. Counter-attacking vigorously, we put them to flight and gave chase, only to be forced to retreat by canister fire from six pieces of cannon . . . Colonel Marbot had been wounded by a lance-thrust in the breast . . . and we were now attacked by infantry and forced to fall back on the centre, whilst yet conducting a rear-guard action. In the course of this retrograde movement, we encountered Marshal Soult, the latter directing us to take up a position near a battery of the Artillery of the Guard so as to give it a degree of support.[7]

8. Just before the house, take a track that angles leftward across the fields and in the process crosses the area in which Domon and Subervie tried to hold back the Prussians. After several hundred yards the track reaches a road where the visitor should turn right. Very shortly the road becomes sunken and heads ever more steeply downhill. About half-way down, some fragments of stone wall will be observed at the top of the bank on the left-hand side of the road. Together with some other remains in the woods beyond, this is all that survives of the chateau of Frischermont, whilst it was presumably from their shelter that nervous German pickets fired the first shots of the battle as Jacquinot's cavalry patrols came clattering down the hill from the plateau above.

H. Chateau of Frischermont

A substantial complex of buildings centred on a fortified manor house dating from the twelfth century, at the start of the battle Frischermont was held by troops from the Dutch Twenty-Eighth (Orange-Nassau) Infantry Regiment. Far too exposed to be held

The exterior wall that is all that remains of the Chateau de Frischermont viewed from the lane to Smohain. It was from this position that the first shots of the battle were fired when the defenders challenged a force of French cavalry that had been sent to explore the Smohain area. (Author's collection)

for any length of time, however, by the early afternoon it had been abandoned without a fight. Eventually garrisoned by troops from Durutte's division, it was evacuated once again when Bülow sent two infantry battalions to secure his right flank. Little damaged by the battle, it was nevertheless demolished in 1857 and replaced by a more modern structure that was pulled down in its turn a century later. Whether Wellington knew that in 1705 it had briefly been the headquarters of the Duke of Marlborough during the Ramillies campaign is unknown.

> *Dominique Fleuret, captain, Fifty-Fifth Regiment of Line Infantry:*
> The regiment was reduced to 400 men . . . These were formed into a single battalion and used as skirmishers . . . We marched against the Prussians, who had moved against our right to cut the army's retreat. We repulsed them twice, but the main body of the Prussian army arrived and forced us to retreat.[8]

The lane from Papelotte to Plancenoit in rear of Durutte's position looking north. It was here that Durutte tried to check Ziethen. (Author's collection)

9. Continue down the hill. Very shortly, a small village is reached. This is Smohain.

I. Smohain

A picturesque village that is now called La Marache, Smohain contains a number of buildings dating from the era, and was the scene of fierce fighting when troops from the divisions of Durutte and Jacquinot pushed into it in the early afternoon and eventually drove out the defenders (at the start of the battle a light company of the Second Regiment of Nassau and a squadron of the British Tenth Light Dragoons). Later in the day it was the scene of a further struggle when the vanguard of Ziethen's I Corps evicted the detachment that had been posted to hold it by General Durutte.

Von Neumann, major, Twelfth Infantry Regiment:
General von Steinmetz ordered me to take my battalion and two companies of *schützen* to the village of Smohain. Here I was to throw out the French . . . Four platoons of the *schützen* moved

on the lower part of the village and threw out the enemy there, while my fusilier battalion, led by its skirmishers, also moved through the village. Both the *schützen* and the fusilier battalion advanced against the enemy skirmishers who fought back ferociously. This struggle continued until the enemy's general withdrawal began, whereupon our cavalry followed up.[9]

10. Having paused at the foot of the hill, turn sharply to the left and follow the track around the outer wall of another courtyard farm complex. It was along this track that Ziethen's corps advanced when it launched the decisive attack that broke Durutte's division at the close of the day. At a crossroads turn right and ascend the track to the crest of the hill. From here an excellent view may be obtained of Papelotte (easily distinguishable by the tower over its main gate, later addition though this is).

J. Durutte's Division

The son of a merchant from Douai, Pierre Durutte enlisted in one of the numerous battalions of volunteers formed to augment the French army in 1791 and 1792. As devoted as he was brave, he distinguished himself in battle after battle and by 1812 had reached the rank of divisional commander. At Waterloo the commander of the right-hand-most division of I Corps, he participated in the general advance mounted by that formation around one o'clock, but did not make use of the same massive columns employed by many of the other troops involved in the attack: instead, his men were formed in eight small battalion columns which were much more adapted to the broken terrain, and therefore made considerable progress, occupying Frischermont, Smohain and part of La Haye and possibly even effecting a lodgement in Papelotte. However, such was the broken nature of the terrain and the nature of the defenders – veteran troops from the Second and Third Battalions of the Regiment of Nassau who had seen much service in the Peninsular War – that he could get no further, despite the fact that the charge of the Household and Union Brigades had only affected one of his battalions. In this area, then, the battle for some time descended into a stalemate that was only ended by the advance of Ziethen's corps at about half-past seven. By this time reduced to half-strength by Durutte's dispatch of one of his two

The woods screening Frischermont looking west from the lane from Smohain to Plancenoit. It was here that Zeithen's corps broke through at the end of the battle. (Author's collection)

brigades to support operations in the centre, the French at first put up some resistance but were quickly overwhelmed.

Joseph Rullière, major, Ninety-Fifth Regiment of Line Infantry:
From three to four o'clock [*sic:* really about one hour later] one began to see movements of the Prussians on the right of our army. Some time later we came under musket fire from their skirmishers. My battalion was set to stop them in which it succeeded. The firefight had raged for half an hour, when General de Labedoyère, *aide-de-camp* to the emperor . . . came to announce it was Marshal Grouchy who was debouching on our right. I remarked to him that . . . it was the Prussians . . . we had opposite to us, and that they had already killed and wounded many men . . . At the same moment, the captain of the *voltigeurs* of my battalion fell wounded with a musket-ball in his thigh. As the Prussians were beginning to show in force, I made him mount my horse, and sent him to the army's hospital.[10]

11. Return to the track from Smohain and pause at the crossroads.

K. Ziethen's Advance

From the position at which the visitor is standing, a good view may be obtained of the ridge along which Bülow's corps had already fought its way earlier in the afternoon. Having cleared Smohain, meanwhile, Ziethen's men found little in their way other than scattered remnants of Mouton's forces which had been pushed back southwards rather than retiring on Plancenoit, and by eight o'clock were assailing his left flank and at the same time pushing past it towards La Belle Alliance, the only resistance which they faced in this respect coming from the battery of 12-pounders of the Artillery of the Guard stationed in the angle of the tracks from La Belle Alliance to Plancenoit and Papelotte.

> *Von Blücher, major, Twenty-Fourth Infantry Regiment*:
> The order came to attack their line outside the village in column, and we beat the enemy back in great disorder, supported by Battery No. 7. Our skirmishers now advanced in an open-order line . . . leaving behind the necessary supports. We moved towards the right flank of the IV Army Corps as their skirmishers had almost run out of ammunition. We shared out our ammunition and then attacked the enemy together with vigour. The enemy . . . fought fiercely before being thrown back. Shortly after that, resistance collapsed and our cavalry followed their flight.[11]

12. At the crossroads turn right and head west. After several hundred yards the track swings left and descends into the bottom of the valley.

L. Ziethen's Advance (continued)

The visitor is now following the main route from Ohain to Plancenoit, this running parallel to the rear slope of the original French front line. Note the open nature of the terrain: almost unchanged since 1815, this ensured that the French retreat was continually harried by Prussian cavalry. As can be imagined, the advance of the Prussian forces in this sector, not to mention along the ridge above, caused complete consternation in the ranks of Napoleon's forces.

The climax of the battle on the right flank: Ziethen's troops burst into the valley behind the original French front line along the axis of the lane from Smohain to Plancenoit. (Wikimedia Commons)

Jean-Baptiste Lemonnier-Delafosse, aide de camp to General Foy:

Masses of troops began to appear from the direction of Saint Lambert . . . As was announced by their cannon, it was the Prussians . . . In response, the emperor cried, 'It is Grouchy: victory is ours!', and sent out his *aide de camp*, Labedoyère, to announce the latter's arrival. On all sides cries went up of 'En avant! En avant!', but orders were lacking, and nothing came for us . . . Much perturbed at this, I wanted to learn the truth of what was going on, and asked General Foy for permission to go and find out. The latter being equally concerned, I rode across the whole width of the battlefield and eventually . . . found the VI Corps of General Mouton and the Young Guard drawn up at right angles to our position and Bülow and his Prussians heading straight for them in such a way that, if they were not stopped, they could not but reach the main road before our centre and left had had a chance to get away. Coming across an adjutant-major . . . named Servatius, I asked him whether Grouchy had really come. 'Grouchy?' he said. 'Does it look like Grouchy?' I now saw dark masses of troops debouching on to the battlefield from the direction of Ohain. It was General Ziethen, who, thinking that they were French, had just attacked the troops of the Prince of Saxe-Weimar and, after a very sharp combat, driven them from a village which they had been defending. Returning at once to General Foy, I gave him the news . . . 'Dreadful! Dreadful', he exclaimed. 'But not a word!'[12]

13. From here, the state of the crops permitting, more adventurous visitors may push straight on along the southern slope of the French ridge and by ascending the steep hill follow the route of those members of Ziethen's corps who advanced directly on La Belle Alliance (doing this will bring the visitor out on to road from La Belle Alliance to Plancenoit near the spot reputed to have been

The counter-attack by two battalions of Old-Guard grenadiers that temporarily cleared Plancenoit of Prussian troops immediately prior to the final attempt to break Wellington's line. (Wikimedia Commons)

Napoleon's command post in the latter stages of the battle: whether this was actually the case is a moot point, but the views that it offers of the eastern half of the battlefield are unrivalled; having reached Napoleon's position, visitors who choose to take this diversion may return to Plancenoit by walking back along the road). Otherwise continue along the track until a point where it angles sharply to the south near a substantial modern property standing in a grove of trees.

M. The Collapse of the French Right Wing

It is often claimed that the French army collapsed on account of the repulse of the Guard. This is true of the French left wing, but on the right, given the configuration of the ground, it was impossible to see anything that was happening beyond the line of the Brussels highway. Here, by contrast, the collapse was the result of the advance of Ziethen from Smohain, this being equally impossible to observe from the French left wing. At the same time, it is in part the division of the battlefield into two separate halves that explains why the British and Prussians have such different views of the end of the battle: from what they could see, for the former the crucial event was the repulse of the Guard while for the latter it was the advance of Ziethen. At all events it is clear that the collapse of I Corps was, if anything, even more rapid than was the case with Reille's men.

> *Jacques Martin, lieutenant, Forty-Fifth Regiment of Line Infantry*:
> Whilst the Old Guard were launching their formidable assault, Napoleon had spread the news through the whole army that Grouchy had arrived and that victory was certain. On all sides the news revived our enthusiasm: the half-destroyed corps of [General Drouet] stirred itself anew; renewed cries of 'Long live the emperor!' rang out along the line from the right where I was to the left where the Guard was making its attack; already the divisions of Durutte and Marcognet were crowning the plateau. Just at that moment, however, an enormous mass of infantry and cavalry hurled itself upon the battlefield. What was it that destiny had brought us this time? Alas, it was not Grouchy, but rather

[Ziethen] . . . Before that torrent of enemies everything gave way. There was no more hope, no more resistance. With Prussian cavalry hemming them in on every side, our [i.e. Drouet's] divisions fell back into the valley. Believing that they had been betrayed, meanwhile, their soldiers dispersed. Of the whole of [Drouet's] corps, there soon remained not a single battalion, not a single company in order, whilst every single gun was in the hands of the enemy. It was a case of who could fly quickest and furthest. And, as for me, I did as all the rest.[13]

14. Continue along the track to the Prussian monument. On the high ground ahead and to the right will be observed a line of modern houses. The left wing of Mouton's second position ran due north just in front of these properties and continued to be manned even as Ziethen's corps flooded across the low ground where the visitor is now standing.

The line of modern houses that marks the left wing of Mouton's final position. The open slopes gave the defenders an excellent field of fire. (Author's collection)

N. Prussia's Vengeance

Heavily outnumbered from the start, the two divisions of VI Corps had been fighting continually for over three hours against ever increasing numbers of enemy by the time the new arrivals came in sight, and yet they managed to win a little more time for Napoleon even now. As such, they are far more worthy of respect usually paid to the largely fictitious 'last stand of the Old Guard'; to paraphrase the emperor himself, however, history is on the side of the big battalions. Meanwhile, the Prussians were wreaking a terrible vengeance on the fleeing French: setting aside the humiliation of the 1806 campaign, the build-up to the invasion of Russia had seen the population reduced to near-starvation by the presence of 500,000 French troops on their territory, whilst the behaviour of many French soldiers had left much to desired.

> *Basil Jackson, aide-de-camp to Sir William de Lancey:*
> Crossing to the left of the *chaussée,* I found myself involved with Prussian infantry streaming from the direction of Frischermont in no military order whatever as they swept onward bayoneting every wounded Frenchman they came upon. Seeing a knot of them standing close to a wall, I rode up and perceived a wounded light dragoon sitting against it, and there seemed to be some hesitation as to his fate, when I called 'Er ist ein Engländer' upon which the men raised their bayonets and the poor fellow was saved. The disorder of the Prussians . . . was so great that I was glad to push on, and soon overtook our Fifty-Second Regiment and with it our glorious commander, but thinly attended.[14]

16. Return to Plancenoit via the Chemin du Lanternier.

TOUR 8: THE ATTACK OF THE GUARD

Time: three hours (up to six if the opportunity is taken to visit the Panorama and the Mémorial 1815). Going: mostly metalled roads or well-maintained tracks, though some patches of the latter may be waterlogged in wet weather; moderate slopes with occasional steeper stretches; some stretches of field walking (optional). See Maps 7–9.

1. With evening drawing on, Napoleon's situation was becoming truly desperate. The infantry of I and II Corps were nearing the end of their tether; the cavalry were no longer capable of decisive action; the artillery was beginning to run short of ammunition; the Prussians were barely being held off at Plancenoit; and there were no reserves left other than the infantry of the Old and Middle Guard – a mere fifteen battalions of which two had already had to be temporarily

Napoleon salutes the ten battalions of the Old and Middle Guard that spearheaded the Army of the North's final attack as they march past La Belle Alliance.

sent to Plancenoit to bolster the much-tried Young Guard – together with one or two batteries of Guard artillery. Realizing that he had only one hope of salvaging anything from what had already turned into a day of disaster – the marginal victory that was all that the French could hope to achieve was scarcely likely to shock Europe into acquiescence, while such were the Army of the North's casualties that France's means of fighting on had been gravely reduced – at about half-past seven Napoleon therefore flung his last reserves into a desperate bid to break Wellington's battered ranks. Begin the tour at La Belle Alliance.

A. La Belle Alliance

As one of the few buildings in the French sector of the battlefield, the inn of La Belle Alliance had quickly been designated as a hospital, and was now crammed with wounded who were being cared for by a hard-pressed staff of surgeons and medical orderlies headed by the famed pioneer of military medicine, Dominique Larrey. That said, whilst there was no deliberate intent of firing on a hospital as such, the more-or-less random fire of the Anglo-Dutch artillery had left it heavily scarred and pock-marked. Other wounded, meanwhile, were trying to make their way to the rear along the Charleroi highway, which was also thronged with men who were trying to slink away or had simply become lost or disorientated in the chaos. Having spent much of the first part of the day further back at Rossomme, the emperor had at some time come forward to the vicinity of La Belle Alliance, a small knoll just to the right of the road to Plancenoit being signposted as the spot from which he watched the last part of the battle. However, whilst the story is certainly not impossible, it is more likely that he took post somewhere in the vicinity of the road junction as this offered a wider view than the knoll.

Octave Levavasseur, aide-de-camp to Marshal Ney:
General Drouot rode up, shouting, 'Where is the Guard, where is the Guard?' I pointed them out to him: they were approaching . . . Just then, the emperor rode past me followed by his officers . . . on the other side of the road. Arriving before the Guard, he said, 'Follow me!', and led them down that road

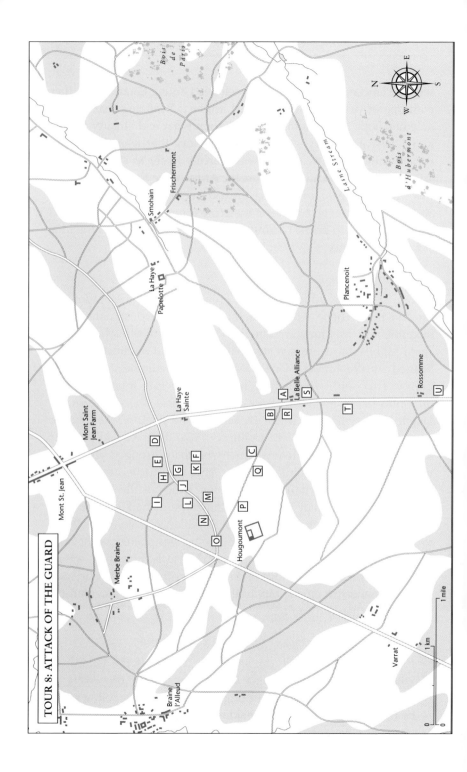

TOUR 8: ATTACK OF THE GUARD

swept by a hundred pieces of artillery. Immediately behind him came 150 bandsmen playing the triumphal marches heard on the [Place du] Carrousel. Very soon the road was covered with the guardsmen marching in serried ranks in the wake of the emperor: the cannon balls and spherical case that raked it bestrewed it with dead and wounded. A few paces more and Napoleon would have been alone at their head.[1]

2. Taking the utmost care, cross the road at the crossing and walk along the western side of the highway to the track that leads across the fields in the direction of Hougoumont.

B. The Track to Hougoumont
At the time of the advance of the Guard, the area to the right in the angle between the Charleroi highway and the road to Plancenoit

The lane from La Belle Alliance to the Ohain Road viewed from near the original French front line. The third echelon of the Guard advanced through the fields immediately to the right. (Author's collection)

was occupied by the three 12-pounder batteries of I, II and VI Corps, together with an additional battery of 12-pounders contributed by the Foot Artillery of the Guard, though this last was tasked not with pounding Wellington's positions but rather keeping the Prussians back from Plancenoit. The point where the track branched off the main road is also the point where Napoleon, who had initially ridden with the columns of the Guard as they advanced from their positions around Rossomme, turned aside: according to many accounts his initial intention was to lead the advance all the way to the Anglo-Dutch positions, the decision not to do so being the result of pressure from his senior commanders, but whether this story has a basis in anything other than legend is a moot point. Whatever the truth, it has to be said that Napoleon's style of command was very different from that of Wellington's: whilst the emperor remained in the rear of his army all day, the duke led his men from the very midst of the fighting.

Hyppolyte Mauduit, sergeant, First Regiment of Foot Grenadiers of the Imperial Guard:

Formed in columns of attack by echelon with two guns loaded with canister positioned in the intervals between them . . . [the Guard] set out to attack the enemy. Headed by Count Friant, the first battalion of the Third Grenadiers took as its alignment the left-hand verge of the main road, while the other units followed *au pas de charge* in the best of orders, taking care to maintain their proper distances . . . Meeting with Marshal Ney near the farm [of La Haye Sainte] the emperor gave him command of the column which already possessed such commanders as Lieutenant-Generals Friant, Roguet and Michel . . . One and all, they marched to their deaths to repeated cries of 'Vive l'empereur!' As they went, they filed past the emperor. The latter had placed himself in the very middle of the road . . . between two batteries that had been given orders to support them. It was almost seven o'clock in the evening. Mingling with the dusk, the smoke was beginning to make it impossible to see anything beyond a certain distance.[2]

The view north along the watershed from the vicinity of the intermediate ridge. The first wave of the Guard advanced towards the Butte du Lion following the direction of the furrows. (Author's collection)

3. Follow the track to a point where it begins to drop downhill.

C. The Watershed

The watershed that ran from La Belle Alliance to the site of the Butte du Lion was an obvious approach for the Guard to take, though doing so meant that the attack would not strike the weakest point in Wellington's line (the stretch of ridge immediately above La Haye Sainte), and would have to brave the full weight of the Anglo-Dutch artillery. To make matters worse, the attack was not even delivered in a single mass, but allowed to fragment into three different elements: first four battalions of the Third and Fourth Chasseurs that advanced directly along the watershed; next, a battalion each of the Second, Third and Fourth Grenadiers that headed for the slopes above La Haye Sainte; and, finally, one battalion of the Third Grenadiers and two battalions of the Second Chasseurs that veered slightly to the left (it will be noted, then, that references to the attack of the Old Guard are misleading: of the ten battalions involved in the attack, only the one battalion of the Second Grenadiers and the two battalions of the

Second Chasseurs belonged to that formation, all the others forming part of the Middle Guard, a scratch force thrown together in 1815 from veterans recalled to the colours). That said, the Guard did not just attack alone, being accompanied by at least one battery of horse artillery and elements of both I and II Corps. As for the repeated claim that the individual battalions attacked in square, this is frankly risible: such formations being completely inappropriate for the task in hand, it is probable that the belief stems from misinterpretation.

Jean de Crabbé, aide de camp to Marshal Ney:
Marshal Soult . . . summoned me. He told me that the emperor had confided his ultimate reserve, all that remained of the Guard, to Marshal Ney to make a decisive attack on the English lines. He had asked for an experienced officer of his headquarters to carry supplementary orders. I reached the rise near the farm [*sic*] of La Belle Alliance where the emperor was located. He was surrounded by a squadron of the Guard Chasseurs à Cheval, jackets and trousers green trimmed with red, and shabraques of the same . . . From this position one could see the whole of the battlefield . . . The emperor was on a chair in front of a table on which some maps were spread . . . General Count Drouot and two *aides de camp* were at his side. He wore his usual grey riding coat over his uniform of a colonel of chasseurs and on his head his legendary hat. Slumped in his chair, he appeared to me both exhausted and angry. One of the *aides de camp* informed him of my arrival. Without even turning to me he said, out of the blue, 'Ney has acted stupidly again. He has cost us the day! He has destroyed my cavalry and is about to destroy my Guard. He manoeuvres like a good-for-nothing. He attacks the plateau obliquely instead of assaulting right at the centre. Go at best speed and order him to modify his march and pierce the centre of the English position in a compact mass.'[3]

4. The state of the crops and ground permitting, visitors may now make their way across the fields in the direction of the Charleroi highway and then turn northwards so as to pick up the track that provides access to La Haye Sainte; in following this last stretch, they will be

The last few yards of the slope leading up to the Ohain Road from La Haye Sainte. Aside from the steep slope, the assault would have been further slowed by the de facto rampart that lined the road. (Author's collection)

taking the same route as the second echelon of the Guard. Otherwise return to the main road, cross over at the pedestrian crossing and then follow the main road northwards past La Haye Sainte to the cross roads. Whichever route is decided on, immediately beside the 'Hotel 1815' ascend the bank at the right hand side of the road.

D. Ompteda's Position

At the time of the Guard's attack, the stretch of the road from the crossroads to the spot where the visitor is standing was held by Ompteda's brigade of the King's German Legion. However, whilst in itself a force of high quality, over the course of the day the former had been used most cruelly: thus, of its four battalions, the Second Light had constituted the original garrison of La Haye Sainte and had lost some 200 casualties in the fighting there, whilst the Fifth and Eighth Line had both been terribly cut up by French cavalry in the course of misguided counter-attacks ordered by the Prince of Orange, the second of which had cost the life of Ompteda; in consequence, the only unit in any sort of order was the First Light, and even that had seen two of its companies suffer heavy losses when they were sent to the help of their fellow riflemen in the farm. Assailed not by the Guard but elements of Drouet's corps who had ascended the slopes from La Haye Sainte, the brigade now disintegrated and fled in disorder.

Captain Georg Baring, Fifth Line Battalion, King's German Legion:
Fresh columns of the enemy again advanced, and nothing seemed likely to terminate the slaughter, but the entire destruction of one army or another. My horse, the third which I had had in the course of the day, received a ball in his head: he sprang up, and, in coming down again, fell on my right leg and pressed me so hard into the deep loamy soil that, despite of all exertion, I could not free myself. The men in the road considered me dead, and it was not until after some little time that one of them came to set me free. Although my leg was not broken, I lost the use of it for a moment . . . An Englishman was charitable enough to catch a stray horse, place a saddle upon him and help me up: I then rode forward again when I learned that General Alten had been severely wounded. I saw that the part of the position which our division had held was only weakly and irregularly occupied. Scarce sensible from the pain which I suffered, I rode straight to the hollow road where I had left the rest of the men, but they had . . . been obliged to retire to the village in consequence of the total want of ammunition, hoping there to find some cartridges.[4]

5. Continue along the bank above the road in the direction of the Butte du Lion, noting in the process its height: in places as much ten feet, this gives a good impression of the depth of the sunken road at the time of the battle. Pause at the edge of the Hameau du Lion.

E. Kielmansegg's Position
The strip of land the visitor has just traversed was held by two Hanoverian brigades. Composed of very raw troops, these units had suffered terribly from the French artillery fire. Thus, first came the Fifth Hanoverian Brigade under Ernst von Vincke: a fresh unit brought over in haste from the left flank, this was composed entirely

The Prince of Orange leads the First Regiment of Nassau forward in an attempt to stem the collapse precipitated by the second wave of the attack of the Guard. (Wikimedia Commons)

of militiamen and had lost two of its four battalions when an order to withdraw to a position of greater safety a few hundred yards in rear of the ridge was deliberately misunderstood by their officers as a means of marching off the battlefield altogether. And, finally, a little further to the west came the First Hanoverian Brigade of Count Friedrich von Kielmansegg, this consisting of three *landwehr* battalions, two light battalions and a rifle company. The record of this force was somewhat better in that they had stood their ground all day under heavy fire, but the result had been terrible casualties, not least when a lucky French cannonball had struck down an entire face of the square formed by the Bremen and Verden battalions, while another battalion – the Lüneburg – had been lost earlier in the day when it had been destroyed by French cavalry while trying to clear the west face of La Haye Sainte. Nor did it help that the troops that hit it were formed not in columns alone, but rather a mixture of column and line known as *ordre mixte* that increased an attacking force's firepower while yet retaining many of the advantages of the column. Not surprisingly, then, the brigade disintegrated and fell back in complete disorder.

Carl von Scriba, captain, Bremen Field Battalion:
   A strong square [*sic:* whilst it would be useful to check the original, if he used the word at all, Von Scriba is almost certainly

using it in the sense of 'block' or 'mass'] of French Guards with several guns advanced towards us, and immediately started firing at us at a heavy rate. Our small troop could not withstand this strong assault for very long. At first our men, full of fury, returned the fire, but, unfortunately, [they] were running out of ammunition . . . All efforts were in vain . . . The gallant battalions . . . yielded, but slowly and calmly. The officers' efforts and encouraging words brought the men to a halt some 300 paces, at most, behind the original position . . . We were just in the process of reforming . . . when His Royal Highness, the Crown Prince of the Netherlands, came up to us [and] praised the battalion's conduct . . . but at the same time insisted on a quick advance . . . Our brave troops, unformed although compact, advanced again, with the prince at their head, shouting 'Long live the Prince of Orange!' At our former position we were received with case-shot from not more than 200 paces away. The men bravely stood fast, as before, but all resistance ceased due to lack of ammunition . . . [and] the remains of both battalions slowly retreated.[5]

6. Cross the road, and walk along the outside of the hedge surrounding the Butte du Lion in the direction of the French positions. At the further corner turn right and, the state of the ground permitting, walk to a point in line with the centre of the Butte.

F. Butte du Lion

Held at this stage of the battle by the British brigades of Sir Colin Halkett and Sir Peregrine Maitland, the area occupied by the Butte du Lion and the various buildings associated with it was the real key to the Anglo-Dutch position. That said, it was desperately vulnerable. Artillery posted further back along the watershed had already been pounding the Allied line for perhaps two hours before the arrival of the Guard, and the bombardment was now reinforced by the battery of horse artillery that had accompanied the advancing infantry. Still worse, while Maitland's troops were some of the best in Wellington's army, being composed entirely of Foot Guards, Halkett's were in large part raw recruits while they had also been very roughly handled at Quatre Bras, so much so, indeed, that at

Waterloo, their four battalions had been merged into two composite formations. Already shaken by the first wave of the French assault (see below), they now broke and fled:

> *Thomas Morris, private, Seventy-Third Regiment of Foot*:
> Hitherto we had only acted against cavalry, but now Napoleon was leading up his infantry in masses, and, as our brigade was literally cut to pieces, the remnant formed up in line four-deep. But the French infantry that were advancing were now so overwhelming in numbers that we were forced to retire. While doing so, General Halkett received a ball through his cheek and, falling from his horse, was taken to the rear. The fire from the French infantry was so tremendous that our brigade divided and sought shelter behind some banks . . . Captain Garland, on whom the command of the regiment now devolved . . . invited us to follow him in an attack upon . . . the French infantry. About a dozen of us responded to the call and such was the destructive fire to which we were exposed, that we had not advanced beyond six or seven paces before every one of the party, except me and my brother, was either killed or wounded.[6]

7. Carry on into the Hameau du Lion, cross the road and pause outside the Rotunda.

G. The Rotunda

The cluster of buildings at the foot of the Butte du Lion is known as the Hameau du Lion. Dating from 1913, the Rotunda in particular houses the famous 'Panorama', this being a somewhat misleading depiction of the French cavalry charges. As for the 141-foot-high Butte du Lion, thrown up in 1826 to glorify the Dutch part in the battle, this offers a view that is oddly disappointing: certainly the whole of the battlefield can be seen at once, but the ground appears much smoother than is actually the case. On the whole, then, if time is short, it is better to spend it in the 'Mémorial du Waterloo', the brand-new museum opened for the bicentenary (see below). Meanwhile, in the wake of the defeat of the Allied front line, various German troops (the Brunswick contingent and the

First Regiment of Nassau) that had been in reserve were also flung into the fight.

August von Kruse, colonel, First Regiment of Nassau:
Napoleon's Guard reached the plateau with our infantry withdrawing only 100 paces. A violent fire fight broke out, and showing as much courage as foresight, the Crown Prince . . . attempted to put an end to it with a bayonet charge. For this honour he thought of the Nassauers. Thus, he brought up the second battalion and led it in column. The remainder of the first battalion joined up with them and the attack was carried out with great bravery. I saw . . . the French Guard start to waver when, perhaps because the Prince of Orange was wounded, a wave of panic hit the young soldiers, and, at the moment of their greatest victory, the battalion fell into confusion and retreated. The remaining battalions in the first line soon followed, leaving only small bodies of brave men on the plateau. I had the *landwehr* battalion and the remainder of the second battalion join them, but in such a way that the enemy fire could have little effect on them.[7]

8. Cross the road to the forecourt of the large white building opposite the Rotunda.

H. The Waterloo Hotel
The building outside which the visitor is now standing housed the battlefield's very first museum and visitor centre. Known as the Waterloo Hotel, this was operated by the sometime cavalry sergeant-major and veteran of the battle, Edward Cotton, who wrote a best-selling book on the battle entitled *A Voice from Waterloo* and was eventually buried at Hougoumont. Much modernised, his hotel is now a café-restaurant-cum-conference centre, and visitors might be amused at the caution displayed by its owners, the latter having chosen to label their establishment as both 'Le Wellington' and 'Le Bivouac de l'Empereur'! Less amusing is the statue of Napoleon that stands in its forecourt: given the better visibility that the position offered than his famous elm, it was at or very near this spot that Wellington spent the majority of the day, much of it under a heavy fire that killed or

The Prince of Orange is wounded in the shoulder at the height of the attack of the Guard. Known to the British army as 'Slender Billy', the prince was not much of a general, but he did show immense courage at Waterloo. (War Heritage Institute, Brussels)

disabled many members of his staff, and the failure to commemorate his courage and leadership is a great injustice. Indeed, even a statue of the Prince of Orange would have been preferable: though the prince is generally much maligned in British sources, he showed great courage and energy at this point in the battle. Moreover, it was Dutch troops who saved the day in this sector: brought up from its positions in reserve around Braine l'Alleud by Wellington, David Chassé's Third Netherlands Division was in reserve in the area immediately to the north-west of the Hotel Wellington when the Imperial Guard struck home, and responded to the complete defeat of the troops to its left (the brigades of Ompteda, Vincke, Kielmansegg and Halkett, the First Regiment of Nassau and the Brunswick contingent) with a bayonet charge that bundled the French back down the slope.

David Chassé, GOC, Third Netherlands Infantry Division:
    When I saw that an English artillery battery positioned on the left . . . of my division had stopped firing, I went . . . to enquire the reason and learned that there was no ammunition.

At the same time I saw the Garde Imperiale advancing, while the English troops were leaving the plateau en masse and moving in the direction of Waterloo. I immediately ordered the battery of horse artillery under the command of Major van der Smissen [*sic:* actually the commander of the battery concerned was an officer named Krahmer] . . . to occupy the height and to direct an emphatic fire upon the enemy column. At this time I also ordered Major-General d'Aubréme to have the brigade he commanded form two squares in echelon and to form a reserve with the foot artillery. I [then] positioned myself at the head of the First Brigade and advanced in close columns at attack pace against the French.[8]

9. Turn right out of the forecourt of the Hotel Wellington and then turn right again into the Route du Lion (in 1815 the lane to the villages of Merbe Braine and Brain l'Alleud). Walk along this road to the car park at the far end, noting on the way the new underground museum known as the Mémorial 1815.

I. Mémorial 1815

Finished just in time for the bicentenary, the Mémorial 1815 is the newest of the various museums dedicated to the Waterloo campaign, and features a variety of displays of which perhaps the most spectacular is a large collection of mannequins dressed in the uniforms worn in the battle. Featured among its exhibits, meanwhile, is the skeleton of a soldier of the Second Line Battalion of the King's German Legion that was discovered during the museum's construction. A hunchback, the man had evidently been mortally wounded by a musket ball that struck him in the chest, and was subsequently identified as very probably 23-year-old Friedrich Brandt (Brandt's physical deformities are mentioned in the regiment's muster rolls while a surviving fragment of the butt of his musket was marked with the initials F.B.). As the Second Line only came within musket range of the French while serving in the vicinity of Hougoumont in the later part of the afternoon, it can be assumed that he was carried to the rear in the hope of getting him medical attention, only either to die in the arms of his bearers and then be abandoned, or to be left with some hard-pressed regimental surgeon who was trying to care for the casualties in the open field. As will be noticed, meanwhile, the car park is built along a slight rise, this more-or-less marking the line occupied by Wellington's dwindling force of cavalry in the last phase of the battle in an attempt to keep the exhausted infantry from running away.

George Farmer, private, Eleventh Regiment of Light Dragoons:
   During the remainder of the day, little else fell to our share than to sustain, as best we might, the heavy fire . . . which the enemy continued to direct against us . . . Nor was it the least disagreeable [matter] attendant on our position that we stood exactly on a spot as enabled us to behold the last struggles of the wounded whose strength sufficed only to carry them a few yards to the rear. There was a long sort of ditch or drain some way behind us towards which these poor fellows betook themselves by scores, and ere three hours had passed it was absolutely choked up with the bodies of those who lay down there only that they might die. Then again, the wounded horses, of which multitudes wandered all over the field, troubled us. They would come back, some with broken legs, others trailing after them their entrails which the roundshot had knocked out, and, forcing themselves between our files, seemed to solicit the aid which no-one had time to afford . . . We were beginning to get tired of this state of things when an order reached us to form line and move off to the left. 'Now then', we thought, 'a charge is before us.' But it was not so: a square of Brunswickers had begun to waver, and, as a failure on that point might have proved fatal, we were brought up to stop it if we could. We drew our swords, cheered, made our horses prance, and the desired end was gained.[9]

10. Return to the Butte du Lion.

J. Halkett's Position
At the time of the assault of the Imperial Guard the ground immediately in the rear of the Butte du Lion was occupied by the British brigade commanded by Sir Colin Halkett, a force, which, as

The eastern face of the watershed viewed from the foot of the Butte du Lion. The second echelon of the Guard advanced parallel to the Charleroi highway through the low ground to the left. (Author's collection)

we have seen, was both of mediocre quality and much reduced on strength. Yet, inadequate as it was, it now found itself facing the right wing of five battalions of veteran troops that constituted that first wave of the French attack.

George Barlow, captain, Sixty-Ninth Regiment of Foot:
   Between six and seven o'clock [*sic*] . . . the Imperial Guard . . . made a most formidable attack. These fellows came up with carried arms in the most determined manner to within seventy or eighty yards of the heights along which our infantry were posted and opened a most terrible fire. Two pieces of cannon accompanied them, and, being opposite our brigade, then formed *en masse*, raked it very severely with grape-shot as did the shells from some distant howitzers. This was indeed the crisis of this most eventful day. Both armies were in close contact and . . . the cannonade really tremendous along the whole line, for the entire artillery of both armies were in full play to support their respective sides in an effort

to decide the fortune of the battle. The sun was now setting very fast and the clouds of smoke from this tremendous firing had so obscured the faint gleams of the declining day that to distinguish friend from foe became extremely embarrassing: some Dutch infantry on our flank [resembled] the French in our front so much that I caught several of our men firing at them. Presently I was surprised with a view of the Duke and all his staff close in the rear. He was pointing in various directions and seemingly occupied in explaining some important arrangement.[10]

11. Walk along the Ohain Road in the direction of Hougoumont. At the far end of the hedges surrounding the Butte du Lion, turn left and, the state of the ground permitting, proceed to the end of the hedge line (take care to do as little damage as possible to any crops that may be in situ).

The bank beside the Ohain Road which sheltered Maitland's brigade looking west. Whether Wellington actually issued the famous command, 'Up, Guards, and at 'em!', is open to doubt, but the sudden emergence of the brigade from the complete concealment afforded by the bank cannot but have come as a terrible shock to the attackers. (Author's collection)

K. The Plateau

Standing at the edge of Butte-du-Lion enclosure, the visitor is situated approximately in the centre of the ground crossed by the first wave of the Guard in its final approach to the Anglo-Dutch line.

Jean de Crabbé, aide de camp to Marshal Ney:
  I found the Marshal in the middle of the Third Grenadiers on the plateau, on foot, bare-headed, his jacket torn, covered in dirt and mud, his bloody sword in his hand. At his side was General Friant, commander of the Guard infantry, and one of my old friends, Colonel Poret de Morvan . . . Reining in my horse . . . I gave the Marshal the emperor's orders, but he replied to me., 'My dear Crabbé, it is too late to change. It is here we must break through or die, and there is no more I can do now.' This was the last time I saw the Marshal, for at that moment the grenadiers came into contact and into hell.[11]

12. Return to the Ohain Road.

L. Maitland's Position

The area to the right of Halkett's brigade was held by Peregrine Maitland's First Infantry Brigade. Consisting of the Second and Third Battalions of the First Regiment of Foot Guards, this was beyond doubt the best infantry formation in the whole of Wellington's army, and now dealt with that part of the assault of the Guard which reached it – the four battalions of the first wave – with consummate efficiency: it was as a result of this action, indeed, that the regiment was awarded the title of the Grenadier Guards, and that the Guards as a whole adopted the bearskin. Ironically, however, the units that hit Maitland's men were *chasseurs* (i.e. in theory, at least, light infantry) rather than grenadiers, whilst, being members of the newly organized Middle Guard rather than the Old Guard, very few of them, if any, had been issued with bearskins!

Henry Weyland Powell, lieutenant, First Regiment of Foot Guards:
  The Duke of Wellington . . . ordered the First Brigade of Guards to take ground to its left and form line four-deep . . . There ran along this part of the position a cart road on one side

of which was a ditch and bank in and under which the brigade had sheltered themselves during the cannonade which might have lasted three quarters of an hour. Without the protection of this bank every creature must have perished . . . Suddenly the firing ceased, and, as the smoke cleared away, a most superb sight opened on us. A close column of grenadiers . . . was seen ascending the rise *au pas de charge* shouting 'Vive l'empereur!' They continued to advance till within fifty or sixty paces of our front when the brigade was ordered to stand up. Whether it was from the sudden and unexpected appearance of a corps so near them, which must have seemed as starting out of the ground, or the tremendously heavy fire we threw into them, *la garde* . . . suddenly stopped. Those who . . . could see the affair tell us that the effect of our fire seemed to force the head of the column bodily back. In less than a minute above 300 were down. They now wavered and several of the rear divisions began to draw out as if to deploy, whilst some of the men in their rear beginning to fire over the heads of those in front was so evident a proof of their confusion that Lord Saltoun . . . holloaed out, 'Now's the time, my boys!' Immediately, the brigade sprang forward. *La garde* turned and gave us little opportunity of trying the steel.[12]

13. Walk along the Ohain Road to the stone marking the position of Mercer's battery.

M. Mercer's Position
Stationed just to the right of Maitland's brigade, Mercer's battery was not directly attacked by the Guard – indeed, such was the thick smoke and his own state of exhaustion that its commander seems to have been all but unaware that any such event had occurred – but it did suffer very heavily from the fire of the artillery brought up to support the attack.

Alexander Mercer, captain, Royal Horse Artillery:
We suddenly became sensible of a most destructive flanking fire from a battery which had come, the Lord knows how, and established itself on a knoll somewhat higher than the

ground we stood on, and only about 400 or 500 yards a little in advance of our left flank. The rapidity and precision of this fire were quite appalling. Every shot, almost, took effect, and I certainly expected we should all be annihilated. Our horses and limbers, being a little retired down the slope, had hitherto been somewhat under cover from the direct fire in front, but this plunged right amongst them, knocking them down by pairs and creating horrible confusion. The drivers could hardly extricate themselves from one dead horse before another fell or perhaps themselves . . . One shell I saw explode under the two finest wheel horses in the troop: down they dropped . . . The whole livelong day had cost us nothing like this. Our gunners too – the few left fit for duty of them – were so exhausted that they were unable to run the guns up after firing; consequently at every round they retreated closer to the limbers . . . The fire continued on both sides, mine becoming slacker and slacker, for we . . . were so reduced that all our strength was barely sufficient to load and fire three guns out of our six.[13]

*The two battalions of **chasseurs** which constituted the third wave of the attack of the Guard briefly stand firm in the face of the advance of Adam's brigade. Though taken completely by surprise, they inflicted many casualties on the Fifty-Second Foot and its fellows before they finally broke and ran. (Wikimedia Commons)*

14. Walk along the Ohain Road to an isolated tree standing on the right-hand side of the road beneath which will be found a shrine to the memory of the Ninety-Fifth Regiment, several elements of which fought at or near this spot as part of Adam's brigade.

N. Adam's Position

The ground to the right of Mercer's battery was held by Frederick Adam's Third Infantry Brigade. Composed entirely of light infantry units, the heart of this force was the largest infantry battalion in Wellington's army, namely Sir John Colborne's Fifty-Second Regiment of Foot. An experienced commander, Colborne was initially well clear of the assault of the Guard and played no part in the repulse of its first wave. From out of the smoke, however, there suddenly appeared three more battalions of French troops arrayed in column one behind the other and advancing on Maitland's Foot Guards along the western flank of the cross-ridge. As the latter were still in some confusion after their rout of the Chasseurs, for a moment the situation hung in the balance, but, in one of the most famous actions of the day, Colborne wheeled his battalion to the left and struck the three battalions full in the flank.

> *William Leeke, ensign, Fifty-Second Regiment of Foot*:
>   When the leading battalion of the . . . Guard was about 400 yards from . . . Maitland's brigade . . . Sir John Colborne. . . moved forward the Fifty-Second in quick time directly to its front. As we passed over the . . . crest of our position, we plainly saw . . . two long columns of the Imperial Guard . . . advancing . . . in the direction of Maitland's brigade, stationed on our left . . . As the Fifty-Second moved down towards the enemy, it answered the cries of 'Vive l'empereur!' with three tremendous British cheers. When the left of the regiment was in a line with the leading company . . . the word of command 'Right shoulders forward!' came down the line . . . The movement was soon completed and the . . . line became parallel to the left flank of the leading column of the French Guard . . . The regiment opened fire on the enemy without halting . . . Here I saw Winterbottom badly wounded in the head . . . Diggle, commanding No. 1 Company . . . desperately

wounded . . . Lieutenant Dawson . . . shot through the lungs; Anderson [lose] a leg; Major Love . . . wounded in the head Lieutenant Campbell . . . severely wounded in the groin . . . Sir John Colborne . . .grazed in the hand and on the foot . . . about 140 of our men . . . killed or wounded . . . in the course of five or six minutes. As we closed toward the French Guard, they did not wait for our charge, but at first somewhat receded from us, and then broke and fled.[14]

15. Continue along the Ohain road to the junction with the track to La Belle Alliance.

O. The General Advance

At the beginning of the attack of the Imperial Guard, Wellington had been close to Maitland's brigade – according to many accounts, indeed, he had taken personal control of the latter's repulse of the second wave – but, as soon as he realized the presence of the column faced by Colborne, he quickly rode down to the position occupied by Adam's brigade, it therefore almost certainly being from this spot that he ordered the general advance that marked the culmination of the day in so far as his army was concerned.

George Farmer, private, Eleventh Regiment of Light Dragoons:

By this time the dusk was closing fast, and . . . the battle continued to rage with unabated fury . . . Over the surface of the ground, shells, with their burning fuses, rolled, bursting here and there with terrible effect. From the mouths of the cannon fire seemed to be poured, while the ceaseless glare of the musketry . . . was terrific. By degrees, however, the sounds and sight of firearms began to be distinguishable where neither before had been observed, and the rumour ran from rank to rank among us that the Prussians had come and had fallen on the right and rear of the enemy. Moreover, that the news was not without foundation was soon apparent from the altered state of things both near us and far away. Our infantry, which up to this moment had fought in squares, formed all at once into line. There was a heart-rending cheer, begun I know not where, but very soon audible over the whole of our front,

The site of Colborne's defeat of the Chasseurs. The Fifty-Second advanced diagonally up the slope to the right. (Author's collection)

and we too were ordered to leap into the saddle and move forward. How can I pretend to describe what followed! On we went at a gallop and . . . shouting fiercely as we went, drove fiercely and without check up to the very muzzles of a hostile battery. A furious discharge of grape met us and thinned our ranks . . . but the survivors, never pausing to look back or to draw bridle, scattered the gunners to the winds, and the cannon were our own.[15]

16. Take the track to La Belle Alliance and continue along it as far as the path leading off to the right in the direction of Hougoumont.

P. The Collapse of the French Left
Confronted by the shocking sight of a large part of the Imperial Guard in full retreat and threatened by advancing British troops – the light cavalry brigades of Sir Hussey Vivian and John Vandeleur, Adam's infantry brigade and part of Hugh Halkett's Hanoverian brigade – the whole of the French left wing now broke and fled, their flight taking them across the fields to the right.

Amidst chaotic scenes, a mixture of Hanoverian infantry from the brigade of Hugh Halkett and British light dragoons set about some defiant members of the Imperial Guard as the French left wing dissolves in rout. (Wikimedia Commons)

Sylvain Larréguy de Civrieux, cadet, Ninety-Third Regiment of Line Infantry:

The army was seized by a sudden panic. Cries of 'Every man for himself! We are betrayed!' rent the air on all sides, and the whole army dissolved in rout. Discipline was completely lost, and the regiments became mixed up in indescribable disorder, merging into mere masses of men who were worked over in every sense by the enemy cannon. Two or three times Marshal Ney appeared amongst us, sword in hand, bare-headed, entirely on his own . . . and shod in massive riding boots that made it very difficult for him to walk, so wet and muddy was the ground. His ringing voice succeeded in rallying a handful of soldiers, but what could even so illustrious . . . a warrior achieve in the face of such chaos . . . The rout continued. Our disorderly mobs fired upon one another, while the wagons and artillery plunging along the main road crushed the dead and dying.[16]

17. Continue along the track to La Belle Alliance until it ascends the watershed linking the positions of the French and Anglo-Dutch armies.

Q. The Advance of Vivien and Vandeleur

As soon as Adam's brigade had clear the track to La Belle Alliance and pursued the fleeing French up onto the watershed, the light cavalry brigades of Sir Richard Vivien, Sir John Vandeleur and Wilhelm von Dornberg were ordered to pass behind the victorious light infantry and charge the French left wing.

Ernst Meier, lieutenant, Second Regiment of Light Dragoons, King's German Legion:

The cannonade was renewed with redoubled intensity . . . One was no longer safe anywhere. Everywhere men and horses were mangled. The horse of Dragoon Wermetch was thrown down next to me: the cannon ball had passed through the entire length of its body . . . In this indescribable rain of balls . . . an *aide de camp* came galloping up and brought us orders to advance. With a few words, Lieutenant-Colonel de Jonquières reminded the men to do their duty, then had us break off by squadrons . . . and drew the regiment ahead of all the other cavalry. Although we had evaded the enemy's solid shot in our advance, we suddenly came under canister fire from two sides, but we

The Duke of Wellington gallops forward into the valley at the moment of victory. By this point in the battle, so many of his staff had been killed or wounded that he was all but alone. (War Heritage Institute, Brussels)

rode quickly on, shouting 'Hurrah!' all the time. In front of us we saw a broad line of French cavalry . . . They were all posted behind a ditch . . . On passing this obstacle we received a volley from their carbines. Noticing that we were not over-awed by this, they turned . . . and fled. Our pursuit was such that we reached them instantaneously, but, being superior in numbers, the enemy soon reformed and wheeled his two wings towards us, and in this way we were attacked from both sides. A desperate affair was now developing: two squadrons of cuirassiers vigorously charged the right flank of the regiment, and Captain von Bülow and Cornet Dranmeister were killed and Lieutenant-Colonel von Jonquières, Captain Harling, Lieutenant Ritter and Cornet Lorenz wounded. In time Major Friedrichs had the rally sounded, and, as soon as we had formed at squadron strength, we threw the cuirassiers into flight.[17]

18. Continue along the track to its junction with the Charleroi highway and cross over to La Belle Alliance using the pedestrian crossing (it is essential to take the utmost care at this point).

R. La Belle Alliance (reprised)
With the French army collapsing in rout around it and more troops (Chassé's brigade and also that of Kempt) advancing from Mont Saint Jean in its support, having crossed the watershed south of La Haye Sainte, Adam's brigade wheeled to its right and attacked the French position at La Belle Alliance, this being garrisoned by the same three batteries of 12-pounders as before, three battalions of the Old Guard that had not been committed to the assault, namely the First and Second Battalions of the First Regiment of Grenadiers and the First Battalion of the First Regiment of Chasseurs, and finally the remnants of some units of the cavalry of the Guard.

Anonymous officer, Fifty-Second Regiment of Foot (?):
Three battalions of the Old Guard . . . stood in squares, supported by a small body of cuirassiers, on the first rise of their position . . . The Fifty-Second . . . closing with the Seventy-First . . . advanced in line, still four deep, upon the

A horrified Napoleon observes the growing disorder that set in around La Belle Alliance as the last attempt to break Wellington's line dissolves in rout. (War Heritage Institute, Brussels)

squares of the Old Guard . . . The squares . . . made no attempt to deploy, but, after opening a heavy fire from their front and flanks . . . with great steadiness . . . commenced their retreat . . . the two right squares directly to the rear on the right side of the *chaussée*, the left square . . . towards Rossomme along the left side of the road . . . Vivian's brigade of hussars came up rapidly in echelon of regiments to the assistance of the Seventy-First. The cuirassiers, worn out as they were, and discouraged as they had reason to be, with much devotedness fronted . . . to protect the squares of the Old Guard, but, a squadron of the Tenth dashing at them, followed immediately by one of the Eighteenth, they were dispersed in hopeless confusion. The compact battalions of the Old Guard were not so soon routed: a part of the Tenth, having rallied after the charge of the cuirassiers, found itself under the fire of one of the squares; the men fell very fast, and there was no alternative

but instantly to retreat or to charge . . .The charge was very
gallantly attempted . . . but, even under such circumstances,
charged home by cavalry on two faces . . . and under a heavy
fire of infantry on [another], the veterans . . . closed well
together, beat off the cavalry with a very destructive fire, and
. . . made good their retreat.[18]

19. From La Belle Alliance walk southwards in the direction of
Charleroi and pause at the monument to Victor Hugo.

S. The Road to Charleroi
As noted elsewhere, of all the monuments on the battlefield of
Waterloo, the Victor-Hugo monument is the least appropriate,
unless, of course, one wishes to admire the elaboration of a version of
Waterloo that is at best misleading, if not wholly mendacious. At all
events, the sense witnessed at the site it now occupies were anything
but heroic. Whilst some credit is due to the Chasseurs and Grenadiers
of the Old Guard for the manner in which they withdrew from the
field, the rest of the Army of the North fled in the utmost disorder.

*Watched by a pair of soon-to-be freed British prisoners of war, Napoleon takes refuge in
a square of the Old Guard in the closing moments of the battle. (War Heritage Institute,
Brussels)*

Toussaint Trefcon, chief of staff, Fifth Division, Army of the North:

It was a little after eight o'clock in the evening. Little by little the firing was dying away while our troops had been driven from most of their positions: as anyone who knew anything about war could tell, the battle was lost. My state not being such that I could remain in action, I was making my way to hospital. On the way I encountered an old cuirassier officer – a squadron commander, no less – whom I had known in Spain. He, too, was wounded and trying to reach the surgeons. Approaching me, he said, 'My poor colonel, what misfortune has befallen us: we are beaten!' Furious with everything as I was, I believe that I answered him with a volley of curses. In response, the squadron commander did nothing but nod his head sadly: he seemed to be in a stupor. Not being able to find anything in the way of medical care, we continued on our way in the direction of Genappe. The road was jammed with fugitives screaming, 'We are betrayed! Run for it!' With everybody trying to elbow their way through the press, the disorder could not have been more extreme: in terms of horror, indeed, it outweighed anything I had seen in the retreat from Russia or the flight from Leipzig.[19]

20. Exercising the utmost care once more, cross the road and walk southwards along the footway, noting the monument to the last combatants of the French army *en route*. After perhaps 300 yards a turning to Plancenoit will be noted on the opposite side of the road. Just beyond it, there is a nondescript private house: this was the residence of Napoleon's guide, Jean Decoster. Opposite Decoster's house, meanwhile, will be observed a low hill. Depending on the season, this may be inaccessible due to either growing crops or very deep ploughing, but at some times of the year, at least, it is possible to reach the hill's summit from the road. Doing so is most worthwhile as it offers an excellent view of the western half of the battlefield, and, in particular, the ground covered by the brigades of Vandeleur, Vivian and Von Dornberg in their ruthless pursuit of the fleeing enemy. Meanwhile, the hill was also the scene of one of the most famous of all the many Waterloo stories that never happened.

The hill on which Cambronne was captured viewed from the west. At the end of the battle the area in the foreground would have been completely covered by fleeing French troops. (Author's collection)

T. The ' Mot Cambronne '

We come here to the capture of the commander of the First Regiment of Chasseurs, Pierre Cambronne. According to legend, summoned to surrender after he and his men were surrounded by Allied cavalry, Cambronne is supposed to have shouted either 'The Guard dies, but never surrender', or the more prosaic 'Merde!', a word that ever since has been referred to as the *mot cambronne*. Throughout his life, however, Cambronne denied that he said anything of the sort, while it is clear that his story was actually distinctly inglorious.

> *Hugh Halkett, GOC, Third Hanoverian Brigade:*
> The moment General Adam's brigade advanced, I lost no time to follow with the Osnabruck battalion . . . During the advance we were much annoyed by the enemy's artillery. The first company . . . broke into platoons, and, supported by the sharpshooters of the battalion, made a dash at the artillery on our right and captured six guns with their horses. Some hundred yards to our right were some troops of hussars

(I believe the Tenth). I rode up to them and got them to charge a column of infantry which was drawing to their left in rear of the French Guards. The charge succeeded admirably and the column dispersed behind some enclosures . . . During our advance we were in constant contact with the French Guards and I often called to them to surrender. For some time I had my eye upon, as I supposed, the general officer in command of the Guards [i.e. Cambronne] . . . trying to animate his men to stand. After having received our fire with much effect, the column left their general with two officers behind, when . . . I made a dash for the general. When [I was] about cutting him down, he called out he would surrender, upon which he preceded me [to the rear], but I had not gone many paces before my horse got a shot through his body and fell to the ground. In a few seconds I got him on his legs again, and found my friend, Cambronne, had taken French leave in the direction from where he came. I instantly overtook him, laid hold of him by the aiguillette, and . . . gave him in charge to a sergeant to take to the Duke.[20]

21. If necessary returning to the road, continue to walk southwards in the direction of Charleroi, passing, first, a petrol station on the left, and, second, a restaurant on the right. A little way beyond the restaurant is an isolated house and, directly opposite it, a tree-lined drive: in 1815 the ground immediately to the right of the drive was occupied by the farm of Rossomme (destroyed by fire in 1895). Continue to a bend in the road with a lay-by fashioned from the original carriageway beside it. At this point, cross the road and either scramble up the tree-lined bank or proceed along the highway a little further south and enter the field just past the substantial brick house, thereupon circling round behind it. Whichever way is chosen, the visitor will find a grassy knoll sandwiched between the road and the western edge of Plancenoit.

U. The Last Stand of the Old Guard

So far as anything resembling the famous 'last stand of the Old Guard' took place, it did so on the knoll on which the visitor is now standing. In brief, after a brief stand at La Belle Alliance, the First and Second Regiments of Foot Grenadiers, slowly fell back through the

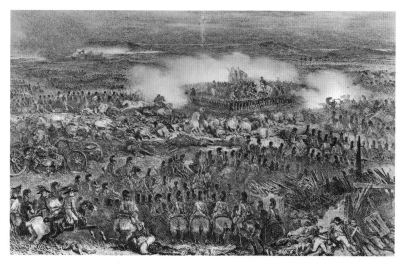

Surrounded by a sea of British and Prussian cavalry, the last battalion of the Guard to retain its order retires from the field. Despite the legend, there was nothing that even remotely resembled a last stand. (War Heritage Institute, Brussels)

fields on the eastern side of the highway until they reached this point. Here, they remained stationary for some while, probably so as to give Napoleon shelter until such time as the means had been found to get him away from the battlefield, but, as every reliable French account makes plain, they did not fight to the last man but rather marched quietly away through the gathering darkness whilst contemptuously brushing aside the disorderly masses of cavalry that was all that now threatened them.

> *Hyppolyte Mauduit, sergeant, First Regiment of Foot Grenadiers of the Imperial Guard:*
> The two battalions of my regiment . . . grew ever more angry at the terrible confusion that marked the battlefield. On all sides our view was obstructed by hundreds of soldiers of every rank . . . searching frantically for some . . . refuge. The drummers had been ordered to beat the grenadier march in the hope that this might offer the army something around which to rally, and at this sound . . . our unfortunate comrades had come surging towards us . . . However, with the interior of our two squares already encumbered with generals and other

officers whose men had been killed or run away, we were very soon reduced to the cruel necessity of denying access to anyone who sought to enter so as to ensure that we did not become the victims of our generosity . . . As for the battery of twelve-pounder guns belonging to the artillery of the Guard that had for the past two hours been flaying Bülow's corps with canister fire . . . it was completely wiped out before our very eyes, all of the gunners choosing a glorious death rather than . . . take shelter in our square, thereby letting the English cavalrymen in with them. 'No quarter! No quarter!' That was what those savages were crying, but . . . their ranks shattered on our bayonets, and for fifty paces around the ground was soon covered with their corpses . . . Subjected to a hail of fire from three sides though we were, we were therefore able to begin our retreat in the midst of the general disorder.[21]

22. End the tour by returning to La Belle Alliance, though visitors who have not seen it before may wish to take the opportunity to visit the command post at which Napoleon spent much of the day: this may be reached by take the more modern of the two lanes that open out from the northern end of the lay-by and then ascending the track on the left.

W. Night
The retreat of the last battalions of the Guard brought an end to the battle. Casualties on both sides had been terrible and the battlefield was a vision of hell, as many as 45,000 dead and wounded and a further 5,000 more-or-less mangled horses strewing an area of no more than four square miles (by comparison, the 68,000 casualties of the first day of the Battle of the Somme were scattered across an area of approximately sixty square miles).

George Farmer, private, Eleventh Regiment of Light Dragoons:
    The ground . . . was literally strewed with the wreck of the mighty battle. Arms of every kind . . . cumbered the face of the earth. Intermingled with these were the carcasses of the slain, not lying about in groups of four or six, but so wedged together that we found it impossible in many instances to

Amidst a scene of utter desolation, the body of a loved one is discovered on the battlefield on the morning of 19 June. The cost of finally putting an end to Napoleon was terrible indeed. (War Heritage Institute, Brussels)

avoid trampling upon them . . . Then again, the knapsacks, either cast loose or adhering to their owners, were countless. I confess that we opened many of these latter hoping to find in them money or articles of value, but not one . . . contained more than the coarse shirts and shoes that had belonged to the dead owners with here and there a little package of tobacco and a bag of salt. And, what was worst of all . . . our spurs forever caught in the garments of the slain and more than once we tripped up and fell over them. It was indeed a ghastly spectacle . . . The dead lay so thick and so crowded together that by-and-by it seemed to us as if we alone had survived to make mention of them.[22]

VISITING WATERLOO

Visiting Waterloo is on one level very simple. Traffic allowing, the battlefield is an hour's drive from the centre of Brussels and is also situated right beside the junction of the N5, today, as in 1815, the main road from Brussels to Charleroi, and the RO orbital motorway, whilst Brussels is, of course, one of Europe's major capitals, and is therefore served by extensive coach, train and air services. Meanwhile, visitors who base themselves in the Belgian capital have a range of excellent hotels at their disposal, though for convenience those in the Rue Fonsny across the road from Midi station (the terminus of the high-speed service from London) cannot be beaten, examples here including the Radisson, the Novotel and the Eurocapital, this being all the more the case in view of the fact that the chief buses to the battlefield – the W and the 365 – depart from outside their very doors. Meanwhile, a slightly quicker route to the battlefield is the train service to Nivelles: in the case of stopping trains, this serves Waterloo itself, but, unless it is first wished to visit the various attractions in the town, it is better to alight at Braine l'Alleud from where a bus – the Wavre service – may be caught to the Lion Mound.

To return to accommodation, hotels are obviously fewer in number in the area of the battlefield itself, but in Waterloo the Hotel Joli-Bois is very pleasant, while on the actual battlefield there is the Hotel 1815, not to mention the flat in the gardener's house at Hougoumont, though the author is reliably informed that this tends to be booked up years in advance.

With regard to museums, the obvious place to begin is the brand-new 'Mémorial 1815' opposite the Lion Mound, whilst the displays in the coaching inn that served as Wellington's headquarters at Waterloo are also well worth seeing, as, indeed, are the memorial tablets in the parish church, a building, alas, that has been much altered and extended since 1815. In view of the somewhat anglo-centric focus of the Waterloo museum, however, admirers of Napoleon might prefer the museum in the house in which the emperor spent the night before the battle at Le Caillou. Finally, at Mont Saint Jean, as well as going to Hougoumont, where there is another museum, all visitors should ascend the Lion Mound at least once, and, in addition, visit the famous Panorama depicting the French cavalry charges, although it has to be said that in neither case is the experience entirely satisfactory: in the case of the former, the view does not give an especially helpful perspective on the battlefield, the net effect in the author's experience being to smooth out the terrain to such an extent as to make it almost impossible to appreciate the topography, whilst, in the case of the latter, there is more enthusiasm for the cause of the emperor than there is for that of historical reality.

Away from the immediate vicinity of the battlefield, there is, of course, much to be seen in Brussels. In the Evère cemetery, there is an imposing monument to all the British dead of the campaign, while Wellington's residence at 54–56 Rue Royale can still be seen along with the nearby Belle Vue palace, a building which he appears to have used as his *de facto* headquarters. Also very atmospheric is the park beside the Rue Royale: this is mentioned in many British memoirs as very much the place to see and be seen in the halcyon days before the battle. Much grimmer, by contrast, are the scenes associated with the Grand Place: here the wounded were laid out by the hundred on straw prior to be being accommodated in hospitals and private residences. Finally, well worth a visit is the Belgian Royal Army Museum. Situated in the Parc du Cinquantaine beyond the EU headquarters, this only has a small display on the Waterloo campaign, but is definitely a must for anyone with a broader interest in military history, the exhibitions on the First World War being particularly good.

Finally, two places that are also worth mentioning, especially for those with access to cars, are Ligny and Quatre Bras. Had space allowed, they would have been included in this guide, but Ligny, in particular, is a complicated site that defies treatment in anything other than considerable length. That said, it is well worth a visit, the place to begin being the Centre Général Girard in the village of itself. Housed in a building that was used as a hospital during the battle, this has an excellent museum and a very good restaurant, and has a very useful walking guide to the battlefield available for purchase. As for the visiting the scenes of the fighting, walking around the streets of the village is a truly an eerie experience, whilst the slopes which

Blücher's men tried to defend are appalling in the lack of shelter that they offer. What comes over above all, indeed, is that the Prussian position was very poor, and that 'Marshal Vörwarts' was very lucky to escape with nothing worse than a marginal defeat. Quatre Bras, by contrast, is much easier to explore. There is no museum and, very sadly, the courtyard farm at the crossroads itself has been demolished. Also gone, meanwhile, is the thick woodland that shielded the Allied right. However, the much fought over farm of Gemioncourt is still there, while a track across the battlefield from the Charleroi highway to the one to Namur provides excellent access to the area of some of the fiercest fighting.

Any visit to the battlefields of the Waterloo campaign, of course, will be much enhanced by further reading. Here there is truly an embarrassment of riches, but it is hoped that readers of this book will also turn to the guide published some years ago by David Buttery, the current volume seeking not to supplant it, but rather to take it further. As to personal recommendations, an all-time favourite is David Howarth's *A Near-Run Thing* and the outstanding short introduction Gareth Glover's *Waterloo: Myth and Reality*; for full details, please see the bibliography. Not covered by this last are the many novels that the campaign has generated, in which context it would be churlish indeed not to mention Bernard Cornwell's *Sharpe's Waterloo*. That said, there are many others including Ian Gale's *Four Days in June*; Robert Brightwell's *Flashman's Waterloo*; Andrew Swanston's *Waterloo: the Bravest Man*; and David Ebsworth's *The Last Campaign of Marianne Tambour*.

In the digital world in which we now live, it would be very wrong to fail to mention websites. Amongst those which offer detailed information on the field are:

Monuments and Memorials of the Napoleonic Era
<www.https://napoleon-monuments.eu/Napoleon1er/index_
    EN.htm>, accessed 17 November 2017.
Project Hougoumont
< www.https.//projecthougoumont.com >, accessed 17
    November 2017.
Waterloo200 (see, especially, Graeme Cooper's guide to walking
    the battlefield),

< www.https.//waterloo200.org >, accessed 17 November 2017.
The Waterloo Association
< www.https.//waterlooassociation.org >, accessed 18
    November 2017.

To all these, meanwhile, can be added the e-guide to the battlefield of which this book is an expanded version. As noted in the preface, full details may be obtained from <https://www.liverpool.ac.uk/csd/app-directory/waterloo/ >.

Let us close with a word about walking Waterloo (and 'walking Waterloo' is very much the operative word: apart from the Lion Mound, Plancenoit, Papelotte, Smohain, and the various sites along the Brussels highway, the battlefield cannot really be explored by car). Aside from the various restaurants in the vicinity of the Lion Mound and the crossroads, facilities on the battlefield are very limited, and it is, in particular, much to be desired that the authorities would install public toilets at La Belle Alliance, Smohain and Papelotte (as it is, these are only to be found at Hougoumont and the new museum). Setting such logistical matters aside, except perhaps at the height of midsummer and perhaps, remembering the experiences of 1815, even then as well, visitors should go well shod and warmly clad. Finally, and above all, in season and out take the greatest care when crossing or walking along the Charleroi highway: the field of Waterloo is furnished with quite sufficient dead without adding to it fools who think it a good idea to try to photograph La Haye Sainte from the pretty much non-existent central reservation.

NOTES

Tour 1: Grand Waterloo

1. B. Jackson, *Notes and Reminiscences of a Staff Officer chiefly relating to the Waterloo Campaign and to Saint-Helena Matters during the Captivity of Napoleon*, ed. R.C. Seaton, London, 1903, pp. 41–3.

2. *Cit.* P. Hofschroer, *1815, the Waterloo Campaign – the German Victory*, London, 1999, II, p. 137.

3. *Cit.* J. Bogle and A. Uffindell (eds), *A Waterloo Hero: the Reminiscences of Friedrich Lindau*, London, 2009, pp. 185–6.

4. Anon., *An Account of the Battle of Waterloo fought on the 18th of June 1815 by the English and Allied Forces commanded by the Duke of Wellington and the Prussian Army under the Orders of Prince Blücher against the Army of France commanded by Napoleon Bonaparte by a British Officer of the Staff*, London, 1815, pp. 32–3.

5. *Cit.* E. Muilwijk, *The Netherlands Field Army during the Waterloo Campaign, III: Standing Firm at Waterloo*, Bleiwijk, 2014, p. 200.

6. T. Morris, *Recollections of Military Service in 1813, 1814 and 1815 through Germany, Holland and France including some Details of the Battles of Quatre Bras and Waterloo*, London, 1845, pp. 152–3.

7. *Ibid.,* pp. 147–51 *passim.*

8. A.C. Mercer, *Journal of the Waterloo Campaign kept throughout the Campaign of 1815*, London, 1870, pp. 325–30 *passim.*

9. E. Cotton, *A Voice from Waterloo: a History of the Battle fought on the 18th June 1815*, fourth edition, revised and enlarged, Mont Saint Jean, 1852, pp. 26–33.

10. *Cit.* Muilwijk, *Netherlands Field Army,* III, p. 147. NB. Puvis' unit was not involved in the fighting at first, but was only thrown in later.

11. S. Larréguy de Civrieux, *Souvenirs d'un cadet*, Paris, 1912, pp. 168–9.

12. R. Gronow, *Captain Gronow's Recollections of the Camp, the Court and the Clubs at the Close of the Last War with France*, London, 1864, p. 103.

13. Larréguy de Civrieux, *Souvenirs*, pp. 167–8.

14. W. Leeke, *The History of Lord Seaton's Regiment, the Fifty-Second Light Infantry) at the Battle of Waterloo together with Various Incidents connected*

with that Regiment, not only at Waterloo, but also in at Paris and in the North of France and for Several Years Afterwards, to which are appended many of the Author's Reminiscences of his Military and Clerical Careers during a Period of More than Fifty Years, London, 1866, I, pp. 29–35.

15. Ibid., I, pp. 42–7.

16. Jackson, *Notes and Reminiscences*, pp. 56–9.

17. H. de Mauduit, *Les derniers jours de la Grande Armée ou souvenirs, correspondence et documents inédites de Napoléon en 1814 et 1815*, Paris, 1848, II, pp. 460–1.

18. *Cit.* A. Field, *Waterloo: the French Perspective*, Barnsley, 2012, pp. 192–3.

19. L. Canler, *Mémoires du Canler, ancien chef du Service de Sureté*, Brussels, 1862, p. 13.

20. *Cit.* Hofschroer, *1815, the Waterloo Campaign*, II, p. 77.

21. *Cit.* Muilwijk, *Netherlands Field Army*, III, p. 171.

22. W. Hay, *Reminiscences 1808-1815 under Wellington*, London, 1901, pp. 177–81. Ponsonby was eventually rescued by John Vandeleur, the *aide de camp* to his brigade commander, John Ormsby Vandeleur: 'Colonel Ponsonby is most desperately wounded, piked through the body and his arm broken by a sabre cut. We were obliged to leave him on the ground till after the battle . . . Immediately it was over, I asked leave to go look for his body among the dead. Everybody said I would never find it, but I was determined to find it and I did, but he was nearly dead . . . I got him on to a horse and brought him in at six o'clock: I was all night looking for his body.'; *cit.* Anon. (ed.), *Letters of Colonel John Vandeleur, 1810-1846*, London, 1894, p. 159.

23. G. Gleig, *The Light Dragoon*, London, 1855, pp. 154–5.

24. *Cit.* S. Monick, ed., *The Iberian and Waterloo Campaigns: the Letters of Lieutenant James Hope, Ninety-Second (Highland) Regiment, 1811-1815*, Heathfield, 2000, pp. 251–4.

25. *Cit.* Anon., *The Battle of Waterloo, Containing the Series of Accounts published by Authority, British and Foreign, with Circumstantial Details, Previous, During and After the Battle, from a Variety of Authentic and Original Sources with Relevant Official Documents, Forming an Historical Record of the Operations in the Campaign of the Netherlands, 1815*, London, 1815, pp. 49–50.

26. J. Kincaid, *Adventures in the Rifle Brigade in the Peninsula, France and the Netherlands from 1809 to 1815*, London, 1830, pp. 341–2.

27. *Cit.* W. Verner (ed.), *A British Rifleman: the Journals and Correspondence of Major George Simmons, Rifle Brigade, during the Peninsular War and the Campaign of Waterloo*, London, 1899, p. 367.

28. *Cit.* ibid., pp. 365–7.

29. C. Hibbert (ed.), *The Wheatley Diary: a Journal and Sketchbook kept during the Peninsular War and the Waterloo Campaign*, Witney, 2000, p. 70.

30. Bogle and Uffindell (eds), *A Waterloo Hero*, pp. 171–2.

31. Canler, *Mémoires*, pp. 15–16.

Tour 2: the French Positions

1. B.H. Liddell Hart (ed.), *The Letters of Private Wheeler, 1809-1828*, London, 1951, pp. 170–2.

2. *Cit.* B. Coppens (ed.), *Waterloo: les combattants racontent*, Paris, 2009, p. 100.

3. *Cit.* ibid., p. 96.

4. P.G. Doulcet de Pontécoulant, *Souvenirs militaires: Napoléon à Waterloo ou précis rectifié de la campagne de 1815*, Paris, 1866, pp. 256–61 *passim*.

5. Mauduit, *Derniers jours de la Grande Armée*, II, pp. 277–8.

6. *Cit.* Field, *Waterloo: the French Perspective*, pp. 192–3.

7. Canler, *Mémoires*, p. 13.

8. J. Martin, *Souvenirs d'un ex-officier, 1812-1815*, Paris, 1867, p. 284.

9. *Cit.* Muilwijk, *The Netherlands Field Army*, III, p. 173.

10. P. Beslay (ed.), *Un officier d'état-major sous le Premier Empire: souvenirs militaires d'Octave Levavasseur, officier d'artillerie, aide de camp du Maréchal Ney, 1802-1815*, Paris, 1914, pp. 295–6.

11. E. Durutte (ed.), 'Les mémoires du Général Comte Durutte', in *Le Soldat Belge*, 1910–11, No. 3, pp. 4–5.

12. *Cit.* A. Uffindell and M. Corum, *On the Fields of Glory: the Battlefields of the 1815 Campaign*, London, 1996, pp. 216–17.

13. C. Bourachot (ed.), *Souvenirs militaires du Capitaine Jean-Baptiste Lemonnier-Delafosse*, Paris, n.d., pp. 217–18.

14. M. de Baudus, *Etudes sur Napoléon*, Paris, 1841, I, pp. 227–8.

15. Mauduit, *Derniers jours de la Grande Armée*, II, pp. 290–3.

16. *Cit.* H. Siborne (ed.), *Waterloo Letters: a Selection from Original and Hitherto Unpublished Letters bearing on the Operations of the Sixteenth, Seventeenth and Eighteenth of June 1815*, London, 1891, pp. 308–9.

17. Mauduit, *Derniers jours de la Grande Armée*, II, pp. 254–8.

18. Ibid., II, pp. 460–1.
19. Baudus, *Etudes sur Napoléon*, I, p. 225.
20. G. Schlumberger (ed.), *Journal du route du Capitaine Robinaux*, Paris, 1908, pp. 210–11.

Tour 3: The Defence of Hougoumont

1. Cotton, *Voice from Waterloo*, pp. 26–33.
2. *Cit.* Hofschroer, *1815, the Waterloo Campaign*, II, pp. 74–5.
3. M. Clay, *A Narrative of the Battles of Quatre Bras and Waterloo with the Defence of Hougoumont*, Bedford, 1853, p. 15.
4. Bourachot, *Souvenirs militaires du Capitaine Jean-Baptiste Lemonnier-Delafosse*, p. 217.
5. *Cit.* Muilwijk, *Netherlands Field Army*, III, p. 147.
6. Schlumberger, *Journal du route du Capitaine Robinaux*, p. 208.
7. Clay, *Narrative of the Battles of Quatre Bras and Waterloo*, pp. 15–17.
8. Ibid., p. 17.
9. Ibid., pp. 17–18.
10. *Cit.* Muilwijk, *Netherlands Field Army*, III, pp. 148–9.
11. Clay, *A Narrative of the Battles of Quatre Bras and Waterloo*, pp. 18–19.
12. *Cit.* Muilwijk, *Netherlands Field Army*, III, p. 147.
13. *Cit.* G. Glover (ed.), *Letters from the Battle of Waterloo: Unpublished Correspondence by Allied Officers from the Siborne Papers*, London, 2004, p. 172.
14. Larréguy de Civrieux, *Souvenirs*, pp. 168–9.
15. A. Lévi (ed.), *Carnet de campagne du Colonel Trefcon, 1793-1815*, Paris, 1915, pp. 190–2.
16. *Cit.* G. Glover, *The Waterloo Archive – Previously Unpublished or Rare Journals and Letters regarding the Waterloo Campaign and the Subsequent Occupation of France, V: German Sources*, London, 2013, pp. 32–3.
17. C. Eaton, *Narrative of a Residence in Belgium during the Campaign of 1815 and of a Visit to the Field of Waterloo*, London, 1817, pp. 270–97 *passim*.

Tour 4: Drouet's Attack

1. *Cit.* B.W. Webb-Carter, 'A line regiment at Waterloo', *Journal of the Society of Army Historical Research*, XLIII, No. 174, June 1965, p. 64.
2. Martin, *Souvenirs*, p. 284.
3. Ibid., pp. 287–8.
4. P.C. Duthilt, *Mes campagnes et mes souvenirs de 1792 à 1815*, ed. C. Bourachot, Paris, 2008, pp. 318–19.

5. Bogle and Uffindell (eds), *A Waterloo Hero*, pp. 166–8.
6. Kincaid, *Adventures in the Rifle Brigade*, pp. 333–4.
7. *Cit*. Verner, *British Rifleman*, pp. 365–7.
8. *Cit*. Anon., *Battle of Waterloo*, pp. 49–50.
9. Monick (ed.), *Iberian and Waterloo Campaigns*, pp. 251–4.
10. *Cit*. Muilwijk, *Netherlands Field Army*, III, p. 171.
11. *Cit*. G. Glover (ed.), *The Waterloo Archive – Previously Unpublished or Rare Journals and Letters regarding the Waterloo Campaign and the Subsequent Occupation of France, II: German Sources*, Barnsley, 2010, pp. 167–8.

Tour 5: Uxbridge's Counter-Attack

1. G. Glover (ed.), *A Lifeguardsman in Spain, France and at Waterloo: the Memoirs of Sergeant-Major Thomas Playford, Second Lifeguards, 1810-1830*, Godmanchester, 2006, pp. 49–52.
2. *Cit*. Glover, *Waterloo Archive, V*, p. 57.
3. *Cit*. Glover, *Letters from the Battle of Waterloo*, pp. 47–9.
4. Bogle and Uffindell (eds), *A Waterloo Hero*, pp. 168–9.
5. Canler, *Mémoires*, pp. 15–16.
6. Beslay, *Un officier d'état-major sous le Premier Empire*, pp. 298–300.
7. *Cit*. Siborne, *Waterloo Letters*, pp. 61–2.
8. H. Ross-Lewin, *With the Thirty-Second in the Peninsula and other Campaigns*, Dublin, 1904, pp. 272–4.
9. *Cit*. Siborne, *Waterloo Letters*, pp. 70–2.
10. Martin, *Souvenirs*, pp. 287–91.
11. *Cit*. Siborne, *Waterloo Letters*, p. 61.
12. *Cit*. C.T. Atkinson (ed.), 'A Waterloo journal', *Journal of the Society for Army Historical Research*, XXXVIII, No. 153, March, 1960, p. 37.
13. *Cit*. Cotton, *Voice from Waterloo*, p. 59.
14. *Cit*. Atkinson, 'Waterloo journal', p. 38.
15. *Cit*. G. Glover, *The Waterloo Archive – Previously Unpublished or Rare Journals and Letters regarding the Waterloo Campaign and the Subsequent Occupation of France, I: British Sources*, London, 2010, pp. 32–3.
16. J. Mistler and H. Michaud (eds), *Lieutenant Chevalier: souvenirs des guerres napoléoniennes*, Paris, 1970, p. 323.
17. Martin, *Souvenirs*, pp. 290–1.
18. J. Tomkinson (ed.), *The Diary of a Cavalry Officer in the Peninsular and Waterloo Campaigns, 1809-1815*, London, 1894, pp. 300–1.
19. Hay, *Reminiscences*, pp. 177–81.

Tour 6: The French Cavalry Charges

1. P. Fleury de Chaboulon, *Les cent jours: mémoires por servir à l'histoire de la vie privée, du retour et de la regne de Napoléon en 1815*, London, 1820, II, pp. 180–1.
2. Leeke, *History of Lord Seaton's Regiment*, I, pp. 29–34.
3. Ibid., I, pp. 34–5.
4. *Cit.* E. Owen, *The Waterloo Papers: 1815 and Beyond*, Tavistock, 1997, pp. 25–6.
5. *Cit.* Glover, *Waterloo Archive*, I, pp. 159–60.
6. Mercer, *Journal of the Waterloo Campaign*, pp. 309–16.
7. *Cit.* Field, *Waterloo: the French Perspective*, pp. 140–1.
8. Ibid., pp. 147–51 *passim*.
9. Glover, *Lifeguardsman in Spain, France and at Waterloo*, p. 53.
10. *Cit.* Field, *Waterloo: the French Perspective*, pp. 149–50.
11. *Cit.* Glover (ed.), *Waterloo Archive*, II, pp. 105–9.
12. Hibbert, *Wheatley Diary*, pp. 65–8.
13. *Cit.* Muilwijk, *Netherlands Field Army*, III, p. 195.

Tour 7: Bülow, Ziethen and Mouton

1. *Cit.* A. Uffindell, *On the Fields of Glory: the Battlefields of the 1815 Campaign*, London, 1996, pp. 219–20.
2. *Cit.* Field, *Waterloo: the French Perspective*, pp. 179–80.
3. *Cit.* Uffindell and Corum, *On the Fields of Glory*, pp. 216–17.
4. *Cit.* Hofschroer, *Waterloo: the German Victory*, II, p. 118.
5. *Cit.* ibid., p. 96.
6. *Cit.* Field, *Waterloo: the French Perspective*, p. 164.
7. C. Thoumas (ed.), *Souvenirs militaires de Victor Dupuy, chef d'escadron d'hussards, 1794-1816*, Paris, 1892, pp. 290–1.
8. *Cit.* Field, *Waterloo: the French Perspective*, p. 165.
9. *Cit.* Hofschroer, *Waterloo: the German Victory*, II, p. 139.
10. *Cit.* Muilwijk, *Netherlands Field Army*, III, p. 173.
11. *Cit.* Hofschroer, *Waterloo: the German Victory*, II, p. 140.
12. Bourachot (ed.), *Souvenirs militaires du Capitaine Jean-Baptiste Lemonnier-Delafosse*, pp. 217–18.
13. Martin, *Souvenirs*, p. 296.
14. Jackson, *Notes and Reminiscences*, p. 56.

Tour 8: The Attack of the Guard

1. Beslay, *Un officier d'état-major sous le Premier Empire*, p. 304.
2. Mauduit, *Derniers jours de la Grande Armée*, II, pp. 418–19.
3. *Cit.* Field, *Waterloo: the French Perspective*, pp. 192–3.
4. *Cit.* Bogle and Uffindell (eds), *A Waterloo Hero*, pp. 196–7.
5. *Cit.* Glover, *Waterloo Archive II*, p. 109.
6. Morris, *Recollections*, pp. 152–3.
7. *Cit.* Hofschroer, *1815, the Waterloo Campaign*, II, p. 137.
8. *Cit.* J. Franklin (ed.), *Waterloo: Netherlands Correspondence*, Ulverston, 2010, p. 116.
9. Gleig, *Light Dragoon*, pp. 155–6.
10. *Cit.* Owen, *Waterloo Papers: 1815 and Beyond*, pp. 42–3.
11. *Cit.* Field, *Waterloo*, p. 196.
12. *Cit.* Siborne, *Waterloo Letters*, pp. 254–6.
13. Mercer, *Journal of the Waterloo Campaign*, pp. 325–30 *passim*.
14. Leeke, *History of Lord Seaton's Regiment*, I, pp. 42–7.
15. Gleig, *Light Dragoon*, pp. 157–8.
16. Larréguy de Civrieux, *Souvenirs*, pp. 172–3.
17. *Cit.* Glover, *Waterloo Archive V*, pp. 16–17
18. Anon., *The Crisis of the Battle of Waterloo by an Eye-Witness*, Dublin, 1833, pp. 20–5.
19. Lévi (ed.), *Carnet de campagne du Colonel Trefcon*, pp. 192–3.
20. *Cit.* Siborne, *Waterloo Letters*, pp. 308–9.
21. Mauduit, *Derniers jours de la Grande Armée*, II, pp. 460–1.
22. Gleig, *Light Dragoon*, pp. 159–60.

FURTHER READING

Adkin, M., *The Waterloo Companion*, London, 2001.

Baker-Smith, V., *Wellington's Hidden Heroes: the Dutch and the Belgians at Waterloo*, Oxford, 2015.

Barbero, A., *The Battle: a History of the Battle of Waterloo*, London, 2005.

Black, J., *The Battle of Waterloo: a New History*, New York, 2010.

Buttery, D., *Waterloo Battlefield Guide,* Barnsley, 2013.

Caldwell, G., *Rifle Green at Waterloo,* Leicester, 2015.

Chalfont, A., ed., *Waterloo; Battle of the Three Armies*, London, 1979.

Chandler, D.G., *Waterloo: the Hundred Days*, Oxford, 1980.

Clayton, T., *Waterloo: Four Days that Changed Europe's Destiny*, London, 2014.

Cornwell, B., *Waterloo: the History of Four Days, Three Armies and Three Battles*, London, 2014.

Corrigan, G., *Waterloo: a New History of the Battle and its Armies*, London, 2014.

Dawson, P.L., *Au Pas de Charge! Napoleon's Cavalry at Waterloo*, Stockton-on-Tees, 2015.

_____, *Charge the Guns! Wellington's Cavalry at Waterloo*, Stockton-on-Tees, 2015.

_____, *Napoleon and Grouchy: the Last Great Waterloo Mystery*, Barnsley, 2017.

_____, *Waterloo: the Truth at Last – Why Napoleon lost the Great Battle*, Barnsley, 2017.

Esdaile, C.J., *Napoleon, France and Waterloo: the Eagle Rejected*, Barnsley, 2016.

Fletcher, I., *'A Desperate Business': Wellington, the British Army and the Waterloo Campaign*, Staplehurst, 2001.

Field, A., *Waterloo: the French Perspective*, Barnsley, 2012.

Franklin, J., *Waterloo, 1815, 1: Quatre Bras*, Oxford, 2015.

_____, *Waterloo, 1815, 2: Ligny*, Oxford, 2015.

_____, *Waterloo, 1815, 3: Mont Saint Jean and Wavre*, Oxford, 2015.

_____, *Waterloo: the Struggle for Hougoumont in the Words of Those who witnessed the Events of June 1815*, Stroud, 2016.

Fremont-Barnes, G., *Waterloo, 1815: the British Army's Day of Destiny*, Stroud: 2014.

Gale, I., *Scotland for Ever! The Scots Greys at Waterloo*, Edinburgh, 2015.

Gillespie-Payne, J., *Waterloo in the Footsteps of the Commanders*, Barnsley, 2004.

Glover, G., *Waterloo: Myth and Reality*, Barnsley, 2014.

_____, *Waterloo: the Defeat of Napoleon's Imperial Guard: Henry Clinton, the Second Division and the End of a 200-Year-Old Controversy*, Barnsley, 2015.

Goldsbrough, R., *The Cavalry that Broke Napoleon: the King's Dragoon Guards at Waterloo*, Stroud, 2016.

Hamilton-Williams, D., *Waterloo: the Great Battle Reappraised*, London, 1993.

Haythornthwaite, P., *Uniforms of Waterloo in Colour, 16th-18th June 1815*, Blandford Forum, 1974.

_____, *The Waterloo Armies: Men, Organization and Tactics*, Barnsley, 2007.

_____, *Picton's Division at Waterloo*, Barnsley, 2016.

Hofschroer, P., *1815, the Waterloo Campaign, the German Victory*, London, 1999.

Howarth, D., *A Near-Run Thing: the Day of Waterloo*, London, 1967.

Hussey, J., *Waterloo: the Campaign of 1815*, Barnsley, 2015.

Lipscombe, N., ed., *Waterloo: the Decisive Victory*, Oxford, 2015.

Logie, J., *Waterloo: the 1815 Campaign*, Stroud, 2006.

Mann, M., *And They Rode On: the King's Dragoon Guards at Waterloo*, London, 1984.

Muilwijk, E., *The Netherlands Field Army during the Waterloo Campaign*, Bleiwijk, 2014.

Paget, J., *Hougoumont: the Key to Victory in Europe*, Barnsley, 1999.

Pericoli, U., *1815: the Armies of Waterloo*, London, 1979.

Roberts, A., *Waterloo: Napoleon's Last Gamble*, New York, 2005.

Sale, N., *The Lie at the Heart of Waterloo: the Battle's Last Hidden Half-Hour*, Stroud, 2014.

Schom, A., *One Hundred Days: Napoleon's Road to Waterloo*, London, 1993.

Simms, B., *The Longest Afternoon: the 400 Men who Decided the Battle of Waterloo*, London, 2014.

Spunner-White, B., *Of Living Valour: the Story of the Soldiers of Waterloo*, London, 2015.

Sutherland, J., *Men of Waterloo*, London, 1967.

Uffindell, A., and Corum, M., *On the Fields of Glory: the Battlefields of the 1815 Campaign*, London, 1996.

Weller, J., *Wellington at Waterloo*, London, 1967.